Bliss *and* Dance

For Karen Sellick, née Bliss,
whose seed of inspiration and
legacy was the driving force
in making this book happen.

Bliss *and* Dance
REVELATIONS ON STAGE

Edited by
Jennifer Jackson

UNICORN

Contents

FOREWORD
Dame Darcey Bussell
7

INTRODUCTION
Jennifer Jackson
8

---

1. Ninette de Valois and Arthur Bliss: Theatrical Experiments for a Modern English Repertory Ballet (1927–37)
Anna Meadmore
12

2. Arthur Bliss and the Contribution Made by Designers in the Creation of his Ballets
Jane Pritchard
26

PART ONE
Checkmate, 1937

3. Deathly Moves: *Checkmate* A Ballet in One Scene with a Prologue
Andrew Burn
36

4. Dancing *Checkmate*
David Bintley
50

5. *Checkmate*: Beyond the Classroom, Choreographic Theatre
Jennifer Jackson
56

PART TWO
Miracle in the Gorbals, 1944

6. *Miracle in the Gorbals*: Revelation on Stage
Paul Spicer
68

7. Englishness of Some Other Sort
Sam Ellis
78

8. Gillian Lynne's *Miracle in the Gorbals*
David Bintley
with Voices of the Cast compiled by Jennifer Jackson
88

PART THREE
Adam Zero, 1946

9. *Adam Zero*: The A–Z of Life's
Experience in Music and Dance
PAUL SPICER
108

10. Revisiting *Adam Zero*:
Spectre of Symbolism and Stagecraft
MICHAEL BYRNE
118

11. Bliss in Bremerhaven:
Sergei Vanaev Reawakens *Adam Zero*
MICHAEL BYRNE
130

PART FOUR
The Lady of Shalott, 1958

12. Early and Late: Bliss's Attraction
to Dance and *The Lady of Shalott*
LEWIS FOREMAN
138

13. From Fragments a Portrait:
Lew Christensen's *Lady of Shalott*
JENNIFER JACKSON
148

14. *Girl in a Broken Mirror*:
Ballet and Music in Education
SUSIE CROW
164

EPILOGUE

15. Remembering Karen Bliss
SUSAN JONES
176

Endnotes 182
Contributor Biographies 188
Acknowledgements 190

Select Bibliography 192
Index 196

Foreword

DAME DARCEY BUSSELL
PRESIDENT OF THE ROYAL ACADEMY OF DANCE
COACH, FORMER PRINCIPAL WITH THE ROYAL BALLET

With any creative project, I find, as a dancer, that the music is always the underlying thread, the motive for dancing, leading you into the narrative. The music shows you the path, and the movement follows with the expression.

This book is about Sir Arthur Bliss's music for dance and the ballets it inspired. Bliss's ballet scores brought him great acclaim in his lifetime (1891–1975). He was commissioned to write four works: three of them were created for Sadler's Wells Ballet between 1937 and 1946, and the fourth ballet, composed in 1958, was danced by the San Francisco Ballet with choreography by Lew Christensen. Bliss worked side by side with the choreographers and dancers; it was his understanding and appreciation of the language of ballet that lit the success of his compositions.

We are reminded here of the spirit of a time of extraordinary creativity, when the style and heritage repertoire of The Royal Ballet was being established and spread beyond Britain. Bliss's rich collaborations with choreographers Ninette de Valois and Robert Helpmann forged new ways of presenting compelling narrative ballet that resonate to this day. Looking closely at these ballets, we also perceive the dance theatre landscape in Britain and in post-war America. We can see reflections of Bliss's own life story – his service to music performance and education, and his passion for harnessing the emotive potential of music through dance.

The book is the result of loving research and analysis by music and dance practitioners and scholars. It interweaves two 'lost' works, *Adam Zero* (1946) and *The Lady of Shalott* (1958), evoking their performance with vivid imagery. It tells of the genesis of the Bliss and de Valois masterpiece, *Checkmate* (1937), and celebrates the unbroken line of productions conveyed via interviews with many of the dancers (in which I am featured as the Black Queen!). Photographs capture the recreation in 2014 by Gillian Lynne of *Miracle in the Gorbals*, working with the dancers from Birmingham Royal Ballet and from her embodied memory as an original member of the cast in 1944. It is a visual feast.

I am a passionate advocate for understanding the influence of past generations on the art of today. The Bliss ballets tackle bold themes and they make compelling theatre; they remind us of the power of dance to move and change us as human beings.

This is a beautiful book – it will educate, entertain and empower artists and audiences alike.

Darcey Bussell as the Black Queen. The Royal Ballet, Royal Opera House, June 1993. Photo: Bill Cooper (ArenaPAL).

Introduction

JENNIFER JACKSON

Sir Arthur Bliss (1891–1975), composer, conductor, musician and diplomat, was at the centre of British musical life for more than fifty years. *Enfant terrible* in the 1920s, he metamorphosed into *bon papa* of the music establishment and Master of the Queen's Music from 1953 until his death. Alongside significant public service, he produced an impressive body of work: orchestral and choral works, chamber music, song, opera, film, theatre and ballet music.

His music emerged from a turbulent period in twentieth-century history, shaped by distinguished service and the loss of a beloved brother in the First World War and the years 'between the wars', when his radical experiments in sound matured into major orchestral works and highly successful collaborations, especially for ballet and film.

The Bliss ballets, composed between 1937 and 1958, fall into a period of his 'high maturity' and were acclaimed in his lifetime.[1] He was commissioned to write four works: three for Sadler's Wells Ballet, the company founded and led by Ninette de Valois. She choreographed the first, and Robert Helpmann made the subsequent two ballets. The fourth ballet, choreographed by Lew Christensen with San Francisco Ballet, was commissioned as the headline event at the opening of a music complex in Berkeley, California, and recalls Bliss's close family ties with the USA.

Born in London to an American father, Bliss met his lifelong companion and wife, Trudy Hoffman, in 1925 in California. Bliss's younger daughter Karen (1932–2020) trained in the USA and with Sadler's Wells Ballet before dancing professionally, and later becoming a distinguished ballet teacher in Oxford. This book testifies to the transmission of the gifts of music and dance through successive generations. The essence of its shape and content emerged at the very first meeting of what became the working group for the book. Karen's passion for the art of dance and music generated the notion of a book that 'thinks like a dancer'. This idea underpins the interdisciplinarity of the structure, which integrates the writing of practising musicians, dancers and scholars about the four ballets – their genesis, creation and historical and cultural moment.

Bliss worked with Sadler's Wells Ballet at a highly significant time, from when the company was building its repertoire and audiences in the 1930s, throughout the war and to the re-opening of Covent Garden Opera House in 1946. His story and that of de Valois intertwine around early Sergei Diaghilev-inspired experiments, collaborative success and their respective roles, serving to establish structures for music and dance practices that endure today. Helpmann's impact on the theatrical brand of ballet forged by these Royal Ballet pioneers is nowhere more evident than in the two collaborations with Bliss. Their vision is echoed in developments in

Arthur Bliss in 1937.
Photo: Gordon Anthony
© Victoria and Albert
Museum, London (Royal
Ballet School Special
Collections).

America where Sadler's Wells Ballet had given a nascent American dance audience the taste for theatrical presentation and high production values. Collaborating with the flamboyant Hollywood designer Tony Duquette, Christensen began a fruitful period of collaboration on psychologically driven and narrative works on the West Coast.

Indeed, all the Bliss ballets are characterised by bold narratives and imaginative, ambitious design. They are a powerful reminder that ballet is a living tradition, a performing art which is collaborative, interdisciplinary, embodied and revealed in performance on the stage.

Bliss wanted to be known to the public by his music,[2] and wrote of ballet as 'an art form in which the composer was free to control his medium'.[3] By looking through the lens of his ballets, this book asks what we might know of Bliss – and of dance as an art form.

The ballets are a prism on truly extraordinary and fascinating stories. While the music is scored and thus a constant across all four, the original choreography exists only in parts. Each ballet is revealed in photographs and essays by music and dance specialists, including the testimonies of dancers, musicians and other creative collaborators.

The opening two chapters by Anna Meadmore and Jane Pritchard set the scene. They highlight the profound influence after the First World War of Diaghilev and the Ballets Russes on the lives of artists involved in the theatre and the fluidity between genres in the social circles within which they moved. Meadmore reveals the depth of the collaboration between Bliss and de Valois, when both were establishing themselves as serious artists and finding opportunities to be seen and heard. Pritchard draws attention to Bliss's involvement in composing for a variety of theatrical productions and she brings her expertise in design for theatre and dance to rich descriptions of the settings and costumes for each of the works for Sadler's Wells Ballet.

After these introductory chapters we encounter the works in four parts in the chronological order of the original productions: *Checkmate* (1937), *Miracle in the Gorbals* (1944), *Adam Zero* (1946) and *The Lady of Shalott* (1958). Each part begins with a chapter from the perspective of a musician, followed by chapters focusing on the dance and its place in Bliss's creative work.

Andrew Burn gives us the fascinating story of the provenance of the idea for *Checkmate* at a dinner party in the 1920s and its realisation in 1937 as a masterpiece of British dance. To follow, David Bintley's vivid description leads us into his experience of working with de Valois, then in her eighties, on his role as the Red King and dancing the ballet himself across several decades. My chapter offers another perspective from inside the work, drawing on interviews with executants from several generations, to analyse the choreography and ponder the enduring nature of this great ballet.

Bliss's biographer, Paul Spicer, weaves moving detail about the personal circumstances of Bliss's next commission into his essay about the score, scenario and first performances of *Miracle in the Gorbals* in 1944. Sam Ellis wrote his doctoral thesis on the music of Arthur Bliss. He contributes a philosophical essay on Bliss's paradoxical position in British music as both a central figure and outsider, seen through this radical wartime collaboration and juxtaposing the notion of the classical pastoral with the urban industrial setting. Gillian Lynne's 2014 production of *Miracle in the Gorbals* is evoked by the testimonies of David Bintley, who as Director of Birmingham Royal Ballet commissioned its recreation, and by the recollections of members of the cast and creative team of working on and performing the ballet.

Paul Spicer invites us into what Bliss considered his finest ballet music, *Adam Zero*, highlighting the imaginative range and appropriateness of musical styles referenced in the score and the challenge of bringing to the stage this allegory of a man's life cycle. The first newly created ballet to be premiered at Covent Garden after the Second World War, *Adam Zero* was performed on a mere nineteen occasions. Michael Byrne's extensive research into the remnants of this 'lost' work results in a vivid evocation of the complex action on stage. His next chapter draws together twenty-first-century iterations of the ballet: Sergei Vanaev's impressive 2015 production in Bremerhaven, Germany, and Andrew McNicol's vignettes choreographed with students and presented at the Robert Helpmann Symposium in 2013.

To introduce Bliss's last commissioned ballet, Lewis Foreman takes us on a journey across six decades to consider how Bliss's feeling for dance manifests in his scores. Then he examines the roots of the ballet itself, the poem by Alfred Tennyson on which it is based, previous settings of *The Lady of Shalott* and the scenario that Bliss developed in collaboration with Christopher Hassall. The premiere of *Lady of Shalott* by San Francisco Ballet transports the reader to a different context for ballet creation: the West Coast of America and a pioneering 'dance dynasty', the Christensen Brothers.[4] My account of another 'lost' choreography by Lew, the youngest of the brothers, includes the recollections of original cast members, interviewed as part of my research in 2024. Bliss's passionate commitment to nurturing both music-making and young musicians continues in the work of the Bliss Trust. Susie Crow's chapter traces the provenance of the only UK performances of *The Lady of Shalott*, in a unique production in 1975 by Leicestershire Schools Symphony Orchestra in collaboration with New Parks Girls' School. Retitled *Girl in a Broken Mirror*, it was the subject of a high-profile Thames Television documentary.

The book closes with a reflection on legacy and on Karen's story. Her own memories of her career, and those of her colleagues and friends who consider her teaching, choreography and active participation in DANSOX at the University of Oxford, are collated by Susan Jones.

It has been an enormous privilege to be so closely involved with this treasured journey of discovery. Some details appear more than once, coloured by the context and focus of the respective authors. I invite you to delve into each chapter as a stand-alone essay, also to read across the whole book to make your own discoveries and to add depth and subtlety to the appreciation of this extraordinary and rich history.

1.
Ninette de Valois and Arthur Bliss: Theatrical Experiments for a Modern English Repertory Ballet (1927–37)

ANNA MEADMORE

The choreographer-director Ninette de Valois (1898–2001) set three of her ballets to the music of Arthur Bliss: *Rout* (1927), *Narcissus and Echo* (1932) and *Checkmate* (1937). These works spanned the decade in which she emerged as the predominant force in early British ballet. *Rout* and *Checkmate*, in particular, represented significant milestones in de Valois' development as a choreographer; they also marked her rising reputation as a director. In 1927 her treatment of *Rout* as a dance work was met with considerable scepticism. The dance critic Arnold Haskell thought it was simply another of those 'frenzied choreographic experiments' in modern dance that he — and other ballet reactionaries — so deeply mistrusted.[1] In fact, Bliss's 'experimental' music for *Rout* had given de Valois the ideal vehicle for testing her theories about how to embed modern ballet as part of the progressive repertory theatre in England. Writing in 1926, she had described ballet as 'a complete theatrical art' founded on a 'classic school', which is nevertheless 'limitless in its adaptability'.[2] Her concept was realised by 1937, when *Checkmate* demonstrated that de Valois had established a national ballet in which classical tradition and contemporary creativity were inextricably linked. Still regarded as her masterpiece, *Checkmate* is occasionally revived as a landmark 'heritage' work.[3]

All three of her Bliss ballets reflected de Valois' growing influence as the founder of an English ballet school and nascent company. Her ambitious enterprise was launched in 1926 as the Academy of Choreographic Art, a private dance studio situated in West Kensington. In January 1931 the Academy was integrated into the newly rebuilt Sadler's Wells

Fig. 1.1: Opening of the Academy of Choreographic Art, March 1926. Most of those present had links to the Diaghilev Ballet, including Anton Dolin and Edwin Evans (back row, second and third from left), Lydia Lopokova (seated centre), Ninette de Valois and Ursula Moreton (front row, first and second on left) and Marie Rambert (kneeling right). Photographer unknown (Royal Ballet School Special Collections).

Fig. 1.2: Ninette de Valois (standing centre) and Ursula Moreton (in black dress, kneeling), with senior students from the Vic-Wells School, *c*. 1931. Photographer unknown (Royal Ballet School Special Collections).

Theatre. De Valois' School and Company were soon dubbed 'the Vic-Wells', reflecting their regular appearances at the Old Vic and Sadler's Wells, the twin repertory theatres managed by Lilian Baylis. From 1940 they became known as the Sadler's Wells Ballet, finally being appointed The Royal Ballet School and Companies in 1956. Thus, within thirty years – a period encompassing great turbulence after the First World War and the vast upheavals of the Second – de Valois had steered the formation of a national institution from a standing start. At every stage, she demonstrated a remarkable capacity for choosing the right colleagues. Bliss, for one, was not only pivotal to her own early career as a choreographer, but also continued to be a staunch supporter of her whole enterprise, eventually serving as a Governor to the Sadler's Wells School from 1947 to around 1952.[4]

Fig. 1.3: Ninette de Valois in *You'd be Surprised*, London, January–May 1923. Later that year she joined the Ballets Russes, and Sergei Diaghilev used this image in his Monte Carlo season programme. Photo: Hana (Royal Ballet School Special Collections).

This chapter looks at the two earliest productions in the Bliss-de Valois triptych. De Valois' danced rendition of *Rout* was made in 1927, seven years after Bliss's *Rout for Soprano Voice and Orchestra* (1920) was first performed in concert. His *Rhapsody* (1919), sometimes called *Rhapsody for Strings and 2 Voices*, was retitled *Narcissus and Echo* for her choreographic interpretation of 1932.[5] Almost a century since either ballet was last performed, both must be approached as 'lost' dance works. Most forgotten dances leave traces behind in the form of music and design, photography and film, dance notation and rehearsal notes. First-hand accounts or critical reviews provide other vital sources. Clues about the qualities of movement lie in the aesthetic norms, dance techniques and performing styles that prevailed at the time they were created. From such

NINETTE DE VALOIS AND ARTHUR BLISS: THEATRICAL EXPERIMENTS FOR A MODERN ENGLISH REPERTORY BALLET (1927–37) | 13

assuredly good,' he wrote, 'to examine critically the great masters of the past … but I fail often to find adequate space given to … the many signs which mark this as a period of very special creativity.'[6] De Valois was equally impatient with those who ignored or resisted the 'very special' post-war burgeoning of creative innovation with which both she and Bliss personally identified. In an article she wrote for *Dancing Times* in 1926, entitled 'The Future of the Ballet', de Valois made a similar appeal to those she called 'the anti-moderns', asking for a more 'cooperative' approach to the explorative work of younger choreographers – among whom she was starting to count herself.[7]

De Valois was seven years younger than Bliss and in her late twenties when she first worked with him in 1927. She had opened her Academy the year before, but was still better known as a Soloist with Sergei Diaghilev's Ballets Russes; having spent two years with the Company from 1923 to 1925, she continued to appear with them as a guest artist until 1928.[8] Her recent activities as the 'movement director' for a variety of dramatic productions – especially for Terence Gray's Festival Theatre in Cambridge and at Baylis's Old Vic – had attracted favourable attention, but she had yet to prove herself as an autonomous creator of modern ballets. By contrast, Bliss's abilities as a composer had already gained considerable recognition. As early as 1921, London's leading music critic Ernest Newman had endorsed his youthful compositions as the products 'of a curiously lively, questing mind'.[9] Diaghilev had been so struck by Bliss's score for *Rout* that he asked him to expand it for a larger orchestra; it was then given as a musical interlude between ballets, under the baton of Ernest Ansermet.[10] This remained a rare accolade for an English composer. Diaghilev's carefully curated programmes of interval music usually featured Russian and French scores; only later did he include a scattering of pieces by Eugene Goossens, Lord Berners, Arnold Bax, Roger Quilter and Constant Lambert.[11] De Valois probably first heard Bliss's *Rout* played during a Diaghilev interlude.[12]

In an article for the *Weekly Dispatch* (July 1921) entitled 'The Rise of Arthur Bliss', the young composer's commission from Diaghilev was hailed as no less than 'the seal of a European reputation!'

Fig. 1.4: Arthur Bliss in his studio flat, London, 1927, featured in *The Lady*, 24 February 1927. Photographer unknown (Bliss Archive, Cambridge University Library).

traces, we can surmise what a long-dormant work might have looked, sounded and felt like. Bliss's short, adventurous compositions inspired de Valois to make equally potent and theatrical dance works: the *Rout* and *Rhapsody/Narcissus* ballets both reflected the era in which they were made and the artistic convictions of their creators.

Backdrop to the Bliss–de Valois ballets: shared influences and ideals

The interwar period saw unsettling sociocultural cross-currents swirling around Europe that caused perceptions and values to change. As a young man in 1921, Bliss had penned an article for the *Musical News and Herald* expressing his frustration with the mainstream press, which he felt was more interested in dead composers than live ones: 'It is

Fig. 1.5: Jacques-Émile Blanche, *Tamara Karsavina*, 1911. This painting hangs in the foyer of the Royal Academy of Dance, London. Photo: Oliver Dixon, Kallaway (Courtesy of Royal Academy of Dance).

Fig. 1.6: Costume design by Léon Bakst (1912) for Vaslav Nijinsky in the title role of *L'Après-midi d'un faune* (*The Afternoon of a Faun*) from a Ballets Russes souvenir programme, undated (Royal Ballet School Special Collections).

The author, who wrote under the pseudonym 'Marcato',[13] then added: 'The next thing, no doubt, will be an Arthur Bliss ballet.'[14] Indeed, Marcato claimed that Bliss was already writing a piece for Tamara Karsavina, one of Diaghilev's greatest stars. It was to be called 'Masque of the Red Death' after the gothic fantasy by Edgar Allen Poe, although this idea never came to fruition.[15] Marcato's article went on to complain, rather wearily, how hard it was, 'when talking of music nowadays', not to 'drag in' the subject of ballet. Yet it also conceded the 'vivifying' effect of the Russian ballet: 'Offered such wondrous feasts for the eye, people have simultaneously been half unconsciously educated to listen in this brief time to such music as it would have taken a generation to accustom them to in the severe walls of the concert room.'[16]

That 'brief time' had begun when the Ballets Russes burst upon the English theatrical scene with its London debut in 1911. Bliss and de Valois were among the generation who felt its impact most keenly upon their own artistic sensibilities. During the Company's twenty-year existence (1909–29), Diaghilev commissioned composers at the forefront of European modernism to write music for ballet – beginning with Igor Stravinsky, whose innovative scores for *The Firebird* (1910) and *Petrushka* (1911) were followed by his revolutionary *Rite of Spring* (1913).[17] Diaghilev's productions achieved a fresh synthesis of the theatre arts, shifting cultural attitudes towards ballet. By introducing new music in tandem with gorgeous designs, fantastical stories, stunning dancers and choreography, the Ballets Russes and its brilliant collaborators unleashed the contemporary theatrical potential of the form, and shaped the aspirations of many young artists.

Bliss's biographer, Paul Spicer, has argued that Bliss's 'lifelong admiration for Diaghilev and his devotion to Stravinsky fed the seeds of his own ballet scores', which were 'amongst the most successful strands of his composition'.[18] Citing the example of *Rout*, Spicer observed that Bliss's youthful musical experiment may have been a 'postscript' to Stravinsky's *Petrushka* score, given that 'the opening of *Rout* is so similar … that they are almost interchangeable'.[19] Bliss himself traced his love for the music of Stravinsky back to his early encounters with the Diaghilev repertoire. In his autobiography, he fondly recalled the 'zest' of student outings to see the Ballets Russes.[20] During a golden year before the outbreak of war in 1914, Bliss often attended their performances accompanied by his friends from the Royal College of Music, Herbert Howells, Eugene Goossens and Arthur Benjamin: 'These evenings were shot through with unexpected excitements,' he wrote, 'as the curtain went up on a Bakst design or the opening notes of a Stravinsky score were heard.

On a return home from such a feast we seemed to board the bus with the dash of a Nijinsky leap.'[21]

As a member of the Ballets Russes, de Valois absorbed the extraordinary combination of 'classical' Imperial Ballet traditions and 'modernist' Nietzschean ideas of total theatre that was the hallmark of a Diaghilev production. Like de Valois, Bliss recognised the artistic value of this fertile tension, articulating it not only in his music, but also in his writing. In his 1921 essay entitled 'What Modern Composition is Aiming at', he identified in the music of Maurice Ravel – one of Diaghilev's great associates – 'the reincarnation of the seventeenth-century spirit under a modern habit, combining … an audacious harmonic scheme with classic clarity of style'.[22] Bliss clearly admired such classically rooted contemporary audacity: 'We live in rapidly moving times,' he continued, 'many mentalities are at work who are not afraid to explore every avenue, who are desperately anxious for progress'; and he insisted that, despite the misgivings of those still 'clinging desperately to the past', the progress he sought was already 'bang in the midst of us'.[23] Bliss and de Valois were each determined to play a part in that dynamic surge of progressive creativity.

Shared networks: Bliss's and de Valois' coinciding professional and social circles

Their links to the Ballets Russes meant that Bliss's and de Valois' professional and social circles often overlapped. A key mutual acquaintance was Edwin Evans, a widely respected critic and musicologist who was a trusted adviser to Diaghilev. Evans had won that trust when he took a public stand in favour of Stravinsky's *Le Sacre du printemps* (*The Rite of Spring*) after the ballet's London premiere in 1913, 'at a time when that work … was regarded by the majority of musicians as an outrage to their ears'.[24] Evans was also an early champion of Bliss's work. In an article for *The Musical Times* (January 1923), he had defended the young composer against carping accusations that 'the rapidity of his success' was owed to 'personal pushfulness', arguing that the public had taken to Bliss's music of its own accord because it so vividly expressed 'the energy of a buoyant personality, bursting with life'.[25] Evans took an equally proactive interest in de Valois' early work. In an appreciation written two years after Evans died in March 1945, de Valois pointed to his exceptional 'practical knowledge of the ballet', before continuing on a more personal note: 'It was to Edwin Evans that I took my first ideas; a busy man always, his work did not deter him from giving much time and thought to the task of helping me to find suitable music for any choreography I wanted to do.'[26] In the ensuing years, Evans would recommend and arrange several scores for de Valois' ballets. It seems likely that these suggestions included Bliss's energetic music for *Rout*, and later the *Rhapsody*, as a suitably theatrical vehicle for retelling the *Narcissus and Echo* story through dance.

Several centres of artistic endeavour with which Bliss, de Valois and Evans were associated had shared connections. *(see Fig. 1.1)* One of these was the Academy of Choreographic Art. De Valois wrote that Evans was 'the first visitor from the music world to be tentatively invited to the studio to see my first effort in choreography'; she recalled her alarm when he afterwards 'left the studio somewhat hurriedly', and her relief when she discovered that 'he had 'phoned the English composer whose work I was using, and told him he should not miss seeing what I was doing'.[27] It was Bliss whom Evans had called, as the piece in question was *Rout*. Bliss clearly approved of what he saw, since he himself played the piano for *Rout* when the London premiere of the ballet took place at the Academy in 1928.

Another locus of mutual interest was the Mercury Theatre in London's Notting Hill, where Marie Rambert had established her Ballet Club in 1931 (called Ballet Rambert from 1935). Rambert had been a member of the Ballets Russes a decade earlier than de Valois (1912–13), and maintained significant ties with Diaghilev himself, as well as close friendships with her former colleagues, Karsavina and Lydia Lopokova. (De Valois herself called the effervescent Lopokova 'the best friend of my life in the theatre'.[28]) Bliss was well-acquainted with Rambert's husband, the playwright Ashley Dukes, who ran the Mercury Theatre as a private subscription club. Members of this eminent set included Lopokova's husband, the economist John Maynard Keynes, and his brother Geoffrey, a

Fig. 1.7: *Rout* (1927), choreographed and performed by Ninette de Valois (centre) and Ursula Moreton (back row on right), with students of the Academy of Choreographic Art. This image may date from performances in 1928 in London, for which Moreton designed the costumes. Photographer unknown (Royal Ballet School Special Collections).

surgeon and scholar. (Maynard became the Treasurer of the Camargo Ballet Society, while Geoffrey Keynes wrote the scenario for de Valois' 1931 ballet, *Job*.) As the choreographer Antony Tudor later observed, 'even a peripheral acquaintance' with Dukes's social circle 'was an honor [sic] and useful'.[29] Each of these distinguished figures would play an instrumental role in de Valois' practical and creative efforts to establish a national ballet.

It was Dukes's translation of a poem by Ernst Toller that had provided *Rout* with its scenario in 1919. As the founder-manager of the Mercury, Dukes acted as an intellectual bridge between a wide spectrum of the progressive theatre arts and the dance-focused work of Rambert, de Valois and, later, the Camargo Society.[30] 'The Camargo' became another important arena in which Bliss's and de Valois' social and professional circles coincided. Evans saw himself as the 'godfather' of this influential Society, with Haskell and Phillip (P.J.S.) Richardson, the editor of *Dancing Times*, as its original 'progenitors'.[31] De Valois and Rambert served on the Society's committee, alongside Karsavina, Lopokova, Maynard Keynes and other key figures in London's tightly knit ballet world. They included Lambert, who would soon conduct the premiere of de Valois and Bliss's *Narcissus and Echo*.[32] Bliss and his wife Trudy were among those who attended the splendid dinner held to mark the official launch of the Camargo Society on 16 February 1930.[33]

Rout (1927): the progress of a ballet – and a company (1927–32)

The progress of de Valois' danced version of *Rout* can be tracked through each of the principal spheres of her activities as a dancer, teacher, choreographer and director. From the outset, she had aligned her Academy with the repertory theatre movement, led by independently minded individuals whose views reflected her own ideological stance and creative theories. Alongside her partnership with Baylis's Vic and Wells theatres, she had embarked on similar alliances with Gray's Festival Theatre in Cambridge and William Butler Yeats's experimental Abbey Theatre in Dublin. During the 1920s, the Academy also performed at Barry Jackson's Royal Court Theatre on Sloane Square and Nigel Playfair's Lyric Theatre in Hammersmith. (Significantly, Bliss had established the Hammersmith Musical Society at the Lyric in 1919.[34]) Each of these like-minded venues gave de Valois and her students the opportunity to perform modern English ballets for unusually receptive audiences.

Bliss and de Valois' *Rout* usually featured in these programmes, and effectively became the earliest signature piece of the pioneering Academy. The ballet was originally performed at Gray's Festival Theatre on 31 January 1927 as part of a short programme of de Valois' choreography, entitled 'Dance Cameos'.[35] It opened with a revival of her 1925 piece, *The Arts of the Theatre*, and concluded with the premiere of *Rout*. A year later, *Rout* was performed at the Academy itself on 22 January 1928, during a private viewing of de Valois' choreography. One of her original students and Company members, Joy Newton, later wrote of her impressions of these monthly in-house performances, when they danced 'little numbers to Bach, Schubert, Stravinsky, Ravel, Poulenc and Debussy, all rather earnestly'.[36] She recalled the London debut of *Rout* as a thrilling occasion, since she was assigned to turn pages for the two pianists, who played on one piano: 'This was not a little alarming,' she wrote, 'the music being decidedly difficult + modern, … [and] the pianists being Bliss himself and Dr Malcolm Sargent!'[37] Another of de Valois' founding student dancers, Beatrice Appleyard, remembered Bliss playing for the rehearsals of *Rout*, which she had found 'enormously interesting and very exciting'.[38]

The next major revival of *Rout* was given during a series of three public matinée performances by the Academy at the Royal Court Theatre (26–30 November 1928). The programme was advertised as 'Ballets for the Repertory Theatre' and featured a mixed bill entirely made up of de Valois' choreography. *Rout* was also taken into the repertoire of the Abbey Theatre, Dublin (22 April 1929), where de Valois had helped to set up a School of Ballet in 1927.[39] For each of these revivals, the number of the cast was adapted according to the resources at hand; the same was true of the costumes.[40] Just as de Valois and her dancers travelled between a range of venues, so the repertoire of small-scale works she created moved with them, and were tailored to suit the circumstances of the moment – theatrical or otherwise. In January 1930 *The Era* reported on a lecture presented by Evans at the Faculty of Arts in London, on the subject of 'Music and the Ballet'. De Valois and her Academy students were on hand to illustrate his main points with 'illuminating demonstrations', until '[t]he evening finished with a choreographic rendering of Mr. Arthur Bliss's "Rout"', for which, the reporter added drily, 'the accompanist's task was no sinecure'.[41]

Rout undoubtedly presented its interpreters, musicians and dancers alike, with significant challenges. Bliss's *Rout for Soprano Voice and Orchestra* lasts a mere seven minutes, but '[w]ithin that short duration', writes Paul Spicer, 'lies the … contrast of musical ideas … different styles, moods and speeds all of which add up to a lively experience'.[42] According to Grace Lovat Fraser, the singer for whom *Rout* was originally composed, 'it bristled with difficulties and gave the singer the most wonderful opportunity for pure musicianship'.[43] De Valois' decision to tackle such a densely complex score may seem surprising given her relative lack of choreographic experience, although she had previously engaged with the shifting rhythms and melodies of Ravel's original piano version of *La Valse* when creating *The Arts of the Theatre* (1925). In line with her belief that artistic experimentation demanded disciplined application, she must have relished the challenge to her own musicality and craftsmanship.

The penultimate revival of *Rout* was at London's Apollo Theatre, on 25 and 26 January 1931, in a programme presented by the Camargo Society conducted by Lambert (soon to become the founding Music Director of the Vic-Wells Ballet). This saw a marked expansion of the piece, which used 'the original scoring of the music [for chamber orchestra] rather than the two piano reduction de Valois had previously used'.[44] For the first time, the cast included five male dancers, one of whom was the young choreographer Frederick Ashton, who 'apparently had trouble adapting to the emphatically rhythmic choreography', of which 'foot-stamping' was a part.[45] Another of the men was Hedley Briggs, an actor-dancer with whom de Valois had first worked at Gray's Festival Theatre. On this occasion, Briggs also performed the spoken 'prologue'.[46]

The final outing for *Rout* was at Sadler's Wells, on 30 January 1932. By that time de Valois was firmly established as a choreographer, with numerous minor ballets to her name, and at least two major works, *La Création du monde* and *Job* (both 1931). Her Company was no longer in its infancy; while it still faced huge uncertainties about its financial viability, as an artistic entity it had started to win round the sceptics.

Rout: the traces of de Valois' choreographic interpretation of Bliss's score

Accounts of de Valois' *Rout* differ in detail and response. The dance writer Mary Clarke recorded that the dancing began before the recitation of Toller's poem, as translated by Dukes;[47] Kathrine Sorley Walker suggested 'the movement began during the poem and continued as the music started'.[48] Either way, the spoken prologue was originally performed by Vivienne Bennett, and Rosalind Patrick later took over the part[49] – both were Academy students who went on to became successful dramatic actors. Neither Clarke nor Sorley Walker were old enough to have seen *Rout* in performance, although their descriptions of the piece carry authority, since both writers had interviewed members of the original cast, including de Valois herself. Each had also consulted contemporary reviews. Clarke echoed *Dancing Times* (February 1928) when she wrote that *Rout* was 'a dance built up of groupings … frequently of a contrapuntal nature, the revolt of modern youth against the conventions of the older generation'.[50]

Fig. 1.8: Rout (1927). For the premiere at the Festival Theatre, Cambridge, the student dancers wore their mauve Academy of Choreographic Art regulation tunics; their in-house nickname duly became 'the purple virgins'. Photo: Vaughan and Freeman (*Dancing Times*).

Sorley Walker wrote that de Valois' *Rout* incorporated 'expressionist movement in its use of the body to depict the sombre or exultant emotions of grief, oppression, defiance and rebellion'. 'It was a group work,' she added, 'building up its effects architecturally or geometrically.'[51]

Clarke also noted (perhaps with her tongue slightly in cheek) that '*Rout* was received with great solemnity and respect by everyone who saw it.'[52] This was in sharp contrast to the way in which Bliss's *Rout* had been received by the press and public in 1920. In his autobiography Bliss wrote that he greatly enjoyed an article in *The Times* headed 'A Musical Rout', which had characterised the piece as one of his 'whimsical excursions', and explained that the composer had called it a rout 'in the sense of a popular jollification'. The reviewer had then declared it was impossible to decide 'whether to describe it as chamber music or programme music, street music, or "Jazz"'. The article nevertheless conceded: '[*Rout*] is exceedingly clever, and proved quite captivating to an audience who belonged to the other kind of rout, the "fashionable evening assembly"'.[53] Only a minority of critics found de Valois' rather humourless treatment of Bliss's boisterous score wholly convincing.[54]

Julia Chatterton in *The Musical Standard* (7 July 1931) tended towards approval; she thought the music itself was 'like an unexpectedly big sea wave, which knocks us over and leaves us gasping for breath … I therefore found myself nearly always in accord with the choreography that most of the critics have spoken ill of.'[55] Cyril Beaumont, a dance writer and publisher, thought it was the best thing de Valois had done, and described it as 'a very clever orchestration of strong movements, based on those of fly-wheels and piston rods, synchronised with the music, the rhythm being emphasised by the beating of the dancers' feet'.[56] This obviously futuristic style of mechanical movement[57] left others feeling more alienated than excited. The theatre director Norman Marshall, a leading figure in Gray's Festival Theatre who later became a great admirer of de Valois' mature choreography, found *Rout* to be 'a harsh, angry, rather pretentious work in which the dancers seemed to have been deliberately and ruthlessly drained of individuality'.[58] Even so, audiences often reacted enthusiastically to Bliss and de Valois' *Rout*, one reviewer reporting that 'the audience applauded until it was tired'.[59]

Clarke's and Sorley Walker's retrospective descriptions of *Rout* appear more balanced than Haskell's, who was vehemently opposed to any ballet he perceived to be 'tainted' by the German Expressionism of Rudolf von Laban and Mary Wigman.[60] Photographs of *Rout* clearly suggest the intensity, dynamic use of gravity and severe angular positions that characterised this form of modern dance.[61] Haskell conceded that de Valois' work was 'modified by a classical ballet training' and her innate theatricality: 'Where a Wigman runs amok,' he opined, 'de Valois rationalises.'[62] At the time she opened her Academy in 1926, de Valois had explicitly 'rationalised' her intention of placing classical ballet's 'infinitely adaptable' technique at the service of modern creativity,[63] but Haskell could not yet see this manifested in her work.[64] He therefore assumed she had 'started out as a rebel against both classicism and its ultra-modern application', with the result, he thought, that not only did *Rout* have 'much sound and fury, signifying nothing', but also '[as] a teacher in those days she seemed to me to drill all the individuality out of her pupils'.[65] Marshall's similar criticism of de Valois' early ballets shows that accusations of dull academicism would continue to be levelled at de Valois and her dancers for several years to come.

Yet, de Valois gave her students weekly composition classes expressly intended to provide them with a freer, more creative, experience of music and dance, outside the strictures of their daily training in classical ballet. She devised choreographic exercises incorporating ideas taken from a number of modern dance movements then emerging across Europe, including the 'naturalistic' movement of

Fig. 1.9: *Rout* (1927). The movement here is strongly 'machine-like' and futuristic. The dancers, in their Academy tunics, are bare-legged, while Figs. 7 and 8 show them wearing tights and shoes. Photographer unknown (Courtesy of Dance Books).

the Hellenistic revival and the stylisation of various expressionist forms. She also drew upon Émile Jaques-Dalcroze's influential method, which was designed to allow a deeper engagement with music through physical movement.[66] Both Appleyard and Newton wrote that these had been their favourite lessons at the Academy.[67] Appleyard's description of *Rout* indicates that one of the reasons she so enjoyed performing the piece was because it used some of the choreographic material that de Valois introduced in her composition classes. *Rout* 'must have incorporated some of the "plastic" work, I think', she wrote. 'We were barefoot and in tunics' *(see Fig. 1.7)* shows that the piece was later danced in long dresses with plimsolls similar to those worn during choreography lessons) and 'we had to count like mad the whole time as the music was all in irregular phrases of 7, 9, 8, 5 hiccup and proceed … for a count of thirteen and so on'. Dancing the piece was 'a complete eye-opener' for Appleyard, who wrote that she had 'never before realised how exciting ballet could be'.[68]

Narcissus and Echo (1932): created for an English Prima Ballerina

De Valois' *Narcissus and Echo* was choreographed five years after she made *Rout*. Premiered at Sadler's Wells on 30 January 1932, *Narcissus* was a short-lived piece, made primarily as a vehicle for Alicia Markova.[69] She created the role of Echo, with Stanley Judson as Narcissus. Ursula Moreton and Marie Nielson were a pair of attendant Nymphs, who accompanied the voices of two female singers. The dancers were among de Valois' longest-standing colleagues: she had known Markova since she joined the Ballets Russes at the age of just fourteen. Judson had been a member of Anna Pavlova's Company and an Associate student of the Academy before becoming de Valois' regular partner at the Vic-Wells. Moreton had acted as de Valois' assistant from 1925/6, and would remain her most constant, versatile colleague for the next forty years. Nielson, an Associate student of the Academy, was a close friend of Lambert's, and had arranged his professional introduction to de Valois in 1928.[70]

Although *Narcissus* was never revived after its first season, it had occasioned the moment when Markova became a regular guest artist with the Vic-Wells. Hers was an exceptional talent, and she carried the mystique of having been Diaghilev's last great discovery before his death. Markova's box-office appeal proved to be of inestimable value to de Valois and the Vic-Wells Ballet, especially at a time when the arts received no public subsidies. With the support of the Camargo Society, Markova had already created the title role of Procris in de Valois' *Cephalus and Procris* (premiered in January 1931), which was set to Evans's arrangement of André Grétry's eighteenth-century music. De Valois had subsequently persuaded the Sadler's Wells board to fund Markova's appearance in her second Bliss piece. For the next three years, Markova was to occupy the crucial position of Prima Ballerina for the Vic-Wells Ballet.

Bliss's *Rhapsody* score must have appealed to de Valois both for its narrative potential and inherent lyricism. She could impose her own scenario on the work, since, as Spicer observes, 'the listener is left to create his own storyline as the singers have no words, singing simply "ah" to their long lyrical lines'.[71] Bliss himself characterised the eight-minute chamber piece as an 'essay in timbre', written for mezzo-soprano, tenor, flute, cor anglais, string quartet and double bass.[72] A fulsome review in *The Musical Standard*, written just after the concert premiere of *Rhapsody* in October 1919, clearly delighted Bliss who quoted it in his memoir fifty years later.[73] It praised the work for its emotional, beautiful, poetic and dreamlike qualities, adding that it had an 'entrancing spirituality' and 'a glamour akin to a Celtic legend'.[74] The sheer 'glamour' of the piece would have made it an ideal vehicle for the cool and elegant Markova. Ralph Vaughan Williams's assessment of Bliss's *Rhapsody* offers a further insight into why the score was so apt for Markova as Echo: he discerned in the work 'a rare and classical sense of beauty',[75] and Markova was then the exemplar of balletic classicism in England.

There are no known images of de Valois' *Narcissus*. Sorley Walker interviewed Markova, who remembered it as 'a very modern ballet', with a black-and-white set by the dancer and designer William Chappell that 'used three levels'.[76] Sorley Walker summarised her findings:

Fig. 1.10: Alicia Markova as the Sugar Plum Fairy, partnered by Stanley Judson, in the Vic-Wells' 1934 production of *Casse-Noisette*. Photographer unknown (Royal Ballet School Special Collections).

Fig. 1.11: De Valois's 1931 ballet, *La Création du monde* (1935 revival), with William Chappell and Ursula Moreton as The Man and The Woman (standing centre). Note the use of different stage levels created by the rostrum and the dancers' layered positions. Photo: J.W. Debenham (Royal Ballet School Special Collections).

The action opened with Echo on the highest level with her attendant maidens below her and Narcisse [sic] lying on stage gazing into a pool created – and this was at the time unusual – by lighting effects. Echo's dancing was barefoot and largely in profile, and in retrospect Markova feels that the choreography had links with Central European Dance. De Valois was obviously employing the style she had already exercised in *Rout*, in *La Création du monde* and in parts of *Job*.[77]

In her memoirs, Markova expanded upon this description, explaining that the levels of staging were 'designed to separate Narcissus from Echo': 'As Echo,' she continued, 'I appeared barefoot in slightly Wigman-esque dances, on the top of the shelf-like setting, with two nymphs half-way below me, and Narcissus obsessed with his reflection in a pool of light on stage level.'[78] A similar account by the dancer Anton Dolin confirms that the movement was performed 'barefoot on different levels', and adds the detail that 'four figures dressed in black and white were posed decoratively on a flight of steps'.[79]

These accounts are surprising, since Bliss's 'poetic' *Rhapsody* score might have suggested a more conventionally balletic choreographic response compared to that of *Rout*. The fact that de Valois created parallel and barefoot movement (rather than turned-out and *en pointe*) for her famously 'classical' Ballerina appears to be counter-intuitive; and yet Markova associated the style of *Narcissus* with European Expressionism. In her memoir, Markova added that Echo's movement was like that deployed by Vaslav Nijinsky in his vision of archaic Greece, *L'Après-midi d'un faune* (1912).[80] The key element she identified – that of moving in profile – similarly points to the influence of the 'antique' style of Mikhail Fokine's Grecian ballets, which borrowed from 'Duncan's pseudo-Greek stylizations'.[81] *(see Fig. 1.12)* De Valois' *Création* and *Job* (both 1931) were also 'barefoot ballets'; as in those works, it seems she had fused Fokine's Hellenic lyricism with angular, expressionistic gesture for her *Narcissus* ballet.

De Valois' much-admired stagings of classical Greek dramas with Terence Gray in Cambridge had shown her how to make use of different levels of the stage, and the lighting techniques pioneered at the Festival Theatre by Gray and his lighting designer, Harold Ridge.[82] For *Création* and *Job*, she had deployed various raised platforms onstage, and introduced scenic effects through new ways of harnessing light. She evidently used these same devices in the staging of *Narcissus*, seen in the layered delineation of the stage space and the pool of light in which Judson's Narcissus gazed at his own reflection. One review of *Narcissus* described 'choreography of stylized restlessness', which 'gave us the queer unsubstantiality of a world of reflected images and false voices'.[83] Growing experience had given her the confidence to explore this antique fable – and Bliss's score – with a bold, but subtle, theatricality.

Conclusion

It seems extraordinary that Bliss's influential work with de Valois, and his equally significant collaborations with Robert Helpmann during the 1940s, is largely absent from his autobiography. Bliss made scant reference either to de Valois and Helpmann, or to the ballets he had made with them. With characteristic courtesy, he apologised in his foreword for omitting to mention every one of his colleagues, saying he had confined his memoir to those who had 'directly or indirectly shaped' his career.[84] While Bliss may not have felt his ballet scores had affected the course of his professional trajectory, they had unquestionably imprinted a sense of heightened theatrical drama within a distinctly British genre of narrative ballet. The ballets created, first by Bliss and de Valois, then by Bliss and Helpmann, permeated the theatrical landscape of the 1930s and 1940s. They laid strong foundations for a bold storytelling tradition in British ballet that has continued through the works of Frederick Ashton, John Cranko, Kenneth MacMillan, Christopher Bruce, David Bintley, Matthew Bourne, Christopher Wheeldon, Cathy Marston and a host of other dance-makers.

Unlike Bliss's later, specially commissioned, ballet scores, *Rout* was not 'conditioned from the first moment of its creation to be a partner of the dance', yet it undoubtedly possessed the same qualities that the musicologist Antony Hopkins identified as the distinguishing features of Bliss's *Checkmate* (1937) and *Adam Zero* (1946), namely, 'strong rhythm, vivid orchestration, dramatic emphasis and a sense of the theatrical'.[85] In a similar way, his *Rhapsody / Narcissus* score naturally lent itself to ballet. Hopkins's views echoed those made earlier by Evans, when he gave his own assessment of Bliss's talent for writing ballet music that enhanced the theatrical impact of the form. Evans cited Bliss's score for *Miracle in the Gorbals* (1944) as an excellent example of 'straightforward ballet music', explaining succinctly that what he meant by this was 'robust when the stage demands it, sensitive in moments of subtlety, and above all, "good theatre"'.[86]

Through his deep interest in dance as theatre, and his lifelong engagement with ballet as a collaborative art form, Bliss acquired an unusual 'practical knowledge of the ballet' (to borrow the term used by de Valois in her posthumous 'Appreciation' of Evans[87]). As a consequence, he was able to harness his considerable talents as a 'daring but accessible innovator',[88] and rose to meet the very specific demands of writing music for narrative ballet. With the towering exception of Lambert, no other British composer-conductor of his generation was able to match that knowledge and ability. And none would leave such a wealth of magnificent ballet scores.

Fig. 1.12: Ursula Moreton (kneeling on right) as a Nymph in Ninette de Valois' 'Grecian' ballet, *The Picnic* (1929), also called *The Satyr* (February 1930) or *The Faun* (December 1930). The asymmetrical costumes by Hedley Briggs suggest what William Chappell's designs for de Valois' *Narcissus and Echo* (1932) may have looked like. Photographer unknown (Royal Ballet School Special Collections).

2.
Arthur Bliss and the Contribution Made by Designers in the Creation of his Ballets

JANE PRITCHARD

As a composer, Arthur Bliss was responsible for three key ballets created in the early years of British ballet. More widely, he was involved in a scene in which composers, artists and choreographers all made contributions to imaginative productions in a style that echoed that established by Sergei Diaghilev's Ballets Russes (1909–29).[1] Bliss was brought into the theatre scene immediately after the 1914–18 war and his contribution recurred over the next four decades. His involvement in dance was sporadic rather than continuous. He fulfilled commissions and took an active part in the creation of the works. The three major ballets for which he composed original scores were all strikingly designed, making a strong visual impact. Indeed, with all three, the librettist, choreographer, designer and composer individually and together contributed to the excitement and quality of the performed works. It may be added that while each has its own narrative, they are all symbolic of wider concerns of their time.

Before looking at the designs for the three major works, it is necessary to register that the ballet scene in Britain changed rapidly in the first three decades of the twentieth century. From formulaic, large-scale, spectacular ballets danced to easily accessible tunes presented in music halls of the first decade, the focus changed to the more imaginative and varied collaborations of the Ballets Russes of the 1910s and 1920s. Nevertheless, ballet continued to play a role in leading variety theatres, now presented by smaller groups of dancers, many of whom were affiliated with the Ballets Russes, and British artists struggled to find their own 'voice', creating a new sense of a national ballet.

Bliss, who like many artists at this time admired performances by Diaghilev's Company (and in particular Igor Stravinsky's music), became involved with these activities. It was through his collaborations with Nigel Playfair who revitalised the Lyric Theatre, Hammersmith, the innovative artist, illustrator and designer for the stage Claud Lovat Fraser (1890–1921) and his wife Grace (1889–1977), an opera singer and costumier, and ballerina Tamara Karsavina that he had opportunities for his first staged works.

In 1919 Bliss was invited to write and arrange the score for Playfair's production of William Shakespeare's *As You Like It*, first presented at the Shakespeare Festival, Stratford-upon-Avon, and then at the Lyric, Hammersmith. Bliss's score was variously said to be based on Thomas Arne's setting of the songs and other eighteenth-century music or on music by William Byrd, Robert Johnson and Giles Farnaby.[2] The music was arranged for an all-female string quartet led by Fanny Wadsworth, wife of the painter Edward Wadsworth, a friend of Bliss. The production of *As You Like It* attracted considerable attention, particularly in respect of the brightly coloured, stylised designs by Fraser. Haldane Macfall in *The Book of Claud Lovat Fraser* noted that Fraser had 'a consummate sense of theatre'.³ He could be regarded as Britain's answer to the Ballets Russes' Léon Bakst. His striking use of colour harmonies to express drama and emotion equalled that of the best designers for the stage and, like Bakst, he took a keen interest in all aspects of stage art. His designs evoked the atmosphere required rather than slavishly putting a 'realist' world on stage. This horrified the Stratford audience. Where was their traditional Forest of Arden complete with a dead deer killed at Hampton Lucy that had featured in the play for so many years? The *Morning Post* complained that the costumes were 'so daring and colouring so extravagant in conception that they seemed, to conservative minds at any rate, all out of key with Shakespeare'. Other critics described the production as futuristic but, as his wife Grace noted in her autobiography, 'the odd thing was that so far were the dresses from being futuristic that they were the most realistic that Fraser ever attempted. The lines and the colours were all carefully copied from contemporary missals, contemporary that is with the supposed date of the action of the play.'⁴

As You Like It was much more enthusiastically received at Hammersmith. The critic at the *Spectator* considered Fraser's designs as 'nearer perfection than any stage production that I have ever seen. Probably Mr. Granville-Barker's production of *Twelfth Night* and the Russian Ballet's *Good-Humoured Ladies* ought to be excepted, but I think that many people will rank Mr. Playfair's production quite as high, and some will prefer it.'⁵

Fraser was assisted in producing the costumes by his wife Grace, who became a skilled costumier, even making many of the costumes for the hunt in scene 3 of Diaghilev's *The Sleeping Princess* (1921). More importantly for Bliss, she was a trained opera singer and her friendship with Bliss, formed during *As You Like It*, renewed her career. As she wrote, his music provided her with 'a great incentive and had exciting possibilities. I greatly admired his work and his experiments with unusual ways of using the voice.'⁶

Fraser was with Bliss in his initiative to form the Hammersmith Musical Society and appeared in Giovanni Pergolesi's *La Serva Padrona* (1733). It was also for Fraser that Bliss created the experimental score *Rout* (1920), initially performed in Baroness Catherine d'Erlanger's ballroom. *Rout* was composed to exploit Bliss's 'theories about the use of the voice purely as an instrument without any literary connotations. There were to be no words, instead only meaningless syllables chosen for their colour values and percussive or soft impact.'⁷ It was originally scored for voice, flute, bassoon, bass, harp and glockenspiel.⁸

Rout was selected as one of the twenty-five symphonic interludes presented by Diaghilev's Ballets Russes during their summer season at the Prince's Theatre in 1921. Here, the vocals were sung by Zoia Rosovska (Rozowska) who played a significant role with the Ballets Russes, singing for *Pulcinella* (1920) and the *Chanson Polovtsiennes* (sometimes used to introduce the Polovtsian dances from *Prince Igor* (1890)), and performing as Leonora in *Le Astuzie Femminili* (1920) and the Mother in *Mavra* (1922). As the evening programme for 4 July 1921 notes, *Rout* had been 'specially orchestrated for full orchestra by the composer', further explaining that '*Rout* is used in the old English sense of revelry'. Bliss 'had wanted to evoke the sound of a carnival overheard at a distance' and gave a soprano 'a medley of made-up words to sing'.⁹ *Rout* is said to show influences from Stravinsky's *Petrushka* (1911), which was performed when *Rout* was sung again on 18 July.

Bliss's first venture into dance came with his orchestration of Christian Sinding's *Fire Dance* (1921). This was arranged as a solo for Laurent Novikoff in a divertissement presented by Karsavina at the London Coliseum for which all the newly created dances were designed by Fraser.¹⁰ This was Fraser's second season for Karsavina and, sadly, he died just as he was completing the designs. The divertissement went ahead as a memorial. It was a series of separate ballet-miniatures that were performed with a setting described in the *Observer* as 'luminous blue curtains, with one straight pillar of a dark shade in the centre, a thing of extraordinary simplicity, yet majesty'.¹¹ Against this, the bright colours of the costumes sung. That for Novikoff in *Fire Dance* was described in the *Sunday Times* as 'a miracle of expressiveness both in its colour and pattern. We can no doubt trace the influence of Gordon Craig in the effective headpiece with its flowing ribbons, but the jagged drapery streaming from the right sleeve is a stroke of original genius, which only needs a little movement to be transfigured into sparks flying upwards.'[12] In many respects these early 1919–21 arrangements and compositions and the links to his collaborators lay the foundation for Bliss's music for ballets.[13]

The role of Russian ballerina Karsavina in the early development of British ballet should be acknowledged. Through her marriage to Henry Bruce she had acquired British citizenship, and she was one of several artists determined that British dancers, designers and composers should be recognised and given opportunities for creativity. After Karsavina left Russia in 1918 she was welcomed back to the Ballets Russes, but it is important to note that she was never a full-time member of the Company. Pre-war, she combined her career at the Imperial Ballet with dancing for Diaghilev; after the Revolution, she balanced a freelance career and motherhood with guesting for the Ballets Russes. In between two seasons in Paris for which Karsavina created the roles of the Nightingale in *Le Chant du Rossignol* (1921) and Pimpinella in *Pulcinella* (1920), both choreographed by Léonide Massine to music by Stravinsky and designed by Henri Matisse and Pablo Picasso respectively, she performed at the London Coliseum in J.M. Barrie's play *The Truth about the Russian Dancers* (1920). For this she devised the dances for herself and her corps de ballet, while Arnold Bax wrote the music and Paul Nash undertook the designs.

Although Karsavina did sometimes turn to Russian designers (Alexandre Benois and Konstantin Somov, for example), she was determined to build up a team of British composers and designers with whom to collaborate. It is perhaps surprising that she did not use Bliss more, but his two years in the USA (1923–5) put him out of her reach for a while. It must have been shortly before Bliss set out for America that he had dinner with the ballerina and Grace Lovat Fraser at which he first came up with the idea for a ballet based on chess, a preliminary version of which, with the pitiless Black Queen as the villain of the game, was worked out. This would eventually become *Checkmate*, choreographed by Ninette de Valois for which Bliss presented her with the synopsis and score.

Checkmate was created in 1937 when the Vic-Wells Ballet needed a new ballet with which to impress audiences on its first visit to Paris, but de Valois knew Bliss and his music having choreographed two ballets to his scores not originally written for dance: *Rout* (score 1920) and *Rhapsody for Strings and 2 Voices* (1919) for *Narcissus and Echo* (1932). *Rout* (1927) appears to have gone through several versions. It was danced at the Festival Theatre, Cambridge, and subsequently presented at de Valois' own Academy of Choreographic Art, the Royal Court Theatre, London, and the Abbey Theatre, Dublin, before it was rearranged for the Camargo Society and the Vic-Wells Ballet. De Valois' *Rout* used not only Bliss's score but also began with Ashley Dukes's translation of a poem by Ernst Toller concerning the resurgent youth movement of Central Europe and was partly danced in silence. At this time Bliss was on the Camargo's advisory panel for music. Was it possible that in creating this ballet to an existing score de Valois was hoping Bliss might compose a new ballet for the Society?

Narcissus and Echo was the short-lived ballet danced by the Vic-Wells to Bliss's *Rhapsody for Strings and 2 Voices* and first presented on 3 January 1932. As with all of Bliss's early ballets, this may be seen as an experimental work. Choreographed by de Valois, it introduced Alicia Markova as ballerina to the Vic-Wells Ballet. Designer William Chappell created a black-and-white structure on three levels with Echo (Markova) dancing in bare feet on the top, while Narcissus (Stanley Judson) below gazed into a pool created by light. The cast was completed by Ursula Moreton and Marie Neilson as Nymphs, plus the two vocalists.[14]

As Antony Hopkins noted, Bliss had a 'flair for highly-coloured and dramatic music',[15] which worked well for choreography by de Valois and Robert Helpmann. *Miracle in the Gorbals* (1944) and *Adam Zero* (1946) with their more elaborate scenarios by theatre director Michael Benthall told more precise narratives, while *Checkmate* had the simpler premise of a game of chess. Nevertheless, *Checkmate* incorporated clear echoes of the 1930s world of political tensions. Its abstract set design was by American-born Edward McKnight Kauffer (1890–1954). He was widely known for his posters, an art form that needed to instantly capture viewers'

Fig. 2.1: Frederick Ashton in his costume as the player who symbolises Death, Vic-Wells Ballet, 1937. Photo: Gordon Anthony © Victoria and Albert Museum, London (Victoria and Albert Museum).

Fig. 2.2: Edward McKnight Kauffer's costume design for Love, for the revival of *Checkmate* in 1947. (Bliss Archive, Cambridge University Library).

attention, while Edward Burra (1905–76) and Roger Furse (1903–72), the designers of *Miracle in the Gorbals* and *Adam Zero* respectively, had far more experience of theatre. Burra had been involved with twentieth-century British ballet from its 1920s beginnings, having befriended William Chappell (dancer, designer and producer) when they both studied at the Chelsea College of Art. He was fascinated by low life and his biographer Jane Stevenson suggests that Helpmann invited Burra to design *Miracle* for his 'unique ability to produce intensely dramatic images of people in cheap clothes'.[16] Furse, who had designed de Valois' light-hearted ballet *The Prospect Before Us* (1940), was associated with drama. He designed for the Old Vic Company and was admired for his designs for Thornton Wilder's *The Skin of our Teeth* (1942). He came from the world of drama inhabited by Benthall and Helpmann and increasingly the film world that Bliss knew.

Checkmate needed to convey pieces of a chess set in motion, and the floor of the production was black and white squares evoking a chessboard but not requiring dancers to move on the squares. The ballet opened with a drop curtain behind the two players Love and Death (initially both performed by men). It showed two disembodied grey-and-white arms and hands apparently floating in a blue sky with a hint of clouds and a star. Six black dots (three on each arm) were linked by a series of black lines, giving the whole a sense of a matrix of destiny or fate. Several versions of this design exist, and it was adapted for the cover of the printed score. The curtain and Bliss's Prologue – The Players, as much as the unmasking of Love and Death as they begin their game, establish the mood for the work with its sense of fate. McKnight Kauffer, like de Valois,[17] recognised that the theme of the narrative and score led to the symbolic drama focusing on 'the part played by Fate in Man's life'.[18] The curtain and players disappeared, and the stage opened up. The backcloth had a brightly coloured abstract design of triangles and abstract shapes in grey, red, blue, black and white on a ground shaded yellow to green on which radiating lines appeared, similar to a Barbara Hepworth stringed sculpture.[19] It was securely a 1930s abstract, anchoring the ballet in the era of its creation while giving it a timeless atmosphere. As can be seen in the photographs by Gordon Anthony of his sister's 1937 ballet, the costumes were originally far more elaborate than the stylised and uniform versions worn today.[20] The original sets and costumes were among the material lost in the Netherlands as the Sadler's Wells Ballet fled from the advancing war in 1940. *Checkmate* was not seen again until it was redesigned for performance at the Royal Opera House in 1947. The streamlined and simplified costumes gave them a more unified look. The changes were both aesthetic and practical (rationing was in force) and one suspects the dancers were relieved that the headpieces became less cumbersome.

De Valois' interest in Bliss's music never waned and she continued to champion him. In 1958 she planned to create a version of his *The Lady of Shalott* as her choreographic swansong. This would have featured ballerina Svetlana Beriosova imprisoned in a glass tower. It was de Valois who encouraged Kenneth MacMillan to use Bliss's Music for Strings for his non-narrative *Diversions* superbly designed by Philip Prowse for The Royal Ballet in 1961.[21]

Burra's experience as a designer was an advantage for the challenge of conveying the tenements of the Gorbals and the Glasgow

Fig. 2.3: The Inhabitants of the Gorbals costumed in everyday clothes against a bleak inner-city setting. Edward Burra's design was typical of dramatic productions in the 1940s. Photo: Edward Mandinian © Victoria and Albert Museum, London (Victoria and Albert Museum).

dockyards that featured in *Miracle in the Gorbals*. He visited the locations, resulting in a masterpiece of a front cloth and an elaborately constructed set. The powerful front cloth 'of the stature of those for *Parade* and *Le Train bleu*'[22] showed the hull of a ship in dry dock surrounded by cranes, which represented the shipbuilding industry of Clydeside.[23] The main set presented the exterior of a twentieth-century slum, which had to convey both a specific place and be sufficiently stylised to suggest the location for miracles. Chimney stacks appeared in the distance and above the Shamrock Bar and Mac's Fish Shop there were functional balconies with open landings on the stairs.[24] As Richard Buckle noted, 'There is a frightening beauty in the blank blackened walls of the huge warehouses and in perspectives of the lighted windows of factories and tenements in dark winter.'[25] Characters needed to enter and exit various dwellings and appear on staircases, and the use of light to focus attention on relationships was clearly important. As with all Bliss's scores for dance, it was divided into short numbers that enhanced the characters and the action.

While Burra created designs for the costumes, given wartime shortages these were often used as a guide and many were adapted from everyday clothes

Fig. 2.4: The Fates (left to right): Palma Nye as the Dresser, Jean Bedells as the Designer and Julia Farron as the Wardrobe Mistress, with David Paltenghi as the Stage Director and Robert Helpmann as Adam as he approaches the winter of his life – all costumed in everyday wear and ballet rehearsal outfits. Photo: Edward Mandinian © Victoria and Albert Museum, London (Victoria and Albert Museum).

that could be found. With the cast wearing 'clothes' and a built set,[26] *Miracle* was a forward-looking work. It was also typical of the 1940s productions that were often bleaker and more dramatic than earlier ones, although a similar but less powerful and shorter slice of urban life had been seen in the work of Kurt Jooss, such as *Big City* (1932).

Adam Zero was 'an allegory of the cycle of a man's life',[27] presented through the creation of a ballet, for which the critic of the *Daily Telegraph* maintained the 'music of Bliss fits every moment perfectly and gives speed, warmth and unity to the action'. The elaborate scenario that Benthall developed with Helpmann's input encouraged Bliss to compose his rich, theatrical score with many changes of mood and characterisation, and this led to the variety in costuming as well as styles of movement and dance. The passing of time was noted in several ways. Bliss's score included details that suggested changes of season. Cyril Beaumont commented that as the Understudies came into focus (with the idea of roles being passed down a generation), 'The music suggests the rustling of falling leaves, followed by a kind of chilling of the air, as though heralding the approach of winter.'[28] Similarly, the production evolves, with scenes and costumes moving on from those evoking Edwardian musical comedies, to dancing to jazz in 1920s dress. Lighting, too, was used to convey the passing of time and the whole work was cyclical, with the stage being reset with ballet barres as at the opening, and the Choreographer about to repeat the scene of the birth of the next Adam.[29]

Short-lived, *Adam Zero* received only nineteen performances. It was ambitious and, as it was the first ballet created by Sadler's Wells Ballet for the Royal Opera House, Furse was required to celebrate the resources of what was then regarded as a large and well-equipped stage. Mary Clarke suggested that the individual who 'had most fun' with the creation of this ballet was the theatre's stage manager Henry Robson, because he had the opportunity to display Covent Garden's stage equipment 'and was responsible for the breath-taking moment when the cyclorama began to move'.[30] Michael Ayrton, too, praised the way Furse handled 'the various traps, the hydraulic bridges and the vast cyclorama',[31] and felt that while his use of the empty stage was impressive, the more traditional elements of the painted set, which was built up, quickly rearranged and removed, lacked the imagination of 1920s and 1930s expressionist sets.

Once again, many of the costumes for the theatre scenes gave the impression of ordinary clothes: everyday wear and ballet rehearsal outfits. The Fates were the Designer in blouse and skirt, the Wardrobe Mistress in chic black dress, the Dresser in overall and headscarf, and the Stage Director in grey lounge suit. In addition, the women in the ballet within *Adam Zero* wore traditional tutus. Adam himself went through a series of changes, many of which were onstage, including adding make-up and swapping wigs as he aged. Finally, there were symbolic elements, not least when the leading woman, now in the guise of the Destroyer, circled the vast empty stage in a scarlet cloak. She enfolded the ageing Adam centre stage, who then vanished – a distinctly Tchelitchevian effect.[32]

PART ONE

Checkmate

1937

3.
Deathly Moves: *Checkmate* – A Ballet in One Scene with a Prologue

ANDREW BURN

As an example of the finest collaboration, *Checkmate* must take high rank among ballets. Arthur Bliss's music, Ninette de Valois' choreography, and McKnight Kauffer's dresses and settings make up a superb whole, telling the story of this game of chess with extraordinary dramatic tension … and conveying an impression of the rich colour and tragic pageantry of a medieval tourney.[1]

This comment from *The Bystander* magazine of October 1937 is as true now, nearly ninety years later, as it was when these talents combined to create a masterpiece of British dance that has remained in the repertory to this day. Its subject, the game of chess as an analogy for conflict between warring powers, also chimed uncannily with the mood of the late 1930s, as the storm clouds of war seemed to be billowing ever nearer. In the struggle between the adversaries, audiences found parallels with the contemporary European situation.

Checkmate had its origins in two of Bliss's favourite enthusiasms: chess and ballet. The former dated back to his childhood, while the latter was fostered by performances by Sergei Diaghilev's Ballets Russes in the years immediately before the First World War. In Bliss's autobiography, *As I Remember*, he recounted that 'I had often thought … when I first saw the splendour of the Diaghilev's ballets, how glorious it would be to have one's own music created anew in the dance'.[2]

It took almost a quarter of a century before Bliss's hopes were fully realised, which is perhaps surprising given that his music has an overtly dramatic character. As he commented:

I have always found it easier to write 'dramatic' music than 'pure' music. I like the stimulus of words, or a theatrical setting, a colourful occasion or the collaboration of a great player. There is only a little of the spider about me, spinning his own web from his inner being. I am more of a magpie type. I need what Henry James termed a 'trouvaille' or a 'donnée'.[3]

During the 1920s and 1930s Bliss's music was heard in dance contexts. In 1927 de Valois choreographed his *Rout*, originally for soprano and chamber ensemble (1920), in a new version that he arranged for piano duet, and in 1932 her ballet *Narcissus and Echo* was danced to his *Rhapsody* of 1919.[4] At Diaghilev's request, in 1921 Bliss had scored *Rout* for an orchestra as an interlude in the Ballets Russes performances, and the same year he orchestrated Christian Sinding's *Fire Dance* for a programme at the London Coliseum presented by the ballerina Tamara Karsavina.[5]

Mention should also be made of *Mêlée Fantasque* (1921), Bliss's first orchestral work to be played in

Fig. 3.1: Ninette de Valois in 1937. Photo: Gordon Anthony (her brother) © Victoria and Albert Museum, London (Royal Ballet School Special Collections).

public, which he conducted at the 1921 Promenade Concerts. It was dedicated 'to the memory of Claud Lovat Fraser, a great and loveable artist', with whom Bliss had collaborated on productions of William Shakespeare's *As You Like It* and *The Tempest*. As Bliss acknowledged in his programme note, he viewed *Mêlée Fantasque* as his first ballet score, in which he aimed 'to convey the rhythmic verve and Bakst-like colour of Lovat Fraser's paintings'. These were 'evoked in colourful episodes', contrasted by 'elegiac passages which hint at the loss of this gifted friend'.[6] As far as is known, no choreographer has created dance to this work.

Karsavina was the most famous of Diaghilev's ballerinas; indeed, Bliss had seen her dance the role of Thamar, with choreography by Mikhail Fokine to Mily Balakirev's eponymous symphonic poem, in the first performance he attended of the Ballets Russes during their 1913 season at the Theatre Royal Drury Lane. As Bliss explained in an article, 'Death on Squares', published in *Great Thoughts* in January 1938, it was while dining at her home around 1923 that the genesis of *Checkmate* occurred. The conversation turned to subjects suitable for ballet; games were mentioned, and 'the idea of the pitiless queen in chess leapt from someone's brain'. Bliss proposed that she would be the 'chief personality … the most powerful and ruthless piece on the board'. Ideas for further characters from this game with its 'fierce and barbaric associations' were teased out. Lovat Fraser's widow, Grace, suggested that the King could be cast as 'an enfeebled old man powerless to protect himself', and again it was Bliss who had the idea of one of the enemy knights being a 'worthy opponent of the Queen. So with these three chief personalities – the ferocious Queen, the helpless King, and the enigmatic fighter, the Knight, we began to construct a scenario.'[7]

The concept, however, lay dormant for some fifteen years until Bliss was asked to collaborate on a new ballet for the occasion of the first visit of the Vic-Wells Company to Paris in 1937. He 'thought immediately of my long-cherished subject of chess'.[8] His proposal was agreed and Bliss set about sketching a scenario. In this he benefited from the expert advice of the theatre director William Bridges-Adams, whom he described as 'a highly imaginative, and at the same time eminently practical, man of the theatre'.[9] During 1936 and 1937, while composing *Checkmate*, Bliss became totally absorbed in the subject of chess and spent hours in the Reading Room of the British Museum studying its history. He was guided, too, by one 'pregnant utterance' of Bridges-Adams: 'This must not … be so much of a divertissement on chess, as the game itself. To make an audience grasp that, you must start from reality and *then* venture into fantasy.'[10] Consequently, Bliss decided 'that early in the ballet the pieces appear one after the other on the gigantic board, and at one precise moment line up in the exact position for starting the game'.[11]

Both de Valois and Edward McKnight Kauffer confessed to knowing nothing about chess. To help them, Bliss 'held sessions in my Hampstead home, during which I moved the chess pieces about on a big chess board and demonstrated their characteristic moves, the Knight's jump, the Bishop's diagonals, the Queen's mobility and the King's tottering shuffle, etc'.[12] As he played the music, he recalled de Valois sitting 'as if turned to stone, a frozen image of concentration'.[13] Bliss also mentions that:

Fig. 3.2: Arthur Bliss, Ninette de Valois and Edward McKnight Kauffer in discussion over a chessboard at Bliss's Hampstead home. Photographer unknown (Royal Ballet and Opera/ArenaPAL).

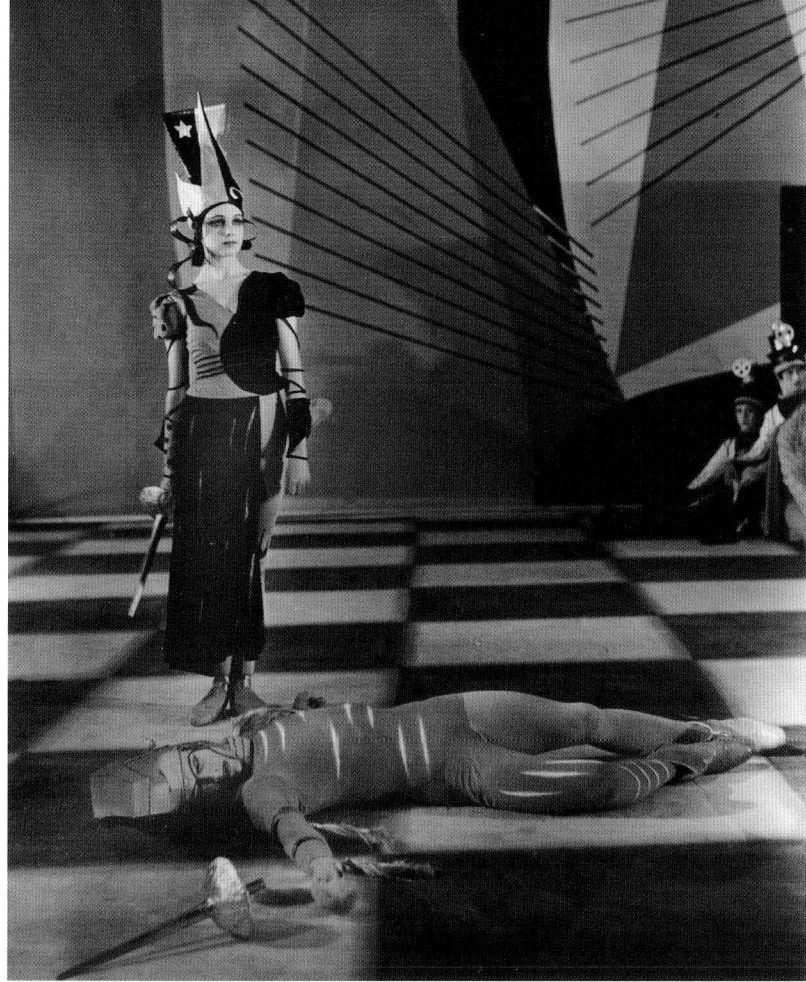

Fig. 3.3: The Red Knight slain. Harold Turner as the Red Knight and June Brae as the Black Queen. Photo: Gordon Anthony © Victoria and Albert Museum, London (Bliss Archive, Cambridge University Library).

Fig. 3.4: June Brae as the Black Queen and Claude Newman and Paul Reyloff as the Red Bishops, 1937. Photographer unknown (Performing Arts Images/ArenaPAL).

Champs-Elysées, was a magnificent state occasion. In *Record Review* magazine of June 1960, Bliss remembered: 'The Théâtre des Champs-Elysées was in gala array. Members of the Garde Républicaine in their uniforms lined the staircases; bouquets decorated the seats of the Diplomatic Corps and French officials; the audience was brilliant and glittering.'[15]

Backstage, however, disaster loomed due to a sudden strike of scene shifters and all was chaos. Nevertheless, as Bliss explained:

> This is where the experience and panache of Bridges-Adams ... shone brightly. Ordering food and wine to be brought backstage, he addressed the scene shifters in fluent Stratford-atte-Bowe French, enlarging on the glories of the French dramatic tradition, and on this unique entente between them and a famous British Company. Mellowed by wine, and astonished at his oration the scene shifters leapt to their feet, the stage was set just in time, and the curtain went up punctually on the first ballet of the evening, *Les Patineurs*.[16]

There were long discussions about the nature of the two players in the game. At first I wanted them shown as huge shadows over the board, but it was eventually decided to have them in the flesh as actors to open the drama. They could be costumed to depict Night or Day, or Alpha and Omega, or Black or White or any other obvious contrast. Finally, we chose Love and Death, and here again my first idea was that, though Death wins the game, Love should be seen setting up another row of pieces, demonstrating that Death's win is no final one.[14]

Bliss dedicated the score of *Checkmate* to the composer and teacher Reginald Owen Morris, an enthusiastic player of chess whom Bliss frequently challenged. During the weeks before the premiere the new work aroused considerable interest in the press, with photographs of the collaborators staring engrossed at a chessboard, as well as of the dancers in their striking costumes taken at outside locations. The premiere on 15 June 1937, at the Théâtre des

THEATRE DES CHAMPS-ELYSEES

SAISON THEATRALE
INTERNATIONALE

Représentations Officielles Anglaises
LE VIC-WELLS BALLET
du Théâtre Sadler's Wells de Londres
Avec l'Orchestre des Concerts LAMOUREUX
sous la Direction de CONSTANT LAMBERT

MARDI LE 15 JUIN 1937

ECHEC ET MAT

(Première Représentation)

Ballet en Une Scène et un Prologue

Musique d'ARTHUR BLISS
Costumes et décors de E. McKNIGHT KAUFFER
Ornements de tête par DORIA PASTON
Tous les costumes ont été exécutés dans les ateliers VIC-WELLS
Chorégraphie de NINETTE DE VALOIS

Les deux joueurs d'échecs	FREDERICK ASHTON, ALAN CARTER
Les Pions rouges	JILL GREGORY, MOLLY BROWN, LINDA SHERIDAN, LAUREL MARTYN, ELISABETH KENNEDY, JOAN LEAMAN, WENDA HORSBURGH, JOYCE FARRON
Premier Cavalier rouge	HAROLD TURNER
Second Cavalier rouge	WILLIAM CHAPPELL
Les Cavaliers noirs	RICHARD ELLIS, MICHAEL SOMES
La Reine noire	JUNE BRAE
Le Roi rouge	ROBERT HELPMANN
La Reine rouge	PAMELA MAY
Les Tours rouges	LESLIE EDWARDS, JOHN NICHOLSON
Les Evêques rouges	CLAUDE NEWMAN, PAUL REYLOFF
Les Pions noirs	MARGOT FONTEYN, MARY HONER, ELIZABETH MILLER, PAMELA MAY, JOY NEWTON, ANNE SPICER
Les Tours noires	LESLIE EDWARDS, JOHN NICHOLSON

Fig. 3.5: Facsimile of the programme for the premiere of *Checkmate* in Paris, reproduced in the piano score (Courtesy of Helen Kotz, Private Collection).

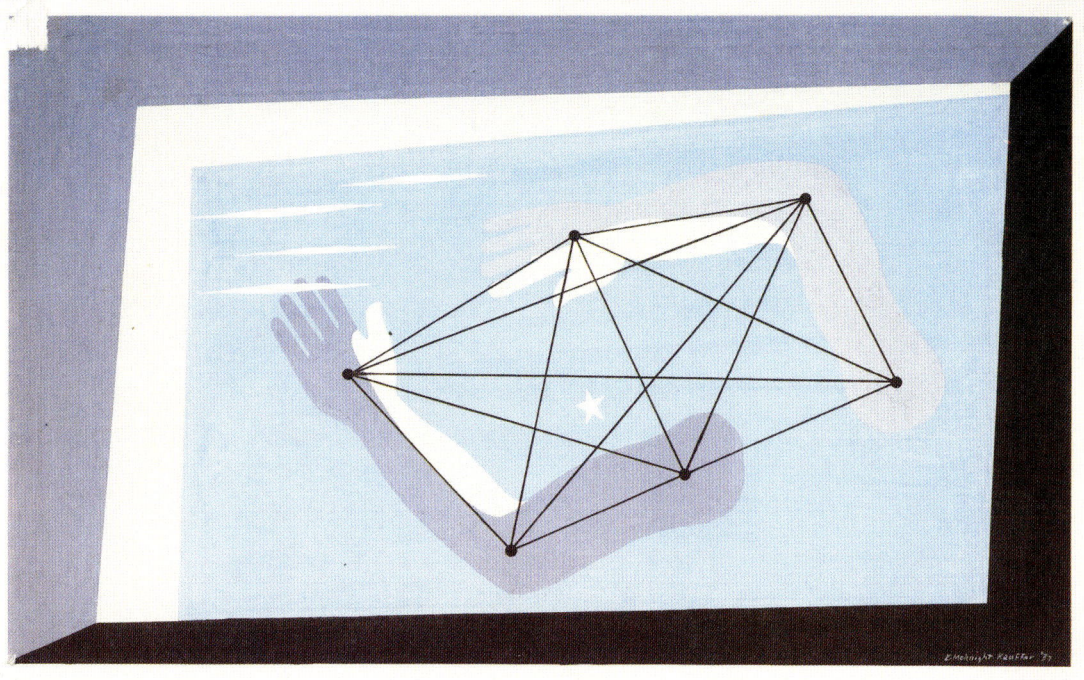

Fig. 3.6: Prologue – The Players: Love and Death are revealed in front of the drop curtain. A postcard of the design by Edward McKnight Kauffer (Royal Ballet School Special Collections).

Checkmate was performed that night by a cast of now legendary dancers, including Frederick Ashton (Death), June Brae (Black Queen), Pamela May (Red Queen), Robert Helpmann (Red King), Harold Turner (Red Knight I), William Chappell (Red Knight II), Michael Somes (Black Knight) and Margot Fonteyn leading the Black Pawns. Constant Lambert conducted L'Orchestre des Concerts Lamoureux.

The first British performance took place on 5 October the same year at Sadler's Wells Theatre, Lambert once again conducting. He was impressed by the score, describing it in the *Radio Times* as 'full-bloodied theatre from start to finish',[17] and Adolf Aber in *The Musical Times* astutely put his finger on the ballet's distinctive attribute:

> The ballet *Checkmate* should actually be characterised as a *dramatic* work above all else, for it is not a ballet in the ordinary sense of the word. Our interest is held by the drama and its representation by pantomime rather than ballet dancing in its usual form. Nevertheless, there are plenty of scenes which give the corps de ballet an opportunity to show their art ... The combination of the two fundamental elements of the work, dramatic pantomime and pageantry, give a vivid impression of Bliss's power of design and the wealth of his musical palette.[18]

Bearing this in mind, it is noteworthy that out of *Checkmate*'s twelve sections of music only three have the word 'dance' in their titles and just one a named dance form – 'mazurka'. In reality, Bliss wrote a score for a dance drama, which, arguably, was why Helpmann chose Bliss as the composer for his ballets *Miracle in the Gorbals* (1944) and *Adam Zero* (1946)

Bliss scored *Checkmate* for standard orchestra forces, with the second flute and oboe doubling piccolo and cor anglais respectively. He omitted tuba, but included harp, and in addition to timpani, an array of percussion to maximise instrumental colour (bass drum, cymbals, small side drum, triangle, glockenspiel, tubular bell tuned to E flat, tam-tam, xylophone, castanets and tambourine). Several of his tempo markings have a contemporaneous quality that guide the conductor and players in realising Bliss's intentions. In the description of the ballet and its music that follows, quotations are taken from both Bliss's stage directions and scenario from the Study Score. Other citations are referenced as endnotes.

Fig. 3.7: Checkmate (1937). Piano score cover, designed by Edward McKnight Kauffer (Courtesy of Helen Kotz, Private Collection).

I. Prologue: The Players
Moderato maestoso

To preface the drama, Bliss 'felt compelled to write … a stern and thoughtful prelude, giving the impression of stress between the opposing forces'.[19] This sombre music is characterised by a brooding viola melody and sinewy chromatic phrases. The curtain rises revealing two players at the start of a chess game, one in gold armour, the other in black. 'The Golden Player slowly removes his visor, disclosing the features of Love. The Black Player slowly strips his gauntlet, disclosing the skeleton arm of Death. Love makes a movement of fear. They turn the chess board once, twice, three times, for move. Love wins, and raising a pawn to his heart, lifts it at arm's length above his head'.[20] Lights dim, a slow curtain descends.

II. Dance of the Red Pawns
Allegro spirito scherzando

A rapid rise of the curtain reveals that, 'The entire stage represents a chess board upon which the red pieces will assemble'.[21] The Red Pawns (Bliss described them as 'light-hearted pages')[22] dance to a carefree woodwind theme, the music of novices that captures their youthful zeal and fervour. Aptly responding to the music, de Valois opted for classical *en pointe* steps. The dance concludes with the Pawns drawn up in a stylistic chess formation.

III. Dance of the Four Knights
Allegro moderato sempre robustamente

'Two Red Knights, fierce and powerful fighters', bound onto the board to an accented string theme that is courageous and masculine. They are joined by Two Black Knights on a 'reconnoitring visit of chivalry'. To leaping, emphatic rhythms, brass alarums and fanfares, they salute and challenge each other to displays of prowess in which 'Red Knight I surpasses them all'.[23] Paul Spicer's description of the Knights 'squaring up to each other in testosterone-fuelled aggressive music' can hardly be bettered.[24] 'The Red Pawns applaud the feats of skill of their Knights and start dancing with them.' With a sudden slackening of tempo to *Larghetto tranquillo*, 'The Black Knights fall on their knees on the approach of the Black Queen':[25] the music is ominous, pregnant with danger; *she* is the most dangerous piece on the board.

IV. Entry of the Black Queen
L'istesso tempo

'The Black Queen enters majestically', goose-stepping her way onto the board, a contemporary allusion that would not have been lost on the audiences of the day. 'The Red Knights and Pawns remain spellbound.' The Black Queen is epitomised by a sensuous clarinet melody offset by harp arpeggios, indicative of both her sexual allure and her deadly, icy nature. She mesmerises the red pieces, especially Red Knight I, 'who, as if hypnotised, follows her across the board'. To a melting violin solo phrase she throws him a rose, while he 'remains gazing at the rose, deep in thought',[26] ensnared by her guile.

V. The Red Knight's Mazurka
Moderato giojosamente - Animato

The stage now empty, Red Knight I, believing he has gained the Black Queen's heart, dances a joyous, athletic solo, de Valois' choreography fitting hand in glove with Bliss's exuberant music. Contrasting with the main theme is a tender idea on woodwind. Towards the end of the dance the music turns sinister as if presaging his doom. A linking passage finishes this section, with oboe and bassoon solos (*a tempo meno mosso e tranquillo*) as 'Three Red Pawns enter from each side carrying the banners of the Red Knights. They take up ceremonial positions to receive the two Red Bishops.'[27]

VI. Ceremony of the Red Bishops
Largamente [misticamente]

A tolling bell and a chant-like fragment on strings, then winds, create a mood of piety for the arrival of the Red Bishops. 'The Pawns lift their banners, and slowly dip them, so as to give the stage the appearance of a chapel. The Bishops bless the kneeling Knights … all remain motionless.'[28]

VII. Entry of the Red Castles
Allegro moderato molto deciso

The blessing is interrupted by the 'long strides' of the marching Red Castles whose movements 'convey the impression that Force is the final arbiter'.[29] Timpani, xylophone, cymbals and bass drum all add vividness to the music. Here, Bliss reused his music to the sequence 'The Building of the New World' from the film of H.G. Wells's *Things to Come* (1936), since he felt the evocation of robotic machinery equally personified the Castles, which he described as 'inhuman and menacing monsters'.[30] Towards the end, brilliant pomp and circumstance fanfares ring out as the Red King and Queen approach. 'During the final section … the Red Knights, Bishops and Castles take up their correct opening chess positions up-stage, facing the audience. The Red Pawns run to meet their King, finally forming a semi-circle down-stage with their backs to the audience.'[31]

VIII. Entry of the Red King and Queen
Grave

Fig. 3.8: *Checkmate* (1937). The Red pieces assembled on the board, upstage of the Black Queen, flanked by her Knights and two Pawns, 1937. Photographer unknown (University of Bristol/ArenaPAL).

To a regal horn solo with florid decoration, 'The Red King enters, borne in a palanquin by four bearers. The Red Queen walks at the King's right side.' Old and feeble, he is the weakest piece of all, as captured by the music's poignancy. 'The King and Queen complete a graceful curve and end on their own squares. The Pawns all bow again together and line up, facing the other row of pieces up-stage. On the last chord the Pawns turn round, adopting a fighting position. A complete set of red pieces in their chess position is thus shown to the audience.'[32]

Even from the very first run of performances, de Valois veered away from some aspects of Bliss's stage directions: for example, the Red King never entered on a palanquin. During the course of successive revivals, other aspects of the staging have changed. Among these is the deadly rose the Black Queen drops to lure Red Knight I. Bliss's scenario simply states 'a rose', which initially was red; later, and more theatrically, its colour became black.

IX. The Attack
Allegro impetuoso e brilliante

The Game begins as two Black Pawns, the two Black Knights and the Black Queen initiate a savage offensive to a forceful brass and wind theme. Rapidly, 'The stage is alive with the intricate manoeuvres of the chess battle.' The corps de ballet alternates with solos of the Black Queen, the latter's sallies accompanied by castanets. As the music slows, massive dissonant chords indicate that, 'A clear opening to the Red King is laid bare and the Black Queen seizes the opportunity. She advances towards the King threateningly.'[33] Her menacing manoeuvre results in the 'check' of the Red King, vividly portrayed by two jabbing chords. In alternating slow and fast tempos, the Red King summons his Bishops to assist him, who intercede with their chant, but are imperiously dismissed by the ruthless Black Queen. The Red King's consort implores mercy in a fragile, pleading oboe solo, but the Black Knights carry her forcibly away (*Allegro virilmente*).

X. The Duel
Maestoso moderato e molto appassionato

'Red Knight I leaps into the arena as champion of his king and faces the Black Queen.' During their battle of wills, Bliss interweaves fragments from previous sections. Finally, Red Knight I has the Black Queen at his mercy. Torn between duty and infatuation, he drops his guard, then hesitates to strike as the Prologue melody resounds through the orchestra, building to thudding chords. In a musical *coup de théâtre*, Bliss indicates a long-held pause of silence as the Red Knight's 'sword drops from his hand'.

The Queen's alluring theme is recalled; the Red Knight turns his back as he takes the rose from his breast to the tender music of his Mazurka. As the music veers sinisterly, she stabs him in the back to a distorted version of his theme. 'The giant figures of the two Players appear, and Death, moving slowly forward, throws his black gauntlet on the corpse.' To doleful cor anglais and flute solos, the body is borne off in a sarabande-like funeral cortège (*Larghetto maestoso*), 'Death leading, Love at the end of the procession'. At the end, 'The Red King, on his throne, is left alone with the Black Queen.'[34]

XI. The Black Queen Dances
Allegro dispettoso

To a tango rhythm, in a steely, cold-bloodied dance, the Black Queen taunts the red monarch, who 'in terror for his life, sits fascinated, as rabbit before a snake'. Her music venomously twists and turns with spite as, to a solo violin passage, she seemingly plays with her victim, finally leaving the stage 'with a gesture of savage triumph'.[35]

XII. Finale Checkmate
Andante poco sostenuto - Allegro vivace e feroce

The King looks for ways to flee, the music alternating between slow, nervy passages and fast violent outbursts, when his means of escape are blocked. To relentless, ferocious music the final onslaught begins with the black forces hounding their quarry with staves, like a baleful morris dance. The King is forced back to his throne, but 'has a vision of himself as a young and strong ruler'. To thundering percussion, 'He draws himself up to his full height and appears majestic as a lion at bay.' Momentarily, 'The black pieces waver.' However, behind him stands the Black Queen, spear aloft. She strikes, plunging it into his back. 'The Red King lifts the crown from his head and falls headlong in the circle of enemy lances and swords.'[36] 'It is Checkmate.'[37]

Fig. 3.9: The original costumes: Pamela May as the Red Queen, pleading with June Brae as the Black Queen. Photographer unknown (Performing Arts Images/ArenaPAL).

Fig. 3.10: Robert Helpmann as the helpless Red King with Sadler's Wells Royal Ballet in 1977. He reprised the role with the Australian Ballet, and his last appearances on stage were as the Red King in Melbourne and Sydney in May 1986, four months before his death. Photo: Leslie E. Spatt (ArenaPAL).

Fig. 3.11: Beryl Grey as the Black Queen with Alan Beale and Bryan Ashbridge as the Black Knights, poised to throw a rose as a challenge to the Red Knight. Arthur Bliss wrote in *As I Remember*: '*Checkmate* has danced itself round a good part of the world since its first performance in Paris, and the Black Queen has become associated in my mind with Beryl Grey, whose beauty and dramatic power have contributed greatly to the success of the ballet.' Photo: Anthony Crickmay © Victoria and Albert Museum, London (Royal Ballet School).

Fig. 3.12: Danielle Brown as the Black Queen and Ricki Bertoni as the Red King in Sarasota Ballet's production in 2017 of *Checkmate*, staged by former Sadler's Wells Royal Ballet Principal Margaret Barbieri, with sets and costumes on loan from Birmingham Royal Ballet. *Checkmate* is a mainstay of The Royal Ballet heritage repertoire, with performances at the Royal Opera House, and by Sadler's Wells and Birmingham Royal Ballet on tour and in their home theatres. It has been staged worldwide by companies in Australia, Hungary, Japan, South Africa and the USA. Photo: Frank Arturo (Courtesy of Sarasota Ballet).

4.

Dancing *Checkmate*

DAVID BINTLEY

As a young dancer with Sadler's Wells Royal Ballet in the mid-1970s, my career path had been marked out quite early by my graduation performance as Doctor Coppelius in *Coppélia* (1870). Even at the age of eighteen I was performing 'old men' roles. But it did not bother me, as the skill set I had was a rarity, I suppose, and if it meant getting bigger parts at a young age, then I was happy with that.

In those days the early ballets of Ninette de Valois and Frederick Ashton were well represented by the Company. The days of *Swan Lake* (1877) and *The Sleeping Beauty* (1890) lay some years ahead and our Company of around forty dancers, based at the old Sadler's Wells Theatre, was a formidable exponent of this smaller, more intimate repertoire. Many of these pieces were conceived for Sadler's Wells and were more impressive there than when transferred to the larger stage at Covent Garden.

Two of 'Madam's' (de Valois) greatest pieces, *The Rake's Progress* (1935) and *Checkmate* (1937), were frequently revisited staples of the repertoire. They came with the added bonus that Madam herself, an octogenarian by then, would often come personally to rehearse us, which was, depending on whether she liked you or not, either wonderful or terrifying. For some reason she liked me, and it was always wonderful. In *Rake's Progress* I began by playing the Tailor, graduated to Man with a Rope and ended up doing the Rake himself over several years of

Fig. 4.1: Sadler's Wells Royal Ballet celebrates the 50th anniversary of *Checkmate* (left to right): David Bintley as the Red King, Roland Price as the Red Knight, Ninette de Valois, and June Highwood as the Black Queen taking a curtain call, 22 April 1987, at Sadler's Wells Theatre. Photo: Roy Jones (ArenaPAL).

Fig. 4.2: David Bintley as the Red King. Sadler's Wells Royal Ballet, 1987. Photo: Leslie E. Spatt (ArenaPAL).

performances. In *Checkmate* I started as a Bishop, was Castle-ed and eventually became King!

The BBC filmed *Checkmate* in 1982.[1] In the rehearsals leading up to it, and in the film itself, Madam was meticulous in putting me through my paces. Was I ever really that young? The film also features superb performances from Margaret Barbieri as the Black Queen and David Ashmole as the Red Knight.

I loved the role of the King and even came out of retirement to perform it with the Company when I was Director of Birmingham Royal Ballet. It was not just the lure of performing a favourite role again; I wanted to pass on to the other casts everything that Madam had imparted to me, and what better way than to get up and show them? Not that I was slavish to Madam's demands. When she first rehearsed me, I thought her approach rather old-fashioned, which I put down to the fact that the ballet had been made in the 1930s and perhaps dramatically she had got 'stuck' there. Maturity later helped me to realise that within Madam's great stylised ballet, modern methods of acting would be completely wrong. I had to find a balance between the inner workings of the King's mind and the stylised, restrictive movements that were the main features of *all* the characters: the *pieces* on the chessboard. And this, I think, is the greatness of *Checkmate*.

Premiered in 1937, the metaphor of the 'good', red pieces, the sympathetic Queen, the courageous dashing Knights, the playful Pawns, the comical, rather stupid Castles and last of all the pathetic, doddery old King, versus the cold, emotionless black pieces under their murderous Queen is all too clear: the good, free forces of liberty standing against the dark, evil shadow of fascism spreading over Europe.

The red pieces assemble in sunlight, full of character and personality insofar as their rigid moves permit them; none can step substantially outside of its role. Their 'humanity' is trapped within the part they must play and the whole ballet breathes this terrible sense of fate. The last piece to arrive is the Red King. He can only stumble towards his throne with the help of the Red Queen, who holds a mirror to her Lord as if to convince him that he is, or was, a mighty monarch. The King, near blind, is unconvinced. He takes his throne with a sigh, summoning the last shreds of his dignity before the battle that is to come.

The ballet is introduced as a deadly game between the forces of Love and Death. Arthur Bliss's music paints this duel in grand, epic and sombre tones before the drop curtain rises on the dance of the Red Pawns. From this point onwards the music is bright, vital and full of optimism. There is genuine excitement in the air and the pennants of the Knights can almost be heard fluttering in the breeze. Only the 'diplomatic' visit of the Black Queen and her sinuous seduction of the Red Knight strike an ominous chord. The music oozes insincerity and lies; like Eve and the serpent, the Knight is seduced not with an apple but with a rose. Then follows the famous Red Knight mazurka. Initially ten minutes long, it was mercifully reduced at de Valois' prompting to a barely manageable three minutes, yet still poses a formidable challenge to a dancer's skill and stamina.

With the board being complete, the black pieces begin to arrive. Over the next few minutes the whole stage will fill, each piece constrained both by its nature but also by the dense stage picture which, like a real chess game, becomes almost bewildering in its complexity. Playing the role of the Red King, sitting above the action and at its heart, the dancer has a grandstand view greater than any audience member. Here, the music grows

Fig. 4.3: David Bintley as the Red King and Claire French as the Red Queen. Sadler's Wells Royal Ballet, 1987. Photo: Leslie E. Spatt (ArenaPAL).

Fig. 4.4: *Checkmate*: Margaret Barbieri as the Black Queen and David Bintley as the Red King, with artists of Sadler's Wells Royal Ballet, Black Knights, Castle and Pawns, at Sadler's Wells Theatre, 1981/2 season. Photo: Leslie E. Spatt (ArenaPAL).

in intensity to a point where it can go no further and then … suddenly ceases. In trembling hushed tones the dancers part and we see a direct path from the Black Queen to the King. Thus threatened, the King, almost as though he were playing the game himself, makes two futile defences using his Bishops and Queen, both of whom are contemptuously dealt with. Enraged by the violation of his Queen, the King throws the Red Knight into single combat with the Black Queen. Following a tense encounter, the Knight is finally victorious and stands poised to kill her. The old, feeble King, sensing victory at last, stands for the first time and in his febrile anxiety urges his champion to despatch the Queen. To thudding timpani the Knight stands, his sword hovering above her exposed breast. Silence. Then the soft, wheedling return of the Queen's seduction music, and the hopeless dejection of the Knight as he turns to the King for forgiveness; his failure complete, he kneels at the throne as shrill, discordant music warns him of the Queen's approach, her two swords whirling like the old image of Boudicca's chariot. Following his death, a funeral cortège is assembled and the Knight is carried off to a hero's burial. Death has triumphed over Love.

The King is left alone to face the inevitable. Any hope he might have of a swift death is soon dispelled as the Black Queen toys with him in a dance of such perfection both musically and choreographically that it ranks in my opinion with any female solo ever written. Violent, then sensual, the Black Queen is utterly unpredictable. One moment strident, the next teasing, she humiliates and emasculates the King as effectively as any Lady Macbeth. Just at the moment when he expects her to finish him … she vanishes.

I loved this 'duet' with the Queen, even though I remained seated within the confines of where I could move, which was nowhere! I shrank into the throne, I tried to slide out of it – first this way, then that. I collapsed into it and when at a dramatic musical point in the dance the Queen brought one of her swords down heavily towards the throne, I always contrived to put a hand in the way, and when the blow landed withdrew it in shock, as though badly cut. The ladies would always apologise profusely after curtain down, or even onstage in a whisper, but I reassured them I had done it on purpose. But the real joy of this moment was the eye contact between us, throughout the dance. I could always tell a great Queen, by how deeply she was into the moment, how much this 'contact' informed the solo.

Another extraordinary musico-dramatic moment now, as an uneasy silence descends and the King, completely alone, looks nervously about the stage. He once more tries to summon up the courage to act his part and face death bravely, but to no avail. The music alternates between the quietly feeble attempts of the King to feel his way towards freedom, and the march-like stridency of the black pieces which cut off his every avenue of escape. Black Pawns, Knights and Castles engage in a truly sickening persecution of the King, whose body is tossed around like a rag doll in the merciless grinding mill of the war machine. The King briefly rallies and, sensing the end, draws himself up and fleetingly shows us the regent he once was, before collapsing again as the Black Queen enters carried aloft. With her shadow magnified and distorted on the backcloth, she drives her sword down into the King's exposed neck, snatching the crown from his head. It is checkmate.

Checkmate is a great ballet and its last great exponent, Sadler's Wells Royal Ballet, revered it as such. De Valois' genius in imbuing the piece with heightened emotion, controlled by the highly stylised language that she developed for the ballet, makes it utterly remarkable. The marriage of de Valois, Bliss and Edward McKnight Kauffer, too, produced a work worthy of the greatest achievements of Sergei Diaghilev.

This article is reprinted by kind permission of The Bliss Society. www.arthurbliss.org

5.
Checkmate: Beyond the Classroom, Choreographic Theatre

JENNIFER JACKSON

Fig. 5.1: Royal Ballet poster, 1993, featuring Darcey Bussell as the Black Queen. Photo: Uli Weber (Royal Ballet and Opera/ArenaPAL).

In 1937, a good decade after the establishment of Ninette de Valois' Academy of Choreographic Art and six years into the growth of the Vic-Wells Company, a ballet based on the ancient game of chess appeared at the right moment. It drew together the talents of a composer at the height of his bold inventiveness, a woman equally bold and secure in her commitment to creating a repertoire with adventurous themes underpinned by classical dance with an English accent, and a designer in Edward McKnight Kauffer whose striking use of colour and line provided the perfect pared-down aesthetic for the work. Arthur Bliss's comment that McKnight Kauffer 'thinks musically'[1] suggests that the collaboration, augmenting the already established partnership between de Valois and Bliss, flowed with imaginative ideas and practical solutions. Added to that heady combination was the Vic-Wells Ballet Company of performers: rising stars and dancers grounded in a particular training and education in the art form, and musical direction from the flamboyant, highly cultured and talented composer-conductor Constant Lambert. His infectious personality fuelled enthusiasm for the theatre as a place of excitement, colour and music; he also

Fig. 5.2: Zenaida Yanowsky as the Black Queen, Royal Opera House, 2007. Beryl Grey coached several generations of dancers in this role, including Darcey Bussell and Yanowsky for their performances with The Royal Ballet in 1993 and 2006/7 respectively. Photo: Johan Persson (ArenaPAL).

had learnt from Sergei Diaghilev that ballet could be an 'intoxicating live creation in which dance, design and music are one'.[2] The combined strong leadership across dance and music inspired the sense of involvement in the youthful mission to make a place for ballet in Britain, which, as de Valois always insisted, was the work of many people.

And there was something to say. The contest between white and black pieces on a chessboard, reimagined as a battle between Love and Death, represents the idea of fate and the inevitability of death. Many years after its creation, de Valois (known to us all as 'Madam') reflected on how, against the rise of fascism and the threat of war, *Checkmate* was an expression of the 'dread' collectively felt.[3] Dame Beryl Grey, renowned for her performance as the Black Queen, saw 'a crumbling monarchy' depicted in the work, and when coaching successive generations of dancers in the role she called the ballet 'prophetic'.[4]

Would this idea for a ballet have had the same impact at any other time? A synthesis of the arts and of circumstance, the forces aligned to give its production potent expression; it is a ballet of and beyond the moment of its creation. To explore what underpins the work's endurance and lasting appeal, different generations of performers share their thoughts and experiences of dancing *Checkmate* and working with Madam. Their voices offer a perspective from inside her great work.

Madam referred to her role as that of housekeeper; she did what was needed to be done to develop the institution. Reflecting on performing *Checkmate* with Sadler's Wells Royal Ballet in the

Fig. 5.3: Sadler's Wells Royal Ballet in 1983 at Sadler's Wells Theatre with Roland Price and David Ashmole as the Red Knights. Photo: Darryl Williams (ArenaPAL).

1980s, choreographer and ballet director Graham Lustig remarks: 'I believe that everyone in the cast felt a sense of reverence. We were the interpreters of one of the very great early ballets – a work that was a cornerstone of the building of The Royal Ballet company.'[5] More than any of her other works *Checkmate* is didactic. Not only is the ballet an outstanding model of choreographic invention and collaboration between music, dance and design, it also nurtures the dancer as an artist and athlete. It offers challenging material for the ensemble – Pawns, Knights, Castles, Bishops – and four contrasting principal roles: a highly unusual female lead in the combative and implacable Black Queen; a virile yet submissive Red Knight; a tender and attentive Red Queen; and a brilliant dramatic vehicle in the Red King. This ballet pushes the dancers' physical stamina, prowess and technical ability. *Checkmate* is a 'tough' ask,[6] but everything needed for the dancer to perform the ballet is held in the choreographic whole, which itself holds firm to the principle espoused by Diaghilev of perfect unity in a created work. Barry Wordsworth, Music Director for Sadler's Wells and later for The Royal Ballet between 1973 and 2015, has championed Bliss's music; he considers *Checkmate* a 'total masterpiece' and a benchmark for all ballet production.[7]

Choreographic language – 'all there in the music'

David Bintley's essay, 'Dancing *Checkmate*'[8], beautifully describes the action and drama from the 'best seat in the house' – his throne as the Red King at the back of the stage. His performance is captured in a 1982 BBC documentary that features Sadler's Wells Royal Ballet in the complete work, filmed on stage and in rehearsals with Madam. The fine cast includes Margaret Barbieri as his Black Queen, David Ashmole as the Red Knight and choreographer-dancer Michael Corder as his second. Barbieri recalls Madam saying that Bliss had presented her with the score and scenario, and that she 'didn't really have to do anything'. The choreography is 'all there in the music'.[9] Musicologist Victor Durà-Vilà suggests that to fully appreciate listening to Bliss's music requires 'strong awareness' of the dramatic action.[10] For Darcey Bussell, as a dancer 'the music is the main artery'; through it 'the narrative is threaded and everything flourishes'.[11] In a beautifully honed

Fig. 5.4: Margaret Barbieri as the Black Queen with Sadler's Wells Royal Ballet. Sadler's Wells Theatre, 1983. Photo: Leslie E. Spatt (ArenaPAL).

Fig. 5.5: Alexandra Ansanelli as the Red Queen and Alastair Marriot as the Red King. The Royal Ballet, Royal Opera House, 2007. Photo: Johan Persson (ArenaPAL).

and resolved relationship between music and dance, Madam's choreography makes the inner logic and life of Bliss's music visible. 'You hear the music and you see the steps.'[12]

Once the curtain rises after the Prologue, the story unfolds entirely through dancing that is firmly rooted in the ballet vocabulary. It is testament to Madam's belief that 'the teachings of the classic school are the sure and only foundation – limitless in its adaptability it consequently proves its power to meet the varied requirements of the theatre'.[13] She dispenses with the convention in classical dance narrative that juxtaposes mime with passages of dancing. Instead, gestures from everyday social behaviour and interaction are intricately woven into the steps and groupings to convey character, human relationships and the power dynamics between the assembled figures. This makes both for very human theatre and for a secure, informed dance text that stands the test of time.

The dance aesthetic is angular, lean and perceptively crafted to convey the ideas. Each of the figures on the board has their 'signature path'. The Red Pawns, acting like a Greek chorus, represent the 'mass mind'.[14] Easily led and obedient to change, they are an ordered group; their interconnecting moves are symmetrical and performed in precise relationship with each other. Their first dance is perky and *en pointe*, full of polite little bows, swift turns of the head and gestures of the limbs that retract as quickly as they are made. With the entrance of the Bishops they are sombre and reverential, and when the Castles stride on, their booted feet deliberate and heavy and their arms weighted and swinging to represent the machinery of war, the Pawns become energised and 'all for the war'.[15] With the death of the Red Knight, their collective gesture of mourning – one hand drooped at the wrist and held in a line of respectful stillness – amplifies the tragedy with simple eloquence.[16]

For the Red King's entrance Bliss had suggested referencing the oriental origins of chess with an

Fig. 5.6: Monica Mason as the Black Queen, Robert Helpmann as the Red King and artists of The Royal Ballet, Royal Opera House, 1971. Photo: G.B.L. Wilson (Royal Academy of Dance/ArenaPAL).

elaborate Chinese chariot. Instead, Madam held firm to the discipline of a dance language; and she made him vulnerable. He enters teetering on the edge of falling, supported by his Queen, while she, sharply attuned to his every move, takes tiny steps forward *en pointe*, contracting to catch each stumble. It is a poignant image, drawing the audience into his plight in the drama.

Corder finds the contrasting 'feminine' and 'masculine' qualities in the music and dance 'thrilling'. He cites how 'the 'slinky, mysterious and threatening' entrance of the Black Queen … makes my hair stand on end!' and the 'very strongly rhythmic, martial and ordered' music so aptly drives and sustains the dance of the four Knights.[17] Barbieri comments on telling choreographic detail for the Black Queen, in the way Madam deliberately draws attention to the female form. 'From the word go she is trying to seduce the Red Knight, and Madam was very insistent on those arms, … [the gesture] comes from under the bosom; it's from her to him, and in the way she looks at him.'[18] Later, on her knees and apparently vanquished, she bends back, opening her arms and breasts to him – in a gesture both of sexual provocation and an appeal for mercy. Her unrelenting clever play is rewarded as he lowers his sword, helpless in her seductive power. In her solo, the intensity of the Black Queen's focus on victory is amplified by the orientation of movement to the back of the stage, towards the King. The audience reads the drama not primarily through facial expression but in the dancer's whole body action, and her back in particular. We are in unusual territory for the ballet stage – the notion of 'romance' is firmly associated not with a traditional love relationship between a man and a woman but with chivalric honour and sacrifice, expressed in terms of 'choreographic theatre'.

Performing the Black Queen – pretend you're a cat!

The first Black Queen was June Brae, but the role is strongly associated with Beryl Grey. She danced it in the first revival in 1947 (after the set and costumes were lost in the Netherlands during the Second World War) and continued to perform the role in subsequent seasons at the Royal Opera House in the 1950s and in the 1963 film. Produced by Margaret Dale for the BBC, *Checkmate* was described as 'a very modern ballet'[19] – twenty-five years after its premiere. The roster of notable Black Queens of this period includes Pamela May, Violetta Elvin, Julia Farron, Gillian Lynne and Svetlana Beriosova.

Monica Mason first danced the Black Queen in 1963 and had just four days to learn the choreography. Too busy to rehearse her in the studio, Madam arranged to meet Mason on stage before her first performance and arrived only five minutes before curtain up, having exited a meeting that was overrunning. She asked if Mason had 'placed' the steps; the answer, 'Yes, I hope it will be to your liking,' was followed with an encouraging, 'I'm sure it will – well – just know what you've got to think about and – pretend you're a cat.'[20] Although somewhat mystified, Mason drew excellent notices for her 'menacing, inhuman' performance of 'hypnotic force', which Clement Crisp wrote 'brought new life to the part; the duel with the Red Knight had a greater inevitability than ever before, and the Red King's death took on the appearance of a sacrifice to a goddess'.[21]

From her first entrance, the Black Queen is menacing – she prowls like a big-game cat onto the stage, poised *en pointe*, the feet etched precisely and noiselessly on their narrow path. Grey references the image of a cat and mouse to evoke the tortuous cruelty of the Queen's play with the life of her weakened opponent, which ends the ballet.[22] It is an image that Barbieri also passes on from her own experience. She describes how, by moving across the board from left to right and systematically up the rows, the Queen is cruelly teasing the king, 'until she gets her sword so it's almost down his nose. And yet she doesn't kill him then. He's backing away – she gets closer and closer, and then – she lets him go – she just walks away. It's a very dramatic moment, because you really are tantalising him, getting so close and saying – okay – I'll give you a few more minutes to live.'[23]

Developing artists

The Sadler's Wells Royal Ballet revival of *Checkmate* in the 1970s presented the opportunity to invite guest ballerinas Maina Gielgud and Natalia Makarova to dance the Black Queen. Rehearsing with Madam, Gielgud describes her attention to stagecraft, the economy and precision of every arm and hand in space, and rhythmic clarity.[24] Critic Fernau Hall remarked that Makarova 'deployed her long arms and legs with silky and demoniacal intensity' and was 'quite unrecognisable' as the Black Queen, a role that was 'very different' from those she encountered in Russia.[25]

Barbieri recalls how, as a Principal dancer renowned for her performances with the Company in *Giselle* (1841) and *Les Sylphides* (1909), she came to the role of the Black Queen. Summoned to the administration office, she encountered Madam:

Fig. 5.7: Svetlana Beriosova as the Black Queen, the most elegant Royal Ballet ballerina of her generation Photo: Tahir Khan (Royal Ballet School Special Collections/ArenaPAL).

Fig. 5.8: Danielle Brown in the Black Queen's solo, with Ricki Bertoni as the Red King in Sarasota Ballet's production in 2017. Photo: Frank Arturo (Courtesy of Margaret Barbieri, Assistant Director Sarasota Ballet).

'Now darling, you're all wrong for this – you're a romantic ballerina. But it will be very good for you to tackle this role. And I'm going to teach you and I'm going to coach you in it.' Barbieri's 'daunting' but 'most amazing' experience working with Madam reveals her perceptive eye for casting and developing artistic potential. Rehearsals were exacting, as every day she demanded a different quality of movement expression: 'she wanted me to be more powerful, to be more feminine, or more seductive … so many different things – it was like trying to find my way in it all.'[26] *Checkmate* went on to become one of Barbieri's signature ballets, and it led to a cherished friendship with Bliss's widow, Trudy, who regularly attended performances. She regarded Barbieri as her favourite Black Queen and mused that her husband might have felt the same.

Barbieri now stages *Checkmate* as part of the varied repertoire at Sarasota Ballet in Florida, where she is Assistant Director. Working with dancers today in the way that had enabled her to understand and excel in the ballet, she looks for potential and takes a 'gamble' in casting. 'Dancers enjoy it just as much as we did; you see them delving into the roles … they get a great deal from it.'[27] Her observation resonates with Bussell's experience of dancing *Checkmate*. Studying the Black Queen's solo as a student, she was struck by the 'strength through the shapes', the unusual transitions from 'pose to jump to pose' in the choreography and how 'fresh and new' it felt. Ideally suited to the movement, she danced the Black Queen in the 1993 Royal Ballet revival and worked with Grey to explore the subtleties of the artistic and expressive dimensions of the role. She remarks on how it nurtured her confidence as a young artist to find her own voice as a woman on stage. 'It wasn't a sexual role at all, but there was something incredibly feminine about it; I didn't associate it at all with a masculine strength – how powerful you could be, with the jumps and because you've got weapons in your hands; it was so much more. I really found that strength, being confident with being just a woman and not trying to be anybody you're not. It gave me the confidence to step into other roles and have that same attitude.'[28]

In 2007 *Checkmate* was part of the programme that marked Bussell's retirement from The Royal Ballet. Zenaida Yanowsky who, like Grey, is tall, elegant and technically strong, was cast as the Black Queen. Working with Grey, then in her late seventies, Yanowsky recalls her impact as a role model and being given permission to explore the nuances in the material. And in response to Grey demonstrating the 'defined and refined' actions of the legs, she remembers thinking, 'Wow, those are good legs!' Always interested in art, the relationship between the design and the choreography played into her finding her way in the role, as she explains: 'an arabesque in [*Sleeping*] *Beauty* or an arabesque in *Checkmate* is still an arabesque, but the energy that goes through, how to utilise the colours of the language, makes the difference for me'. Dancing *Checkmate* was also a valuable lesson in Company style. Growing up in the Canary Islands as the daughter of professional contemporary dancers, Yanowsky was schooled in a variety of different dance genres and on joining The Royal Ballet 'had to work hard to integrate myself into the style'. Coached by then Director Monica Mason, she recognised vital information embodied in this work: the 'stylistic history was very powerful – I could see it – I didn't have it myself, but I understood it; it was my goal'.[29]

Schooling

Musing on the relationship between the personal and impersonal in de Valois' achievements, Patricia Linton points to the significance that, in this, one of her 'most successful ballets, human tensions and characters ... are represented by the impersonality of chess pieces'.[30] Madam was emphatic about the way she wanted the ballet to be approached. While insisting on the dancers' individual engagement and effort, she said: 'You are creatures of fate – you are being moved ... If it becomes too personal it loses character ... You have got to put a lot of flesh and movement into it. But it mustn't be broken up into a highly personal reading of it.'[31]

From the classroom on, dancers learn to orientate their bodily actions in relation to an imagined grid: 'the dancer's square'. This enables a precise relationship within the stage space and to each other, between different groups and with the time taken for each step. The stage floor for *Checkmate* is marked out in squares like a chessboard and is a perfect grid for exploiting the ballet vocabulary for dramatic effect. As well as laying the foundations for representing character, the geometric logic of the choreography sustains the dancers physically and enables them to meet its demands. Not a chess player herself, Madam was not constrained by the need to adhere to the prescribed moves of each of the pieces; Barbieri recalls, however, that she was 'quite fanatical and pedantic about [how] you are working your way up the chessboard'.[32] Obeying the rules of the forms is

Fig. 5.9: The Duel: Zenaida Yanowsky as the Black Queen and Bennett Gartside as the First Red Knight. The Royal Ballet, Royal Opera House, 2007. Photo: Nigel Norrington (ArenaPAL).

Fig. 5.10: Ninette de Valois rehearses Beryl Grey on the set of the 1963 film of *Checkmate*, directed by Margaret Dale. Photo: Anthony Crickmay © Victoria and Albert Musuem, London (Royal Ballet School Special Collections).

essential for their harmonious function in supporting the dancer, apparently without effort. Barbieri explains that in making sense of the inner structures of the choreography, she learnt to navigate the 'exhausting' progression of the role of the Black Queen, when 'having danced the whole of the rest of ballet, you come off stage, five seconds later you're back on, high kicks – into your solo'.[33]

Checkmate's precise space–time framework leaves little room for the choreographic text to morph too far from the original. Choreologist Jacquie Hollander notated *Checkmate* in Benesh in 1972,[34] working from the dancers' recollections of the ballet and later in close collaboration with Madam, who entrusted her with staging subsequent revivals. Hollander comments on how 'deceptively simple' the classroom material appears. With its emphasis on *épaulement*,[35] direction and precision, Mark Silver observes a clear link to the Cecchetti schooling that he encountered in Madam's classes and Richard Glasstone's teaching at The Royal Ballet School.[36] The 'sharp' footwork and '*petit batterie* underneath swift changes of direction' and multiple turns,[37] present particular challenges for dancers who are not trained in the English School. Hollander observes that some Russian-schooled dancers, accustomed to large stages and expansive moves, often struggle. The power of the 'very contained' aesthetic lies in the attack and accuracy employed to achieve specific line and dynamics. Conforming, for example, with the height of the leg extensions is not arbitrary, and the line of the swords held in parallel indicates the thrust and direction of the weapon.[38]

Hollander comments on the impact of Madam's use of simple means for the work of the ensemble. In The Attack, the steps and the formations on the stage are straightforward, advancing and retreating, and often mirroring each other. She teaches each group separately before assembling the full Company in rehearsal: 'Putting the Attack together, I was almost always in tears, because of the electricity in the studio – when they suddenly realised that they had opponents, and this *was* a battle … you can see them lighting up and the music just gets them … we would all just collapse in a heap after it.'[39] As dancer, director and choreographer Stephen Jeffries observes, 'Madam could solve problems almost mathematically, with interweaving of the different characters. She did that brilliantly.'[40]

Finding its own way – over time

Chapter 2 looks in detail at McKnight Kauffer's design contribution to the success of this ballet. The loss of the original designs enabled him to rethink aspects of the set and costuming for the 1947 revival. Over subsequent revivals, the use of breathable, malleable fabrics has rendered costumes and headdresses lighter and movement easier for the dancers. Shifts of emphasis in dance training and taste have crept in. Little gloves once worn by the Pawns were dismissed by Madam as 'too fussy'.[41] The Red Knight's heeled character boots worn in the 1963 film were replaced by the soft leather ankle boots of a classical prince for the 1971–2 revival, when Rudolf Nureyev danced the Red Knight to Monica Mason's Black Queen.

Madam loved Nureyev and what he brought to her Company. Did he influence the change of footwear from cumbersome character boot to elegant ballet boot so that he might better articulate the classical roots of the dancing? Although an unlikely casting (and not his favourite role), Nureyev's Red Knight had impact. A young Silver was captivated by the intensity of his dark reading – his embodiment of sex, and the drama of love and death in the contest between the Red Knight and Black Queen.[42] By contrast, when he tackled the role, Corder relished the challenge of bringing to it the characteristic clarity of line and musicality of his English classical schooling.[43]

De Valois considered *Checkmate* (1937) her great ballet.[44] She thought that *The Rake's Progress* (1935), arguably her other great work, was 'more open to interpretation', while *Checkmate* was 'easier to keep in its original state'.[45] Unlike Bliss's other three ballets with commissioned scores, the dance element of *Checkmate* survives. The choreographic text has hardly changed, withstanding shifting trends in artistic focus and public taste over time, passed down over successive generations of performers and recorded in Benesh notation, as well as on film and video. For Bussell, the originality, the fine balance between drama and dancing, the strength of the choreography, its challenge to the dancers and relevance as a whole Company work ensure that *Checkmate* will last.[46] Audiences witnessing a twenty-first-century production will see the same ingredients, freshly cooked.

De Valois advocated evolution not revolution; she saw the importance of preserving work for future study and championed the use of notation.[47] She did what was necessary to ensure that *Checkmate* would maintain its form as an expressionist ballet rooted in *danse d'école* – a model of the interrelationship of innovation and tradition in the creation of a new kind of 'choreographic theatre'. In its embodiment of her values and philosophy, *Checkmate* is the ballet that Madam seems destined to have made.

Fig. 5.11: The Red Knight hesitates. Rudolf Nureyev with Monica Mason as the Black Queen and Robert Helpmann as the Red King. The Royal Ballet, Royal Opera House, 1971. Photo: Leslie E. Spatt (ArenaPAL).

PART TWO

Miracle in the Gorbals

1944

6.
Miracle in the Gorbals: Revelation on Stage

PAUL SPICER

Miracle in the Gorbals (1944) was a remarkable collaboration between Michael Benthall, who created the scenario, Robert Helpmann, the choreographer, Arthur Bliss as composer and the artist Edward Burra. From Bliss's perspective, it was given considerable impetus on a number of fronts. First, and perhaps most importantly, it marked the return after a long wartime separation of Bliss's wife Trudy and his two daughters, Barbara and Karen. They had had to remain in the safety of the USA while Bliss returned to England in 1941 to work for the BBC, eventually becoming its Director of Music in September 1942. His tenure was only ever intended to be a stopgap both for him and the organisation as his work as a composer had to be put on hold during this time. Trudy and the girls arrived on 5 November 1943 after a separation of two and a half years, signalling Bliss's resignation from the BBC and eventual departure on 31 March the following year. *Miracle in the Gorbals* is dedicated 'To Trudy, Barbara and Karen – thanksgiving for November 5th 1943'.

If this was one considerable impetus for Bliss, the other was quite simply his need to compose. The fact that he had had a complete break during 1942 producing no new works at all meant that he was hungry to compose and impatient to get going on fresh material. Helpmann's invitation to write the music for *Miracle in the Gorbals* was exactly the commission he needed. Helpmann had danced the role of the Red King in Bliss's earlier ballet *Checkmate* (1937), which was a resounding success, and Helpmann knew that he would be the perfect partner in this new collaboration.

The whole realisation of this project was cutting-edge and was not without its critics. There had long been a question in the Helpmann ballets with

Fig. 6.1: Robert Helpmann in 1943. Photo: Gordon Anthony (Royal Ballet School Special Collections/ArenaPAL).

which Bliss was associated about whether they were actual ballets or dance-dramas; some felt they were not ballets at all but effectively mimed dramas. But Arnold Haskell, writing about *Miracle* stated:

> In dance-drama there is a definite story, the story is important and dictates the whole treatment, there is more *recitative*-dancing than *aria*-dancing, i.e., more movement that develops character and action than familiar set pieces. *Adagios*, variations. Let us scotch that absurdity once and for all, that such works as *Hamlet* and *Miracle in the Gorbals* have more acting than dancing in them. It is all dancing and can be nothing else. There is no such thing in ballet as detached acting. Did not Fokine say that the dancer must be expressive from head to foot, that even the movement of an eyebrow was dancing?[1]

He concluded that '*Miracle in the Gorbals* must stand or fall on its merits as a ballet and it must always be remembered that ballet is a visual art.'[2]

One of the principal differences between *Miracle* and so many earlier ballets is its contemporaneous setting; it grew from the detailed scenario conceived by Benthall during his posting to an anti-aircraft gun battery in Glasgow early in the war. The Gorbals, while no longer the lawless, desperate slum area for which it had gained such a terrible reputation, was nevertheless still notorious for its overcrowding, poverty and prostitution. It is notable that in asserting that the area now had no issues of violence, all of Glasgow's representatives, from the Lord Provost to the police, resented their city's image being reflected in such a negative way. But, in the end, all this was good publicity for a ballet the storyline of which was about far more than this one characteristic.[3]

Bliss was an obvious choice as composer, not only because he had already demonstrated his sympathy with the medium through *Checkmate*, but also because he was a natural composer for stage and screen and seemed to come alive with a libretto or scenario to represent musically. In fact, he almost never composed anything without an idea being presented to him as what he called a *donnée* – something that fired his imagination and got his creative juices churning. In this case, working 'with Benthall's full scenario, with Robert Helpmann and with Burra's designs spread out before him',[4] Bliss could allow his descriptive imagination to bring the highly dramatic story to life.

Bliss was not only the composer on this project, but through his extensive knowledge of art (he was an avid collector, as his father had been before him) he was also able to relate the style of the great Greek artist El Greco (1541–1614) to the stage characters involved, suggesting a study of the hand shapes that are so characteristic of the subjects of the paintings.

Fig. 6.2: Studio of El Greco, *The Agony in the Garden of Gethsemane*, 1590s, National Gallery, London (NG3476). (The Yorck Project [2002], *10,000 Meisterwerke der Malerei* [DVD-ROM], distributed by DIRECTMEDIA Publishing GmbH).

Fig. 6.3: Robert Helpmann in a study of hand gestures based on the painting style of El Greco, 1944. Photo: Baron (ArenaPAL).

This led to Helpmann's own experiment with adopting the highly expressive hand shapes at key points in the drama.

Before the First World War, when post-Cambridge he was studying with Sir Charles Stanford at the Royal College of Music, Bliss had regularly been in the audience for Sergei Diaghilev's productions at the Theatre Royal Drury Lane in London. Here, he witnessed the inspirational new ballets by Igor Stravinsky, which, after the war, he wanted to emulate in his own compositional style. Aged twenty-seven he, like everyone of his generation, had to make up for those four lost years of his life. He needed people to sit up and take notice of him.

Bliss's response to this was his early 'experiments in sound', as he called them, inspired by Stravinsky and which were a world apart from the works of nearly all his British contemporaries. Compositions like *Madam Noy* (1918), *Rhapsody* (1919), *Concerto for Piano, Tenor, Strings and Percussion* (1920) and *Rout* (1920) all led to a natural conclusion in the large-scale *Colour Symphony* of 1922, commissioned by Edward Elgar for the Gloucester Three Choirs Festival of that year. At last people could see where these earlier *amuse-bouches* were heading. *Rout* caught the attention of Diaghilev, who asked Bliss to score it for a larger orchestra so it could be included in his Ballets Russes programmes as interlude music. So began Bliss's intimate association with the stage, and with ballet in particular.

It was also Bliss's heightened sense of the pictorial that made him such a brilliant composer for the theatre and film. In between *Rout* and *Miracle in the Gorbals* came highly influential film scores, notably that for H.G. Wells's *Things to Come* (1935), which is still regarded as one of the most important film scores in the early history of film. This led to other films: *Conquest of the Air* (1937) and *Caesar and Cleopatra* (1944), the latter in the same year as *Miracle*. More followed. The enormously successful ballet *Checkmate*, developed with Ninette de Valois and Edward McKnight Kauffer for performance in Paris in 1937 by the Vic-Wells Company, ensured Bliss's burgeoning reputation. This, and the personal connection with Helpmann, made Bliss the ideal composer for *Miracle in the Gorbals*. If not unique in British music at the time, his was certainly an unusual and distinctly contemporary-sounding voice and his varied compositional style brilliantly reflected the highs and lows, the drama and tension, of Benthall's scenario. Another key consideration in

Fig. 6.4: Robert Helpmann as the Stranger, Pauline Clayden as the Suicide and David Paltenghi as the Official. Note the hand shapes and the influence of Helpmann's study of El Greco as suggested by Arthur Bliss. Photo: Edward Mandinian (Royal Ballet School Special Collections/ArenaPAL).

Fig. 6.5: Reproduction of the original front cloth depicting the Clydeside docks in Birmingham Royal Ballet's recreation of 2014, designed by Adam Wiltshire after Edward Burra. Photo: Bill Cooper (ArenaPAL).

THE SADLER'S WELLS BALLET

PRINCE'S THEATRE
LONDON

Director NINETTE DE VALOIS
Orchestra (Leader: John Fisher)
Conducted by CONSTANT LAMBERT

THURSDAY, OCTOBER 26TH, 1944

MIRACLE IN THE GORBALS

(First Performance)

Music by ARTHUR BLISS
Décor by EDWARD BURRA
Scenario by MICHAEL BENTHALL
Choreography by ROBERT HELPMANN

Scene - The Gorbals, Glasgow

The Suicide	PAULINE CLAYDEN
The Lovers	MOIRA SHEARER AND ALEXIS RASSINE
A Beggar	LESLIE EDWARD EDWARDS
A Street Boy	GORDON HAMILTON
The Official	DAVID PALTENGHI
The Prostitute	CELIA FRANCA
The Stranger	ROBERT HELPMANN

Julia Farron, Moyra Fraser, Palma Nye, Joan Sheldon, Gerd Larson, Jean Bedells, Elizabeth Kennedy, Jill Gregory, Gillian Lynne, Paula Dunning, June Vincent, June Appleton, Avril Navarre, Anthony Burke, Franklin White, Henri Denton, Eric Hyrst, Douglas Stuart, Brian Earnshaw, Allan Baker, Peter Skinner, Stanley Holden

Costumes executed by GRACE KELLY
Scenery painted by ALICK JOHNSTONE

A Ballet in One Scene:

I. Overture
II. The Street
III. The Girl Suicide
IV. The Young Lovers
V. The Prostitute and the Boy
VI. The Official
VII. The Discovery of the Suicide's Body
VIII. The Suicide's Body Is Brought In
IX. The Stranger
X. Dance of Deliverance
XI. The Official and the Prostitute
XII. Intermezzo
XIII. The Slander Campaign
XIV. The Conversion of the Prostitute
XV. Finale – The Killing of the Stranger

Bliss's make-up was his hybrid birthright: he had an English mother and an American father. Not only this, but his wife Trudy was American and he spent a number of years in California, where she came from and his father lived until his death. It is easy, therefore, to see the source of his inspiration for the remarkable jazz-inspired, new-world melody Dance of Deliverance in *Miracle*.

It was essential that scenery and costumes should immediately suggest the nature and atmosphere of the work, and both, together with Bliss's music, did this with conspicuous success. The artist responsible for the design, Edward Burra, as Haskell remarked, was 'a master in finding beauty in drab and sordid surroundings'.[5] *(see Fig. 2.3)* Set in the gritty reality of Glasgow's most notorious slum, *Miracle in the Gorbals* tells the story of an extraordinary event in a community plagued by poverty, prostitution and crime. A solitary young girl's despair leads her to suicide, and into the shock of her death a mysterious stranger intrudes. His action in bringing her back to life first enlivens but then unsettles the community, and he is murdered.

The clear similarities with the miracles of Jesus Christ and his ultimate death provide additional heft to the scenario, especially given the nature of the environment in which it all takes place. Helpmann said, 'I wanted to do *Miracle in the Gorbals* because its religious theme – what would happen to Christ if He came back into a modern world – seemed to match what I felt at the time about the state of man.'[6] All Bliss's ballets shared this characteristic of visceral drama, which was so different from the romantic fantasies often associated with the ballet genre; hence the term 'dance-drama'.

It is easy to understand why Bliss enjoyed writing music for ballet so much. When writing for film, music is the servant of the director's will and whim, which led to a number of unhappy situations between Bliss and his directors over the years. But with ballet of the period, music was the central element around which the choreography was moulded, and although there were obvious limitations – such as the duration of scenes where the stamina of the dancers has to be calculated – nevertheless, the composer was able to express himself in the way he felt moved in relation to the given scenario.

The Overture sets the general mood and Bliss prepares us for the weighty emotional thrust of the story about to unfold. Burra's great painted front cloth of a ship in dry dock rises to reveal the street scene bustling with activity and its variety of humankind: youngsters playing, fighting and being admonished by a Minister (Official),[7] toughs looking on, a Prostitute looking for trade, a fish-and-chip shop – all the febrile atmosphere with its lurking possibilities for trouble.

Into this a solitary young girl appears – someone obviously not of this neighbourhood – who is at the end of her tether; she sees the drunks and the hopeless types all around her, and cannot see a future for herself. She makes a decision to end it all in the river. Bliss, at the start of this scene, makes reference to Frédéric Chopin's 'Funeral March' (third movement of the second Piano Sonata), giving the audience a heads-up as to what is about to happen.

Another reason that the music is key to the whole enterprise is the variety that it brings to not only the aural, but the visual scene too. The scene that follows is almost surreal in this gutter-like environment, showing a pair of lovers, whose mutual engagement lifts the spirit of the time and place and in Bliss's gentle waltz with its long-breathed melodic lines transports us to another time and place altogether. The moment is shattered by a heavily discordant warning chord and the Prostitute, annoyed that a potential client is being seduced into a relationship, tries to woo him away before the Minister intervenes. While Bliss's music for the Prostitute's attempted seduction still has the waltz at its heart, it is full of discordant harmony and interrupted moments. A fight ensues, but the Minister emerges as the self-satisfied master of the situation.

Fig. 6.6: The Dance of Deliverance: Michael Somes as the Stranger (lifted), Pauline Clayden as the Suicide (in the foreground with arms raised). Sadler's Wells Ballet, Royal Opera House, 1946. Photo: Roger Wood (The Royal Ballet and Opera/ArenaPAL).

Fig. 6.7: The Stranger enters with quiet authority. Robert Helpmann with David Paltenghi as the Official (Minister) at his feet and leaning away. Sadler's Wells Ballet, Royal Opera House, 1946. Photo: Roger Wood (The Royal Ballet and Opera/ArenaPAL).

The fight that follows is brilliantly represented by Bliss. An angry orchestra throws musical figures around its various sections, with the brass and percussion hurling themselves into the fray. It is a short scene, but visceral in its vivid energy. Now, a completely different kind of energetic music almost frightens in its intensity, and it builds and builds as the rumour of something terrible spreads like wildfire around the street and the crowd gathers. Once again, the music changes to an almost funeral brass elegy as the body of the drowned girl is carried in. The Minister tries to resuscitate the girl, but it is hopeless. Bliss's music is weightily expressive as he directs the emotion of the stage and the audience to what has happened.

The next scene is a pivotal moment as a Stranger enters with such a quiet authority that even the Minister, who initially tries to confront him, feels his power and kneels. Bliss writes a series of variations for this scene, dark in character, but with the feeling of the constancy of a thematic thread binding the music and giving the overarching sensation that something of enormous significance is about to happen. The dead girl is brought back to life, and the extraordinary Dance of Deliverance follows.

Although this is a riotous celebration of the restoration to life of this young girl with the whole cast brought into a frenzy of dance, the overt Americanisms of Bliss's music here tell us that this is his personal 'dance of deliverance' from the years of

Fig. 6.8: The Prostitute and the Suicide following the murder of the Stranger and leaving him in the arms of the Beggar. Julia Farron as the Prostitute, Pauline Clayden as the Suicide, Robert Helpmann as the Stranger and Leslie Edwards as the Beggar. Sadler's Wells Ballet, Royal Opera House, 1947. Photo: Merlyn Severn (Royal Ballet School/ArenaPAL).

separation from his family left in America for all that time. The free-wheeling jazz idiom of the music is enhanced by Bliss's instruction to the drummer that he or she should 'play in an ad-lib style' using various rhythms (four variations) as detailed in the score. It is a real tour de force.

It is the Minister or Official who is central to what follows. He is so deeply resentful at having his authority usurped in this dramatic fashion that he determines to find a way to undermine the Stranger's miraculous powers. Bliss's music turns from unbridled joy to discordant chaos as the Minister (I am continuing to call him this despite the change in his title for reasons of 'tact') forms his plan to discredit the Stranger by sending him to 'save' the Prostitute. In the meantime, he poisons the mind of the crowd by getting them to watch out for him coming from the building with the Prostitute, inferring that he had been 'using' her. The same technique Bliss used for the start of the suicide rumour is used at the beginning of this scene. A halting but quickly repetitive figure becomes a frenzied ostinato as the rumour of the Stranger being with the Prostitute spreads.

When the Prostitute appears, she has completely changed and has obviously been deeply moved by her 'conversion' by the Stranger. Bliss's music is lyrical and expressive. This only incenses the Minister further; he now acts on his anger, gathering youthful tough guys, the Razor Gang, to attack the Stranger. He understands what is happening and offers no resistance; the Stranger is murdered in cold blood. Bliss knows just how to describe this in music and his emotional response is electrifying: the scurrying strings, the agonised brass chords that build to reflect the sense of mounting terror and the pounding timpani magnifying to a horrifying climax when the murder is done. All this Bliss composed brilliantly. His sense of drama was such a key part of his creative arsenal.

The murdering group scatters, leaving the Prostitute and the Suicide to join the Beggar in mourning this extraordinary Stranger. Bliss's coda – moving funereal music – sees the girls comforting each other but then departing in case they are implicated in the crime. This leaves just the Beggar holding the body of the Stranger in his arms.

The premiere of *Miracle in the Gorbals* took place at the Prince's Theatre in London on 26 October 1944. One of the most haunting reflections on the early performance was written by the eighty-five-year-old Buss Jackson who remembered seeing it as a nineteen-year-old in 1944: 'That first night the girl, danced by Pauline Clayden, achieved perfection in an adage, a wonderful combination of technique, timing and inspiration – an ecstasy, which has remained with me to this day. After the grim end, possibly as a relief from tension, the "gods" went wild!'. By contrast, on seeing the ballet and the similarly enthusiastic reception to performances on the Sadler's Wells Ballet tour of America in 1949, the influential impresario Lincoln Kirstein bemoaned a lack of choreographic invention: 'The Gorbals program. Well mother. All is forgiven, but *never* do it again.'[8]

For all the contemporary press chatter about whether the work was ballet or dance-drama, it remains one of Bliss's most successful and powerful stage works, as the wonderful 2014 recreation by Birmingham Royal Ballet showed most clearly.

This chapter has developed research originally undertaken for the author's biography of Sir Arthur Bliss (Ramsbury, Wiltshire: Robert Hale, 2023), where all the ballets in this book can be appreciated in the context of Bliss's wider compositional output.

7. Englishness of Some Other Sort

Sam Ellis

Arthur Bliss occupies a paradoxical position in British musical history. Though often perceived today as a central figure – his long career crowned by establishment roles such as Master of the Queen's Music – he consistently operated with a sense of detachment from the musical mainstream. His artistic versatility, shaped by extensive travel and expressed through genre-defying adaptability, set him apart from many of his contemporaries. *Miracle in the Gorbals* (1944) offers a compelling lens through which to explore this distinctiveness, revealing how Bliss's collaborative instincts and personal relationships created a sense of rootedness that transcended institutional boundaries.

The ballet itself reflects the cultural and artistic tensions of the interwar period from which it emerged. Its neoclassical approach, influenced by historical and allegorical sources, aligns Christ with the image of the Good Shepherd, an archetype steeped in pastoral tradition. This pastoral dimension is juxtaposed against the ballet's grim, urban setting: an industrial landscape representative of Britain's rapid modernisation and its associated social anxieties. By exploring this interplay of pastoral and industrial elements, we can better understand Bliss's artistic vision, his response to the cultural milieu of interwar Britain and his distinctive place in twentieth-century British music.

The extramusical context of Bliss's work, particularly in his mature compositions, was profoundly shaped by his experiences during the First World War. The war produced a decisive break with past certainties, leaving Bliss, like many of his contemporaries, searching for a new aesthetic and philosophical grounding. While he did not wholly embrace modernism, its ideals and experimental spirit influenced his work. However, as we shall see, a modernist impulse in Bliss's music often coexisted with a reverence for historical forms and classical sensibilities.

Bliss's outsider status is particularly striking in relation to British pastoral traditions. While his work sometimes engages with pastoral themes, it does so not through nostalgic or Arcadian idealism, but via a more structured, classical outlook. This singular blend of modernist inclination, neoclassical form and selective pastoral reference reveals Bliss's distinctive artistic identity and his layered negotiation with tradition.

Bliss the outsider

Bliss's outsider status – rooted in his upbringing, education and personal choices – was a defining factor in his art. This 'otherness' was both a circumstantial reality and an intrinsic element of his creative philosophy. Indeed, it was in his distance from the mainstream that Bliss found freedom to challenge conventions and cultivate his distinctive voice.

Fig. 7.1: Children playing in the Gorbals district of Glasgow, the grim urban setting for *Miracle in the Gorbals* (1944). Photo: Bert Hardy, 1948 (Picture Post/Getty images).

Fig. 7.2: David Paltenghi as the Official and Celia Franca as the Prostitute in the 1944 premiere of *Miracle in the Gorbals*. Photographer unknown (Royal Academy of Dance/ArenaPAL).

The First World War irrevocably altered Bliss's personal and artistic trajectory. Emerging from the conflict at the age of twenty-seven, Bliss found himself confronting the loss of both time and opportunity. The war had derailed his early career, delaying his artistic development and fostering a heightened awareness of mortality. The death of his brother Kennard left a lasting imprint on Bliss's psyche. Like many artists who experienced the war's horrors at the front lines, Bliss's sense of loss was personal, intimate and reflective.

Naturally, the war shaped the cultural and artistic responses of its survivors. Samuel Hynes, in his book *A War Imagined* (1990), describes a generation 'drugged by war at the moment when they might have been learning the experimental gestures of their time', left uncertain of their place in a world that no longer resembled the pre-war order.[2] Bliss's post-armistice music reflects his sense of displacement, but also a conscious effort to rebuild meaning and purpose. His experience of confronting death and disorder appears to have deepened his commitment to developing a clear musical intention and a personal artistic philosophy.

Markers of otherness

Bliss's sense of otherness extended beyond his formative years and personal losses. Throughout his career, he remained detached from many of the dominant musical circles of the time. He was notably removed from the Kensington set, centred around Charles Villiers Stanford and Hugh Allen at the Royal College of Music. This social dislocation was amplified by Bliss's unconventional influences and relationships.

He studied under Stanford – joining a list of eminent pupils – although their personal relationship was strained. Stanford, a staunch proponent of the

His heritage itself defied categorisation. Born to an English mother and an American father of New England descent, Bliss perhaps lacked the secure English identity that many of his contemporaries enjoyed. His father's eventual return to the USA underscored this sense of geographical and emotional displacement. Bliss's formative years at Rugby School, an institution still influenced by Thomas Arnold's reformist ethos, also shaped his intellectual and artistic outlook.[1] It was here that Bliss's interest in French music, unusual at the time, was first cultivated.

Robert Whitelaw, a teacher at Rugby, instilled in Bliss a lifelong fascination with classical civilisations and particularly the works of Homer. This early immersion in ancient cultures would later inform his neoclassical inclinations and his fondness for mythological and allegorical themes. At Cambridge University, where he studied both music and history, Bliss further deepened his appreciation for classical models, building a foundation that remained evident in his music throughout his career.

Fig. 7.3: In *Miracle in the Gorbals*, historical and allegorical themes are combined directly with contemporary concerns. Robert Helpmann as the Stranger with the Inhabitants of the Gorbals in a postcard from the 1944 production. Photo: Edward Mandinian (Royal Ballet School Special Collections/ArenaPAL).

Germanic musical tradition that dominated English conservatoire culture, reportedly dismissed French Impressionism – particularly the works of Claude Debussy and Maurice Ravel – as 'eunuch music'.[3] Bliss's admiration for French music, cultivated during his youth and early travels, therefore marked him as an outlier within an establishment that valued Brahmsian technical rigour above all else.

Bliss's Catholicism, particularly as a convert, further underscored his outsider status. In an era when Anglicanism remained the cultural and religious norm among the British artistic elite, Bliss's affiliation with Anglo-Catholicism aligned him with a minority tradition, though one that resonated with other artistic figures of the period. Importantly, however, this outsider position does not appear to have been a source of sustained anxiety for Bliss. On the contrary, it seems to have emboldened his artistic choices and reinforced his willingness to forge his own path.[4]

Later, Bliss's outsider persona took on a paradoxical quality. His appointment as Director of Music at the BBC – a role that positioned him at the heart of Britain's musical establishment – was met with some suspicion and mistrust. Colleagues described him as 'mercurial',[5] and his tenure was marked by an unwillingness to conform to expectations. Similarly, his knighthood and appointment as Master of the Queen's Music – a role redolent of a certain cultural conservatism – stand as semi-ironic markers of a man who had spent much of his life on the periphery of the very establishment he came to represent.

Bliss's life and career were shaped by his experiences abroad, which profoundly influenced his musical style and artistic worldview. Though born in London, he was never fully anchored to the city; rather, he embodied the now-familiar notion of the global citizen. In Bliss's case, this rootlessness was not a limitation but an opportunity to draw inspiration from diverse cultural and artistic sources.

In the months following the Armistice, London seemed a natural locus, a place for recovery and artistic reinvention. However, Bliss also made two formative visits to Paris either side of Christmas 1919: with its vibrant post-war cultural scene, Paris offered exposure to modernist trends that were reshaping European art and music. The influence of French repertoire, first encountered during Bliss's schooldays, found renewed expression during this period. His writings from this time, particularly his essay 'What Modern Composition is Aiming At', articulate his growing alignment with neoclassicism, especially the music of Igor Stravinsky and the artistic ethos of Jean Cocteau and Les Six.[6]

Bliss's time abroad extended beyond Paris. His travels to California in the 1920s, where he met his wife Trudy, and his unplanned residency in the USA from 1939 until 1941, further expanded his cultural horizons. In many ways, Bliss's cosmopolitan life reflects a constant negotiation between 'somewhere' and 'anywhere', between his inherited British identity and his exposure to the global artistic community.[7]

Miracle in the Gorbals: pastoralism meets the modern city

Miracle in the Gorbals occupies a singular place within Bliss's oeuvre, serving as both a synthesis of his artistic preoccupations and a powerful response to the cultural and social realities of wartime Britain. As a ballet, it combines Bliss's interest in historical and allegorical themes with the ability of art to engage directly with contemporary concerns: urban poverty, moral decay and spiritual redemption.

The creation of *Miracle in the Gorbals* was a collaborative process involving some of the most innovative figures in mid-twentieth-century British art. The scenario was written by theatre director Michael Benthall; the choreography devised by Robert Helpmann; and the set design crafted by Edward Burra, whose dark, expressionistic aesthetic deeply influenced the ballet's tone and atmosphere.[8] Helpmann, in particular, brought a raw dramatic energy to the production, intensifying its stark portrayal of life in the Gorbals.

The narrative is both simple and profound. A Christ-like figure – a nameless Stranger – arrives in a decaying, poverty-stricken urban environment. His miraculous resurrection of a young girl ignites a mixture of hope, fear and suspicion among the local residents. The Stranger's presence unsettles the fragile social order, exposing the community's spiritual emptiness and moral ambiguity. In the ballet's tragic conclusion, the Stranger is betrayed and murdered, leaving the community to grapple with the implications of his brief but transformative presence.

Bliss's score plays a central role in conveying the ballet's emotional weight and thematic complexity. His customary use of stark orchestral textures and jagged rhythmic patterns evokes the harsh realities of urban life, while moments of lyrical beauty suggest the possibility of redemption and transcendence. In this way, Bliss created a soundscape that mirrors the ballet's juxtaposition of despair and hope.

The industrial pastoral

Eric Saylor, a leading scholar of twentieth-century English music, has identified in two works by Ralph Vaughan Williams, the one-act opera *The Shepherds of the Delectable Mountains* (1921)[9] and the ballet *Job* (1930), the theme of redemption through loss. In the former, a pilgrim figure must cross the River of Death to reach the Celestial City. For *Job*, humiliation gives rise to peace. In both works, 'the protagonists achieve some measure of deliverance or relief from suffering by losing something crucially important'.[10] Similarly, in *Miracle in the Gorbals*, the sacrifice is by a single protagonist, the Stranger,

Fig. 7.4: Karl Parsons, *Jesus Christ the Good Shepherd*, 1913. © The Stained Glass Museum, Ely Cathedral.

whose death represents the promise of salvation for the entire community. However, unlike the more idealised settings of Vaughan Williams's works, the world of *Gorbals* is a remarkably unsanitised, unsentimental depiction of modern urban life.

The setting of Glasgow's industrial Gorbals district marks a rejection of the idyllic rural landscapes often associated with pastoralism. Instead, the ballet explores the pastoral in a strikingly modern, urban context. The tension at the heart of *Miracle in the Gorbals* lies in its interplay between the pastoral tradition – so central to British cultural identity – and the harsh realities of contemporary industrial existence and brutalities of war. While traditional pastoralism idealises rural life as a space of simplicity, harmony and moral clarity, Bliss and his collaborators offer a more complex vision.

In the scenario of *Gorbals*, the Stranger functions as a pastoral protagonist. Peter Marinelli identifies three archetypes of pastoral figures: the classical, representing humanity in universal terms (often a shepherd); the romantic, embodying heroic individualism; and the modern, personifying the emblematic worker or child.[11] The Stranger aligns with the classical model, serving as a symbol of humanity. While the figure of Christ is transposed from its rural, primitive setting in the Holy Lands to the industrial decay of the Gorbals, the Stranger nevertheless retains his representation as Jesus the Good Shepherd. This transposition underscores a reimagining of the pastoral: rather than an escape from modernity, it becomes an intrusion into it. The Stranger's presence in a fractured community highlights a collective alienation from nature and spiritual roots, while also suggesting the possibility of redemption even in a landscape of industrial poverty.

Bliss's relationship with the pastoral in *Gorbals* may initially seem at odds with his artistic voice, often marked by a neoclassical accent and a position outside the pastoral mainstream. Saylor, however, observes a classical element within the British pastoral tradition itself. He draws connections between 'visions of rural England' and 'classical depictions of Arcadia', noting how Victorian-era British culture was deeply informed by ancient Greek ideals.[12] While rejecting a nostalgic pastoral idyll, Bliss and his collaborators engage with this classical lineage by presenting a figure of pastoral simplicity – rooted in the archetypal Good Shepherd – in a thoroughly modern, industrial setting.

This reinterpretation aligns with some of Bliss's earlier works, such as *Morning Heroes* (1930), in which themes of sacrifice and spiritual renewal are explored in modern contexts. In *Morning Heroes*, Bliss set Wilfred Owen's poetry to music, where survivors of war confront a 'damaged world they have inherited rather than the utopia they were promised'.[13] The parallels with *Gorbals* are clear: both works grapple with the dissonance between idealised visions of redemption and the gritty realities of human suffering.

The Gorbals district itself – associated even now with industrial poverty and urban decay – becomes a modern counterpoint to Arcadian landscapes.[14] Pastoralism is thus reimagined as a mode of critique rather than escapism. By bringing the figure of the Good Shepherd into the heart of an urban-industrial wasteland, *Miracle in the Gorbals* appraises modernity's alienation from nature and spirituality while affirming the enduring power of redemption. The Stranger's sacrifice bridges the ancient and the modern, the pastoral and the urban, illustrating the potential for grace and renewal even in the bleakest of circumstances.

Spiritual redemption in a secular age

In an era marked by war, industrialisation and social upheaval, *Miracle in the Gorbals* grapples with questions of faith and human nature that resonate far beyond its immediate setting. Indeed, the Christ-like Stranger at the heart of the ballet encapsulates the exploratory themes of spirituality and morality. The Stranger's miraculous resurrection of the young girl serves as a powerful symbol of hope and renewal. However, the inhabitants' reaction to the miracle – ranging from awe and gratitude to suspicion and hostility – reveals the fragility of their faith and their inability to accept the possibility of redemption.

The ballet's tragic conclusion, in which the Stranger is betrayed and murdered, has deliberate echoes of the Passion narrative of Christ's

Fig. 7.5: The climactic killing of the Stranger, representing the moment the Gorbals community rejects the pastoral figure of the Good Shepherd and reverts to industrial-era violence. Photo: Edward Mandinian © Victoria and Albert Museum, London. (Victoria and Albert Museum).

Crucifixion. Yet unlike traditional religious works, *Miracle in the Gorbals* offers no clear resolution. The Stranger's death leaves the inhabitants as lost and broken as they were at the outset, their brief encounter having failed to transform them.

This ambiguity reflects the cultural and spiritual anxieties of wartime Britain. The devastation of the Second World War had shattered many of the certainties that had once underpinned British society, leaving most communities wrestling with questions of meaning and faith. In this context, *Miracle in the Gorbals* can be seen as both a critique of moral instability and a meditation on the possibility of redemption in a secular, industrialised world.

Miracle in the Gorbals is a distinctive and powerful score which, as a collaborative enterprise, nevertheless stands as a synthesis of Bliss's artistic influences and thematic preoccupations: as we have seen, it combines modernist and pastoral elements, engages with contemporary social issues and explores spiritual themes. In its stark portrayal of urban poverty and spiritual longing, the ballet challenges the assumptions of the pastoral tradition, offering a vision of redemption that is both modern and profoundly human. Bliss's music brings this vision to life, creating a work that is resonant in its exploration of the human condition.

Gorbals within the Bliss canon

Bliss's engagement with ballet reflected a willingness to embrace interdisciplinary forms of expression. This openness was consistent with his remarkable versatility as a composer, evident in his contributions across nearly every musical genre: chamber works, a symphony, concertos, songs, orchestral movements, choral compositions, film scores and opera. His ballet scores, particularly *Checkmate* (1937) and *Adam Zero* (1946), exemplify his ability to blend music, movement and narrative into cohesive dramatic statements, further showcasing his artistic adaptability.

However, *Miracle in the Gorbals* is qualitatively different to the other ballets on which Bliss worked. *Checkmate* employs allegory and abstraction to explore themes of power and conflict; *Adam Zero* examines the arc of human life through the lens of myth; *The Lady of Shalott* (1958) addresses the youthful tension between longing for experience and fear of its consequences. *Gorbals*, by contrast, is firmly rooted in a contemporary, recognisable world. Its setting in the industrial heart of Glasgow reflects a deliberate engagement with modern social realities, while its narrative grounds spiritual themes in the struggles of ordinary people.

The early success of *Miracle in the Gorbals* demonstrates Bliss's ability to collaborate effectively with other leading artists of his time.[15] His partnership with Helpmann and Burra – whose set designs, as we have seen, contributed much to the ballet's gritty aesthetic – confirms the interdisciplinary nature of the work and its grounding in contemporary artistic movements. Together, Bliss and his collaborators created a ballet that was as visually arresting as it was musically compelling.[16]

The cultural and social context of *Miracle in the Gorbals* is also essential to understanding its significance. First performed in 1944, the ballet reflected the anxieties and hardships of wartime Britain. The Gorbals, a symbol of urban deprivation, perhaps served as a microcosm of the broader social challenges facing the nation. At a time when communities across the country were grappling with loss and uncertainty, *Gorbals* presented a powerful exploration of frailty.

The moment of the ballet's composition highlights the role of art as a means of processing collective trauma. By addressing human vulnerability, *Miracle in the Gorbals* may have provided a space for audiences to confront the emotional and spiritual toll of war. Bliss's music, with its combination of modernist dissonance and pastoral lyricism, offered a stark portrayal of suffering and a glimpse of transcendence. The depiction of a Christ-like figure entering a world of betrayal served as a reminder of the possibility of renewal.

Gorbals in context: British modernism and the arts

Miracle in the Gorbals exemplifies Bliss's ability to synthesise seemingly disparate elements – pastoral and industrial, myth and modernity, spiritual and secular – into a cohesive artistic statement and stands as a testament to interdisciplinary collaboration.

Bliss's position as an outsider within British musical culture underscores the distinctiveness of his approach. As the critic and historian Frank Howes observed as early as 1966, Bliss's work resists easy classification within the pastoral tradition, aligning him with composers like Edward Elgar and William Walton, who embodied an 'Englishness … of some other sort'.[17] Bliss's impulse towards classical and mythological models suggests that his pastoralism, where present, was a reflection of modern imagination rather than an idealised past. This is a nuanced engagement with classical traditions that reveals the ongoing relevance of the pastoral, even in settings as unorthodox as the Gorbals.

The interplay of past and present is central to Bliss's neoclassical aesthetic, which provided him with an anchor amid the fluidity of his heritage and the challenges of modernism.[18] Andrew Blake's classification of Walton and Constant Lambert as small-'m' modernists captures this balance: Bliss too fits this category, resisting the firmer rejection of tradition associated with capital-'M' modernism, while continually seeking to adapt and reinvigorate the vernacular.[19] The collision of the pastoral and the industrial in *Miracle in the Gorbals* becomes, in this sense, a microcosm of Bliss's broader project:

an effort to reconcile the aesthetic and philosophical ruptures of the twentieth century.

Ultimately, *Miracle in the Gorbals* embodies Bliss's mature artistic vision, rooted in tradition yet unflinching in its engagement with the present. It is a work that transcends its immediate historical context, offering a profound meditation on human vulnerability. The enduring resonance of this ballet lies not only in its bold reinterpretation of the pastoral, but also in its testament to the transformative potential of art as a dialogue between the past and the modern world.

Fig. 7.6: Robert Helpmann as the Stranger in the 1946 Sadler's Wells Ballet revival of *Miracle in the Gorbals*. Royal Opera House. Photo: Roger Wood (Royal Ballet and Opera/ArenaPAL).

8.
Gillian Lynne's
Miracle in the Gorbals

DAVID BINTLEY

WITH VOICES OF THE CAST
COMPILED BY JENNIFER JACKSON

As a keen student of ballet history I was always fascinated by three works produced by the Sadler's Wells Ballet during wartime: Frederick Ashton's *Dante Sonata* (1940), Ninette de Valois' *The Prospect Before Us* (1940) and Robert Helpmann's *Miracle in the Gorbals* (1944), much photographed and warmly remembered by that older generation who had danced in them. Later, as Director of Birmingham Royal Ballet, I found not only that I had the resources to try and rescue these 'lost' pieces, but also a sense of duty in trying to get that older generation, some of them approaching their nineties, to see what could be remembered. In the case of *Dante*, the amazing Pamela May and, in particular, Jean Bedells, both original cast members, were able to recall virtually the entire work. At one point I was called in to 'stitch' one section to another – not that I can recall where now – but the rest is Ashton, and an Ashton we had never known before: barefoot, expressionistic, searingly felt and full of the anxieties prevalent in wartime Britain in 1940. The ballet fell out of favour in the post-war years, but when resurrected in 2001 its timeless relevance was felt once more as the London premiere took place on the very evening of the 9/11 attacks in America.

Sadly, de Valois' *The Prospect Before Us*, interesting though it was, had not aged as well. Most famous for Helpmann's portrayal of theatre manager Mr O'Reilly and his drunken dance, Madam's comic

Fig. 8.1: Gillian Lynne with Delia Matthews in rehearsal at Birmingham Royal Ballet studios, October 2014. Photo: Andrew Ross (ArenaPAL).

Fig. 8.2: Gillian Lynne with the Minister and the Razor Gang in rehearsal (left to right): Brandon Lawrence, Valentin Olovyannikov, Max Maslen, Iain Mackay, Jonathan Caguioa, Rory Mackay, Yasuo Atsuji. Photo: Andrew Ross (ArenaPAL).

Fig. 8.3 (overleaf): The cast of *Miracle in the Gorbals* in performance with Cesar Morales as the Stranger and showing the re-creation of the designs by Adam Wiltshire after Edward Burra. Photo: Bill Cooper (ArenaPAL).

ballet might have lifted spirits in the early 1940s but remains something of a curate's egg for modern audiences not quite attuned to the period.

In 2014 I presented a BBC film about the Sadler's Wells Ballet during the Second World War, entitled *Dancing in the Blitz*. I had the very great pleasure of talking with many of the surviving artists from that time, among whom was the wonderful dancer and choreographer Gillian Lynne. Gillie told me that she and former Royal Ballet dancer David Drew had long wanted to revive Helpmann's *Miracle in the Gorbals*.[1] Gillie had been in the original cast, and David in the 1958 revival, and they had done a fair amount of research into the production. Like *Prospect*, however, much of the work couldn't be remembered and it would be necessary to 'stitch' together the many photographs of the piece. My feelings were that this hadn't worked too well with the de Valois piece and most of the surviving cast members said that, to be honest, there wasn't much choreography in the ballet anyway! It was Helpmann's superb acting and the committed performances that he got from his cast which had made the ballet such a success in 1944. Gillie was in agreement. She felt that in some way she carried 'Bobby's' spirit within her, and that instinct, plus her lifetime of skills as a theatre director and choreographer, would be a better way to make the piece live again. Gillie sent me a recording of Arthur Bliss's score and we set to looking for a designer who could realise the stunning original designs by painter Edward Burra.

Gillie's way of creating the choreography was different from the outset. Most choreographers working in narrative will tend to build a character through the steps, in collaboration with the dancer. Full-blown interpretation and emotional investment come later. Not with Gillie. From day one she insisted that every character conform to the idea that she had already fixed in her imagination. She demanded that once the dancer 'had' the character, then the steps would come, and creative rehearsals

Fig. 8.4: The full company in rehearsal. César Morales as the Stranger and Delia Matthews as the Suicide, with Iain Mackay as the Minister in the background. Photo: Andrew Ross (ArenaPAL).

were conducted in a semi-religious atmosphere. Not only was she intolerant of the tension-relieving tomfoolery that's the norm in most rehearsals, but even lapses of attention didn't go unpunished. She was also very reluctant to give her second cast any time, frustrating them and making the pressure on the first cast relentless. Some weeks into the creative process, and at the instigation of a few of the 'covers', I tried to impress on her both their frustration and my opinion that she might learn something about the piece by seeing a fresh 'take'. Gillie's impressive work in the musical theatre was legendary, but in that world one rarely has the benefit of multiple casts and the different interpretations that can slowly mature a work and reveal its different facets. She was very sweet in her reply, yet never put a single person who wasn't in her first cast into rehearsal or performance.

In many ways Gillie's working process paid off. The performances were uniformly committed, accurate and powerful. I couldn't help feeling, however, that the frisson of development, the interpolation of some slight difference in interpretation, was somehow missing. The shows had something of the quality-controlled sterility of a modern-day musical, lacking the spontaneity that a lifetime of watching ballet performances has led me to anticipate. Many ballet audiences assume that the show they are seeing is the same every night. How wrong they are! Every performance is different, unique, and one can't tell as the curtain goes up whether it will be a workaday experience or a truly great event. Nonetheless, a week before the premiere the entire workforce of Birmingham Royal Ballet (and the cast of *Cats*, who were performing at the Birmingham Hippodrome) were all invited to a 'showing' of the finished work in the rehearsal room. In all my years in dance I've never witnessed the level of performance and commitment to a piece of such high melodrama in the rehearsal room, without costume or make-up or scenery to 'hide' behind. Gillie, in her reimagining of *Miracle*, had done what Helpmann did in his original. She had not so much created a choreographic masterpiece, but had drawn performances from the dancers of such commitment, energy and belief that the work really did, in her words, live.

One addition Gillie made to the production is very telling: as the lights go down, and immediately before the first doom-laden strains of Bliss's score, she has the 'all clear' siren sound faintly throughout the auditorium. This immediately reminds us that the year is 1944, and yet the war fades from our consciousness as the story that unfolds seems to engage us in a much deeper, spiritual conflict, with the ballet depicting the return of Christ and his murder once again by fallen humanity.

The characters in *Miracle* are vivid and charged with emotion, as is the hyperrealistic depiction of the mean, violent and impoverished Gorbals area of Glasgow during wartime. When first staged in 1944 the ballet was startlingly contemporary and pointed so much towards the future that the distinguished critic Arnold Haskell even wrote a small book on it, musing on how it would change choreography in the future.[2] The music, too, with its references to modern dance music idioms, is bang up to date. Bliss's fingerprints are all over the score. After the wonderful success of *Checkmate* (1937), it was natural that Helpmann would want to work with a composer of such brilliant gifts, who seemed a natural for music drama. It wasn't to be the last time that the two creative masters would work together, as they went on to collaborate on *Adam Zero* in 1946. Now there's a ballet ripe for rediscovery!

This article was first printed in the Bliss Society magazine www.arthurbliss.org

Fig. 8.5: The Razor Gang with the Minister in performance (left to right): Brandon Lawrence, Valentin Olovyannikov, Iain Mackay, Max Maslen, Rory Mackay, Yasuo Atsuji. Photo: Bill Cooper (ArenaPAL).

" Voices of the Cast

Gillian Lynne's *Miracle in the Gorbals* was premiered at the Birmingham Hippodrome on 8 October 2014. It was the second ballet in a triple bill entitled *Shadows of War* that began with Kenneth MacMillan's *La Fin du Jour* (1979) and closed with David Bintley's *Flowers of the Forest* (1985). David's writing was the starting point for conversations with several members of the cast and creative team[3] about their experience of recreating the ballet.[4]

Paul Murphy (Conductor)[5]
Jeremy Kerridge (Assistant to Gillian Lynne)[6]
William Bracewell (The Lover)
Ruth Brill (an Old Woman)
Laura Day (an Urchin)
Iain Mackay (The Minister)
César Morales Anderson (The Stranger)
Delia Matthews (The Suicide)
Michael O'Hare (The Beggar)
Marion Tait (an Old Woman)

They talked with immense passion and honesty about the very 'different' kind of creative process with Gillie: her vision of how to bring the ballet back to life; her preparation before coming into the studio; how she drew you into the work; the depth and detail of characterisation; individual responsibility and being a Company; theatre and the art of storytelling and – central to the process – the music.

Their reflections and the rehearsal and performance photographs speak eloquently of how Gillian shaped the choreography and the impact on their artistic practices. Writing in 2014, Sarah Crompton remarked on what was revealed to her in exploring this 'lost' work: '[A]s time has gone on, narrative and emotion are things ballet-makers have become more self-conscious about. There was a time when people believed that dance could do anything, as Birmingham Royal Ballet proved when they recreated Robert Helpmann's *Miracle in the Gorbals* from 1944, an oddball reminder of the kind of social realism that was once normal in dance but now seems rare'.[7]

First Steps

Delia: The first thing was that Gillie sat us down in the studio. She played the entire score – music was integral to the whole ballet, so we listened to it, and then we spoke about all the characters. One of the things she got us to do was to learn how the characters walk, just walk across the room, making a pathway for all the classical ballet steps. So, you had that body language of the character in place.

Fig. 8.6: Finding the character in everyday movements. Photo: Bill Cooper. (ArenaPAL)

Ruth: The way she cast the ballet was like nothing I'd ever encountered in a ballet company. She knew the look and essence she needed for each character in the ballet. She spent the first half an hour of the casting call just walking around us and watching us talk to each other.

Laura: What was really important to her was getting the right combination of people in the right places, and that was really even before we had done any steps.

The Score

Paul: Bliss was very proud of his writing for the theatre – and those three scores are standout works of British music. I love *Checkmate*, but for me *Gorbals* was on a more spiritual plane than *Checkmate*. It develops more naturally – it's almost as if he were writing a forty-minute symphony, as it alternates between menacing, powerful and beautiful. You enter into its substance immediately. There's no warm up; you're in the mood of the piece right from the beginning. The orchestra enjoyed playing it immensely. It poses a lot of questions musically that you've got to try and solve.

Iain: We listened a lot to the music. We listened without doing. We listened with intention, to understand. It wasn't that she didn't want us to count it, but she wanted us to feel it, to link the gestures to the music, which I think in the end really drove the piece.

William: A lot of the reconstruction inspiration came from the music … such a clear thematic score. You could sit and just listen to the music and probably understand the story.

Creative Process

Ruth: We were all very clear that we were recreating and reviving something from the past. All was explained. Gillie had some of her own memories and we had some references to draw from: key images to inspire the designs and settings, cast lists, scenario. But there were also many gaps. It felt like Gillie was 'creating' with us; she navigated the past and also used her creative licence to make it her own.

Marion: Jeremy was like the dance captain, and they would work it out together before coming into the studio.

Jeremy: I would meet up with her in her home, or even her hotel room when we were actually in Birmingham creating it. She'd choreograph and show what she wanted. I would be the dancer in many different roles.

Ruth: We also had so much fun working with Gillie. The drama and intensity were balanced with fun and laughter in the studio.

Fig. 8.7: 'Research, research research': Gillian Lynne and Jeremy Kerridge in rehearsal with Delia Matthews as the Suicide. Photo: Andrew Ross (ArenaPAL).

Fig. 8.8: 'It was fun'. Gillian Lynne with Michael O'Hare as the Beggar, César Morales as the Stranger and Marion Tait in the background. Photo: Andrew Ross (ArenaPAL).

Fig. 8.9: The Company crowd around Iain Mackay as the Minister as he tests the pulse of the Suicide's body. Photo: Bill Cooper (ArenaPAL).

Company of Individuals

Iain: It was like being on a movie set some days, which I just loved. As soon as Gillie called 'action' on the scene, there was nobody allowed to not give 150 per cent. I don't mean in terms of the dancing; it was the intention. She was very demanding in the most inspiring of ways. She spent a lot of time on the small moments, so one example, when I check the pulse, to see if the woman is dead. Gillie was really laser-focused, to make sure that the story happened.

Ruth: She didn't stop until it was perfect … but when it was right, we could feel it. She was such a theatrical being. Dynamics, pace, details and theatrical clarity were everything.

Fig. 8.10: The Dance of Deliverance. Photo: Bill Cooper (ArenaPAL).

Iain: It felt uncomfortable, I think, the process. But we embraced it; she brought us all together. As a Company we were pushed in a way that we hadn't been, to engage with the content, to engage with a narrative, to engage with the characterisation. There were no Principals – every single person had to make that score, that story and those movements come alive.

Delia: We were so invested in our characters that it was really easy to play off one another. She really created that environment … we were all really in it together.

Ruth: The sense of community was so strong. It felt like we were bringing back to life an important work, a piece that held an important place in dance history. I felt deeply connected to the rest of the cast on stage. We were all 100 per cent committed to the work.

Fig. 8.11: Yvette Knight and William Bracewell as the Lovers. 'Every gesture, big or small, emerged from the character.' Photo: Bill Cooper (ArenaPAL).

Characterisation

Jeremy: Gillian would work so precisely and intricately with detail, with each character, and you would know exactly what she meant and what your relationship was.

William: In the role I played, there was a clear love story between a young couple, and he was tempted by another woman. The way Gillian, and everybody, approached it, was that every gesture was really important. Quite small changes could say something different. So, I began to understand the importance of very, very small moments, and what a difference small gestures – or big gestures – can make to getting across the character, in quite a short space of time. That was something I really enjoyed.

Laura: I remember Gillian showing these very particular poses, especially with the hands. She would go round and tweak a little finger from one of us to get their position right.

Fig. 8.12: The Minister is threatened by the Stranger's authority. Iain Mackay, César Morales and Delia Matthews as the Suicide. Photo: Bill Cooper (ArenaPAL).

Cesar: The role of the Stranger was very interesting and personal. She guided me a bit in how the role should be, but what she wanted to see was me not following steps or exact directions but what I would create with my own feelings. That was the starting point. The challenge was to be simple, and with not many steps, to transmit to the audience this very special, different and strong energy, like no one else on that stage.

GILLIAN LYNNE'S MIRACLE IN THE GORBALS | 101

" Storytelling

Delia: It was really freeing to focus — pretty solely — on the character and to be given the opportunity to play around with that. I learned a lot from it.

Iain: We sometimes forget because — certainly in my case as a Principal — the technicalities of roles can become sort of a focus. She really drilled back to that feeling of the art of storytelling, that art of dance linked to the music.

Fig. 8.13: Delia Matthews as the Suicide. Photo: Bill Cooper (ArenaPAL).

Fig. 8.14: Iain Mackay as the Minister and Elisha Willis as the Prostitute. Photo: Bill Cooper (ArenaPAL).

Fig. 8.15: The Inhabitants of the Gorbals crowd around the Stranger, the Minister and the Suicide. Laura Day wears a black beret (fourth from left), Ruth Brill wears a pink knitted hat with pom-pom (fourth from right) and Marion Tait, standing beside Ruth, wears a crocheted shawl. Photo: Bill Cooper (ArenaPAL).

Laura: The drama came first and that was what we rehearsed. Not the steps. We mainly rehearsed repeatedly to get right those really dramatic moments — particular[ly] in the crowd scenes. [She'd say] go from the start of 'Panic'. I was the Urchin who ran on having seen the body, and started to spread the message around the community. There is, in the music, this like *diddle le diddle le dum, diddle le diddle le dum*, and that was just one rhythm. And stand alone. And again. And the panic in the music started to build. This was reflected in the chaos and the panic as it passed around, because there was someone in the river. This was where Arthur Bliss's music really came into it, because the music did have that natural arc, and not just an arc over the overall piece, but actually each scene.

Marion: The costume day. There was a room in the theatre, Plymouth, and they had rails and rails of costumes and we just picked things. It was wonderful! And I said, oh I fancy that skirt. There were three of us who were these old hags — we were going to wear clogs and I couldn't because of my bunions. They found this huge pair of boots about two sizes too big, so I wore those, and it all added to the character.

Fig. 8.16: The Stranger is murdered by the Razor Gang. Photo: Bill Cooper (ArenaPAL).

"Vision

Iain: What I remember most about the whole process was the depth and connection that Gillie felt with the music. It was from the very first moment we started in the studio: every movement, every breath, every gesture, every look of the eye was connected to the score, and in a way that – we as a Company, and certainly myself as an artist – I hadn't really had before. And it wasn't prescriptive, but it was still deliberate. There was a vision that she had, that she wanted to bring back to life.

William: I think it was a piece of dance and it was a piece of drama and putting those two words together is a useful way to understand what you're about to watch. I feel like we perform dance-dramas at The Royal Ballet every season. You could call *Mayerling* or *Romeo and Juliet* a piece of dance-drama.

Fig. 8.17: The Suicide and the Prostitute, transformed, mourn the Stranger, held in the Beggar's arms. Delia Matthews, Elisha Willis, César Morales and Michael O'Hare. Photo: Bill Cooper (ArenaPAL).

Jeremy: It was a tribute to Robert Helpmann. He inspired her. He wanted real emotions, real reactions and real, you know, reasons to come on stage. Nothing was false, nothing was fake.

Michael: It would be interesting to see what the response to the 2014 recreation would be today. I think its themes of the tensions within a tight-knit community and its reaction to a stranger in its midst are relevant to all generations.

PART THREE

Adam Zero
1946

9.
Adam Zero: The A–Z of Life's Experience in Music and Dance

PAUL SPICER

Robert Helpmann, choreographer of and dancer in *Adam Zero* (1946), was one of the true originals whose influence moved British ballet forward, modernising the form and expanding attitudes towards it. Writing in 1949 he said:

> Of course the work of every choreographer reflects his personality to an extent. Miss de Valois, Mr Ashton and myself all show different characteristics of our own in our ballets, as well as certain racial similarities. I tried myself, when I began to compose ballets, to strike a style particularly suited to British dancers and to get away from some previous conventions just as Fokine did when he created *Petrouchka*.
>
> I had never seen a Diaghilev ballet as I lived in Australia until after Diaghilev's death, so its modernistic productions of the 'twenties did not influence me. In fact I took the 'dramatic' ballet further along the lines suggested by the choreography of Ninette de Valois. I tried to translate a Shakespearian theme in *Hamlet*, and to bring British ballet in touch with modern slum life in *Miracle in the Gorbals*. *Adam Zero* was an exercise in various dance styles and expressionistic stage production, with a symbolic contemporary background implied in some scenes.[1]

One of the difficulties Helpmann had to face was the attitude of dance critics of the day and their 'wildest assumptions as to a choreographer's "influences"'.[2] In this case, he was accused of 'lifting' the *Adam Zero* birth scene from Antony Tudor's *Undertow* (1945),

Fig. 9.1: The cover of the piano score for *Adam Zero* designed by Roger Furse, published by Novello, 1946 (Courtesy of Helen Kotz, Private Collection).

Fig. 9.2: Robert Helpmann as young Adam. Sadler's Wells Ballet, 1946. Photo: Baron (ArenaPAL).

Fig. 9.3: Robert Helpmann as successful Adam. Sadler's Wells Ballet, 1946. Photo: Baron (ArenaPAL).

Fig. 9.4: Robert Helpmann as Adam in old age. Sadler's Wells Ballet, 1946. Photo: Baron (ArenaPAL).

even though *Undertow* had not yet been seen in England and the scenario of *Adam Zero* was written in Holland in 1944, months before *Undertow* was produced in America.

I start this chapter with these personal reflections of Helpmann's because, despite the inevitable hostile reaction he knew he would face from sections of the press, as he did with *Miracle in the Gorbals* (1944), he followed his path with a sure-footedness and sense of destiny that marked him out as groundbreaking. Arthur Bliss saw this very clearly and it is notable that the two ballets he composed for the Benthall/Helpmann partnership brought from him what he felt was his best music for the stage – and especially that for *Adam Zero*. Bliss was himself a force of nature. An extrovert personality, coupled with a deep sensitivity and a feeling for life that was particular to those who had so narrowly avoided death themselves in the hideous conflict of the First World War, gave him a real feeling for the dramatic. Michael Benthall's realistic or psychological scenarios that so frustrated sections of the press found a willing partner in Bliss.

Adam Zero came hot on the heels of *Miracle in the Gorbals*, which had been staged highly successfully by the Sadler's Wells Ballet in October 1944. Wanting to build on this, Benthall and Helpmann devised *Adam Zero* for the same Company, with Helpmann not only as choreographer, but also as principal dancer taking the central character of Adam. It was premiered at Covent Garden on 10 April 1946.

The scenario was based on an imaginative approach to the life cycle of a man, hence A–Z, *Adam Zero*, with design by Roger Furse.[3] Adam's world was represented by the creation of a ballet on stage with key players in the various scenes representing key figures in his life. Thus 'Omnipotence' was the Stage Director, 'Adam's Fates', the Designer, Wardrobe Mistress and Dresser, and the 'Choreographer' was the woman in Adam's life who was both his lifeblood and ultimately his destroyer, eventually becoming the figure of benevolent death. Despite being falsely accused of stealing from the choreographer Tudor, Helpmann did acknowledge that the staging of *Adam Zero* was influenced by a play, Thornton Wilder's *The Skin of our Teeth* (1942), and even more by Japanese Noh plays he was reading at the time.[4] In one of these the stage represents the world, and Helpmann developed the ancient concept of shifting scenery, applying make-up and so on in front of the audience through the medium of a ballet rehearsal. Also key to the representation of the different stages of Adam's life were the different styles of dance: 'primitive for the man's youth, classical for his prime [and] jazz and jive for his degenerate middle age'.[5]

All this was, of course, a wonderful musical

Fig. 9.5: Adam and the Fates: showing the Covent Garden stage early in Adam's life cycle, and gradually being filled with scenery as Adam grows up. Sadler's Wells Ballet, Royal Opera House, 1947. Photo: Merlyn Severn (Royal Ballet School/ArenaPAL).

palette of opportunities for Bliss, who felt that it was his most varied and exciting ballet score. The actual staging must have been as surprising for audiences as it was impressive. Bliss summed up the scene in his autobiography:

> There was an unexpected moment at the raising of the curtain when Adam's birth was depicted: the audience saw the whole of the huge Covent Garden stage right back to the far wall, completely empty except for the protagonists. Then, as Adam grew in manhood the stage was gradually filled with scenery, only to empty again, bit by bit, as he approached old age until finally he was left alone, with the figure of Death, on the bare boards. It was a splendid role for Helpmann, and might have had a long run if an early

accident had not sent him from the cast. Early in his life cycle he had literally to leap into life, hurling himself from a height into the supporting arms of his friends. After a few performances there was a miscalculation, and he was sufficiently hurt to have to retire.[6]

This accident and the mixed reaction to the show were among the factors that led to its early demise, something which deeply disappointed Bliss as much as Helpmann and the team.[7]

The rather depressing storyline that 'man is born, makes a success in his own particular sphere, loses his position to a younger generation, sees his world crumble before his eyes and only finds peace in death'[8] is actually given life-enhancing music by Bliss. His personal zest for life cannot have found sympathy with this pessimistic view of what life holds for the average person and 1944 was a key moment for him, professionally. Leaving his post as Director of Music at the BBC that year saw the end of a period in which his composition had been almost non-existent and his own music had to be restricted in the broadcast schedules so that there was no feeling that he was taking advantage of his position. It was therefore a great relief to him to be able to return to what was, after all, his central vocation. The following year, May 1945, saw the end of the war and this was the happy background to Bliss's work on *Adam Zero*, the first new ballet to be performed after the reopening of the Royal Opera House.

Scene by scene – the musical canvas

There are seventeen musical movements and fifteen danced scenes, with a rounding-off Fanfare Coda that bookends the Fanfare Overture with which the work begins. Each scene is between one-and-a half and four-and-a-half minutes in length, the latter being the extended Dance with Death.

It is notable that in the score Bliss had written over the music for the first scene, the Fanfare Overture, is a quotation from William Shakespeare's *As You Like It*: 'All the world's a stage, And all the men and women merely players; They have their

I. Fanfare Overture
II. The Stage
III. Birth of Adam
IV. Adam's Fates
V. Dance of Spring
VI. Love Dance (Awakening of Love)
VII. Bridal Ceremony
VIII. Adam Achieves Power
IX. Re-entry of Adam's Fates
X. Dance of Summer
XI. Approach of Autumn
XII. Night Club Scene
XIII. Destruction of Adam's World
XIV. Approach of Winter
XV. Dance with Death
XVI. Finale: The Stage is Set Again
XVII. Fanfare Coda

exits and their entrances; And one man in his time plays many parts.' This was, of course, a reflection of what Helpmann was to have to do throughout the ballet and one of the fascinating elements of this work is the way the music provides a choreographer with a canvas on which the dance can be created. Andrew McNicol, the young and highly successful choreographer, in a discussion about recreating scenes from *Adam Zero* for the 2013 Helpmann Symposium, remarked that '[a] huge attraction was the music – there was so much to explore and experiment with, solely in the music … then being able to experiment in the studio, which stimulated more and more ideas'.[9]

So it is that the music provides the essential building blocks for the whole choreographic edifice, and Benthall's overarching scheme gives Bliss a colourful canvas on which to paint his musical scenery. The score seems to demonstrate a reflection of Bliss's own attitude to life. The completely empty stage seen as the curtain rises through the opening

Fanfare is a reminder that our birth is entirely serendipitous: we might be born kings or paupers, and what we do to fill that empty stage is partly down to circumstances and, of course, what we do through our own efforts to fulfil our potential. That is the key to the storyline of this ballet, and also the challenge for the choreographer.

Among the most successful elements of the musical score are the opening and closing Fanfares. Bliss composed a large number of Fanfares during his career, and especially after becoming Master of the Queen's Music in 1954, but the Fanfare Overture is full of impending drama. Its long pedal points and dramatic brass interactions gradually fade and slow as the curtain rises to point the audience to something they may have never seen before in a ballet: the Covent Garden stage, enormous but almost empty save for the initial protagonists. This leads to the first danced scene, The Stage. The music has an almost extraterrestrial quality to it as the questions grow as to how the stage will be filled. Bliss achieves this by evoking a kind of 'heaven and earth' scoring, where pairs of chords are set high and then low in alternating pairs. There is something of a pre-birth feeling, as if we imagine the baby floating in his mother's body before his birth – the subject of the next scene. Here, Bliss maintains the high and low chords but introduces a floating string melody that portrays a serene stillness which seems to reflect a motherly protection presaging the turbulence to come, like the calm before the storm. Adam will experience the highs and lows with which we are all familiar as we move through life.

The composer's role is fundamental not only in creating the vehicle in which the dancers move, but also in the interpretation of the scenario. Thus, we are being presented with Bliss's feelings for the progression of Adam's life. It is therefore significant that these early movements are so full of a sense of the portentous, signalling the end right at the beginning. The dance of Adam's Fates, the next scene, shows this very clearly. The imaginative start with the metallic hammering of high- and low-pitch steel bars gives an almost supernatural sound to the presence of the Fates (Designer, Wardrobe Mistress and Dresser), but then the rest of the orchestra introduces a dark, and rather busy element to the scene as these crucial figures begin their work. Bliss does this by the use of jagged, dotted rhythms that are given some melodic element; however, these are also sharply edged. We feel that all is not well with Adam's world to come.

Despite this, the Dance of Spring lightens the mood as Adam begins the process of growing up. There are some wonderfully luminous moments in the score, although if compared with other musical evocations of spring, a prime example being Maurice Ravel's unrivalled score for his ballet *Daphnis and Chloe* (1912), Bliss's feels rather heavy-handed. One might think that his view of spring is that of the joyful and very English extrovert as compared with Ravel's decidedly introvert, Francophile approach. Bliss gives us a riotous, earthy dance with a great deal of heavy brass and percussion out of which one can easily see where the Night Club Scene comes, much later in the ballet. A contrasting central section has dancing wind and strings before the whole scene ends brilliantly with a kind of musical scurrying away. There is humour in this and music that would not be out of place in parts of Felix Mendelssohn's *A Midsummer Night's Dream* (1842).

Adam's first encounters with love give Bliss the opportunity to paint a more luxurious picture in a beautiful emotionally driven Love Dance, the longest scene so far. The addition of a harp into the orchestration adds much to the warmth of the orchestral sound.

The Bridal Ceremony is replete with bells and we now find Adam at the height of his potential as he achieves power, the title of the next scene. Adam's Fates re-enter and, once again, the slightly menacing atmosphere is conjured as we are pointed to what is in store – but that is still some way ahead and the end of the scene has a thrillingly triumphant feel as Adam rejoices in his current success. This continues into the Dance of Summer. But the *coup de théâtre* here is the final chord, which moves from a penultimate major chord to an unsettling minor one. This heralds the Approach of Autumn and the start of Adam's decline. The cor anglais melody that haunts the Approach of Autumn sets a powerful atmosphere of regret. There could be no greater contrast from this to the Night Club Scene that follows. This has the middle-aged Adam trying to keep up with the younger set in a seemingly endless

Fig. 9.6: Adam literally leaping into life, as he hurls himself from a height into the supporting arms of his friends. Sadler's Wells Ballet, Royal Opera House, 1946. Photo: Roger Wood (Royal Ballet and Opera/ArenaPAL).

Fig. 9.7: Love Dance: Adam's first encounter with love. Robert Helpmann as Adam and June Brae as his lover. Sadler's Wells Ballet, Royal Opera House, 1946. Photo: Roger Wood (Royal Ballet and Opera/ArenaPAL).

Fig. 9.8: Dance with Death: Robert Helpmann as Adam and June Brae as Death. Photo: Edward Mandinian © Victoria and Albert Museum, London (Royal Ballet and Opera/ArenaPAL).

orgy of boogie-woogie. Even the considerable length of the movement (for such an energetic ballet scene) suggests Adam's reluctance to admit his age and move on. But it is a vivid score featuring saxophones, piano and an array of percussion including temple blocks, cow bells, sleigh bells and xylophone to give it an enhanced authentic dance-band sound. Bliss, also, remarkably, uses a guitar in this movement, although how this would have been heard in the general mêlée is not certain. He directs that it should be played 'in modern dance time' – perhaps suggesting a feeling of 'raciness' in the rather sleazy music. This movement was arranged much later (1970) for three hands at two pianos for Phyllis Sellick and Cyril Smith and renamed Fun and Games.

Reality hits hard in the next scene, the Destruction of Adam's World, as his life moves relentlessly towards its winter. It is worth pausing the musical commentary here to reflect on the way Helpmann dealt with the ageing Adam. We are reminded in Richard Cave and Anna Meadmore's tribute to Helpmann that, 'This experimental work incorporated changing costumes, make-up and scenery in view of the audience so that the action would be continuous.' They observe from photographs that Helpmann used 'minimal application of sketched facial lines [which] sufficed to suggest the central character's advancing years, aided only by a short, white wig. The economy was, perhaps, determined by the fact that Helpmann's make-up was at times "performed" in view of the audience – in itself an intriguing idea, and clearly integral to the concept of the whole work.'[10]

This transformation of the individual as his life progressed was integral to the drama of the scenario. The Approach of Winter is realised by Bliss almost as a ticking clock, with heavily repeated beats throughout; sometimes off-beat, they clearly represent the passing of time as well as mirroring the deterioration of both body and spirit. This leads naturally to the Dance with Death, which is perhaps the most impressive movement in the last part of the work.

It starts with hammer blows from timpani (directed to be played with two sticks) and bass drum and soon turns to consolation as Bliss quotes Walt Whitman's words in the score – 'Lovely and Soothing Death, serenely arriving'[11] – writing what feels like a folksong to the rhythm of the text. At the end it is clear that *Adam Zero* indicates not just an A–Z of a life but that Adam's life has added up to nothing. This point is made plain in the choreography as the Stage Director displays a zero on the blackboard that had been introduced at the start of the ballet to account for the value of life. After Adam's death, the last danced scene sees the stage re-set for the next 'Adam'. The whole score

Fig. 9.9: The blackboard, which had been introduced at the start of the ballet, accounts for the value of life and will display a zero. Robert Helpmann as Adam and June Brae as Death. Photo: Edward Mandinian © Victoria and Albert Museum, London (Royal Ballet and Opera/ArenaPAL).

concludes with a shorter version of the opening fanfare as a Fanfare Coda, and the curtain falls.

One of the criticisms levelled at Bliss's music for *Adam Zero* was the variety of styles he used throughout. This was a major issue with his opera, *The Olympians* (1949), but in this ballet, the styles used were entirely appropriate in the evocation of the changing ages and fashions of Adam's life. When listened to purely as music, one finds a natural progression that adds significant colour to the whole arc of his life. In this, Bliss was right to consider that this score was one of his finest. He had a real feel for the stage and still had one further ballet score, *The Lady of Shalott* (1958), to write, twelve years after the premiere of *Adam Zero*. It should not be forgotten that writing for these works is not at all the same as writing an operatic scene or a symphonic movement. Every progression must be considered in terms of dance movement and the length of each scene carefully measured so that the dancers are not over-exerted. Not only did Bliss master the demands with great skill, but he also had a natural feeling for dance as both an art form and discipline. It is notable that his younger daughter, Karen, became a professional dancer, so perhaps there was something in the Bliss genes.

Fig. 9.10: Arthur Bliss dedicated the music for *Adam Zero* to Constant Lambert. They are pictured here together in 1946 studying the score. Photographer unknown. © BBC (Bliss Archive, University of Cambridge Library).

Bliss always needed what he called a *donnée*, or an idea on which to hang his musical score. It was an extraordinary feature of his creative life that these ideas seemed always to come when he needed them. Even as early as 1922 when he wrote his *Colour Symphony*, his first major work, the idea came from finding a book on heraldry and using the associated colours as moods for each movement. The difference with the four ballets was, of course, that his *donnée* was the scenario. In some respects, this removed a layer of concern as he could simply absorb and reflect the storyline, whether his own, as in *Checkmate*, or as presented to him, and it may partly account for these scores being among the best of his output and some of the music with which he, personally, was most satisfied. Another angle here is the nature of the scenarios for these ballets, which without exception have tragic outcomes. For someone of Bliss's optimistic and outgoing nature it seems strange that these scenarios should elicit some of his best music. It is worth reflecting, however, that Bliss himself was no stranger to tragedy and that the shadow of everything he had passed through in the First World War, together with the loss of his favourite brother, Kennard, was a constant background to his creativity. These ballets, perhaps, gave Bliss a further emotional outlet for his deeply remembered experiences, the expression for which was distinct from a work like *Morning Heroes* (1930) – his overt requiem both for his brother and all those who lost their lives in the war.

Bliss dedicated the score of *Adam Zero* to the conductor and composer, Constant Lambert. Lambert was one of Bliss's great collaborators; he conducted the initial performances of *Adam Zero* as he had for *Checkmate* and *Miracle in the Gorbals*. Bliss was an accomplished conductor in his own right and the distinguished violist, Bernard Shore, for many years Principal Viola of the BBC Symphony Orchestra, wrote that 'Arthur Bliss and Constant Lambert share the honour of being the most efficient composer-conductors. Both are first-rate, with all the technique and experience necessary for the task their own music sets them.' But he goes on to say that 'Constant Lambert is also completely master of the orchestra, he conducts other men's music as admirably as he does his own and possibly with more care … His strong rhythmic sense and clear stick, together with his innate musicianship, makes him a refreshing personality to the orchestra.'[12] The scholar and critic Edward Dent applauded Lambert as 'the best all-round musician we have in this country … always unquestionably safe in scholarship, style, interpretation, sensitive understanding and complete professional accomplishment whatever he undertakes'.[13] It is no surprise that Bliss valued working with him so much. Lambert was such an insightful interpreter of Bliss's intentions as well as being so sympathetic to the needs of the dancers that they formed a creative partnership through these ballets and other works. The last word must therefore go to Bliss himself: 'Constant Lambert is almost kaleidoscopic in his talent. A sensitive composer, a brilliant pianist, an acid critic, and an accomplished conductor. His influence on English music is liberal and compelling.'[14]

Adam Zero was revived in Bremerhaven in 2015,[15] but lives on principally through its recorded concert suites.

As for Chapter 6 on Miracle in the Gorbals, *the material in this chapter is developed from the author's wider research for the biography of Sir Arthur Bliss (Ramsbury, Wiltshire: Robert Hales, 2023), which places the ballets in the wider context of Bliss's complete compositional output.*

10.
Revisiting *Adam Zero*: Spectre of Symbolism and Stagecraft

MICHAEL BYRNE

As this is my most varied and exciting score, I am disappointed that it has fallen into oblivion.[1]

The celebrated British composer Arthur Bliss lamented within the pages of his autobiography the disappearance of *Adam Zero* from the stage, performed a mere nineteen times by the Sadler's Wells Ballet between 1946 and 1948 at London's Covent Garden. Two years after collaborating with choreographer Robert Helpmann and librettist Michael Benthall on the gritty wartime dance-drama *Miracle in the Gorbals* (1944), Bliss reunited their creative forces – alongside designer Roger Furse – to produce *Adam Zero*, the first original ballet mounted at the Royal Opera House following the end of the Second World War.[2]

The ballet's narrative unfolded as a complex Shakespearean allegory about the 'seven ages of man', relying on the metaphor of a dance company making a new work to convey the recursive nature of life – a proverbial 'ballet within a ballet'. Helpmann extolled Bliss's 'brilliant' music, expressing regret at the production's short history and his deep desire to see it made anew: 'It had marvellous things in it, *Adam Zero* – to my mind, it was never done enough, and I am seriously thinking of reviving it.'[3] Benthall had in fact predicted the dance-drama would not endure, noting that 'this is a ballet which has been planned on a grand scale to be played only in large opera houses, requiring a big company and two leading dancers of exceptional acting ability, and for these, if for no other reasons, is not likely to stand the test of time'.[4] No film or dance notation of the staging exists, rendering the ballet irrecoverable and unable to be remounted in any form resembling its original instantiation. And yet, despite the ballet's evanescence, it remains essential to elucidate the 'marvellous things' from Helpmann, Bliss, Benthall and Furse's post-war conception, as well as signal the contemporary iterations that have resulted since.

When *Adam Zero* premiered on 10 April 1946 at the Royal Opera House – a mere six weeks after the grand revival of *The Sleeping Beauty* – many lauded the stage spectacle, dramatic performances and vivid music, but bemoaned its thematic incomprehensibility.[5] 'At curtain-fall they applauded for five minutes, while bouquets floated to the stars. Why? Because *Adam Zero* … was understood by nobody but recognised by everybody' as a 'tremendous entertainment' – 'mad and freakish', 'ancient and modern', solemn and preposterous'.[6] One reviewer distilled the collective sentiment by calling the ballet 'exciting to the eye, entertaining to the ear, and a trifle confusing to the intelligence'.[7] The playbill attempted to ameliorate – with limited success – the complexities of the *mise en scène* by including a brief programme note and outline of the dancers' roles. *(see below)* However, to truly vivify the characterisations of the Sadler's Wells Ballet company members on stage, revisiting the 'ballet bulletins' of Mancunian librarian and balletomane Lionel Bradley has proven invaluable when reconstructing the ballet's dramatic action.[8]

Bradley's attendance at many *Adam Zero* performances over several years and his assiduous post-ballet documentation has enabled newfound levels of production specificity, illuminated further by cross-referencing the historical photographs of Baron, Edward Mandinian, Merlyn Severn and Roger Wood.[9] While Bradley's accounts are sometimes imprecise and vague, drawing upon his ballet diaries has allowed for the most extensive retelling of *Adam Zero*'s forty-minute theatrical arc to date.[10] This chapter, therefore, examines a network of archival relations – diary entries, performance photographs, musical scores, reviews and lesser-known interviews – resulting in an expanded articulation of the ballet's multilayered plot on stage, followed by critical reflections on the production's successes and shortcomings.

ADAM ZERO

A Ballet by MICHAEL BENTHALL
Music by ARTHUR BLISS (by permission of Novello and Co.)
Scenery and Costumes by ROGER FURSE
Choreography by ROBERT HELPMANN

The Stage Director		DAVID PALTENGHI
The Choreographer	('Creator and Destroyer')	JUNE BRAE
The Principal Dancer	('Adam Zero')	ROBERT HELPMANN
The Designer	('His fates')	JEAN BEDELLS
The Wardrobe Mistress		JULIA FARRON
The Dresser		PALMA NYE
The Ballerina	('His first love, wife and mistress')	JUNE BRAE
The Understudies	('His son and daughter')	ALEXIS RASSINE
		GILLIAN LYNNE
The Character Dancers	('His cat and dog')	PAULINE CLAYDEN
		GORDON HAMILTON
The Mime	('His spiritual adviser')	LESLIE EDWARDS

'An allegory of the cycle of man's life from birth to death and rebirth in a new function. Man is born, makes a success in his own particular sphere, loses his position to a younger generation, sees his world crumble before his eyes and only finds peace in death.'[11]

The dramatic action of *Adam Zero*

Shortly after Bliss's Fanfare Overture envelops the auditorium, the curtain ascends to reveal the expansive Royal Opera House stage, stripped bare except for a few discarded pieces of scenery propped against the back wall. In the foreground, the Stage Director (David Paltenghi), dressed in a grey lounge suit and glasses and with greying hair, wipes clean a blackboard – a symbolic storytelling device used throughout the ballet to calibrate the ascent and decline of a man's life through a series of chalked 'pluses' and 'minuses'. Across the stage lie seven or eight couples in blue and brown practice clothes, awaiting the start of their 'rehearsal'. A central spotlight illuminates the Fates – the Designer (Jean Bedells), the Wardrobe Mistress (Julia Farron) and the Dresser (Palma Nye), each dressed distinctively – gathering and removing a large scarlet cloak, tights and a white shirt. Stagehands, comprising members of the ballet and production crew, introduce various props to the stage with supervision from the Stage Director.

Action erupts as the men of the corps de ballet (led by Anthony Burke, Henry Danton and Peter Franklin White) carry two ballet barres forward, signalling the start of daily class and preparatory stretching. Meanwhile, the Choreographer (June Brae), also defined as the Creator and Destroyer, enters purposefully in a flowing sulphur-yellow dress and deliberates on a new ballet. She performs an act of 'proverbial birth' by throwing herself to the ground, writhing, relying on the movement of

Fig. 10.1: Birth of Adam: Stage Director David Paltenghi observes June Brae, who portrays both the Choreographer and Creator in this scene. Sadler's Wells Ballet, Royal Opera House. Photo: Edward Mandinian © Victoria and Albert Museum, London (Royal Ballet and Opera/ArenaPAL).

Fig. 10.2: Dance of Spring: Adam, Robert Helpmann, with his First Love, June Brae. Sadler's Wells Ballet at Covent Garden, 1947. Photo: Merlyn Severn (Royal Ballet School/ArenaPAL).

Fig. 10.3: The Fates, Palma Nye, Jean Bedells and Julia Farron, loom over Adam, Robert Helpmann, and his First Love, June Brae, while the Mime/Spiritual Adviser, Leslie Edwards, confers a blessing. Sadler's Wells Ballet, Royal Opera House, 1948. Photo: Roger Wood (Royal Ballet and Opera/ArenaPAL).

the surrounding Company members to mask the arrival of the Principal Dancer, Adam Zero (Robert Helpmann). The Stage Director removes a blue cloth to reveal Adam curled up in the centre of the stage, semi-naked on the floor. The Fates encircle the 'newborn', measuring him with red string from a spool before the section of flooring on which they stand rises 3.7 metres. A curved staircase leading to a doorway is wheeled into position and connected to the elevated platform with a railing. While props and scenery continue to arrive (including a bench, sofa and other architectural flats), nothing rivals the unfurling of the cyclorama, curving majestically across the rear of the stage.

The Choreographer has left by the time the male corps de ballet appears in plus fours and boiler suits, with the women sporting short skirts and blouses. Adam hurls himself dramatically from a great height into the arms of the expectant corps de ballet men standing in a double row below.[12] *(see Fig. 9.6)* His vigorous dance with the men transitions upon the sighting of the Ballerina, His First Love (June Brae), among the corps de ballet women. Romance blossoms between the pair, with Adam and his paramour performing a tender *pas de deux*, 'radiant and absorbed in mutual wonderment' – an 'awakening of love'.[13] The Mime, Adam's Spiritual Adviser (Leslie Edwards), confers their union with ceremonial flair, enrobed in an ecclesiastical gown, grey wig and biretta given to him by the Stage Director and the Fates. Following the marriage, the couple ascend the stairs, disappearing through the doorway while the Spiritual Adviser slumps on a nearby bench to sleep. During the course of the ballet, Adam appeals to him during moments of crisis, to which the Spiritual Adviser responds with a performative blessing before retreating to his slumber.

The narrative suddenly adopts a more political tone as three men in black tights, brown jackets and bowler hats emerge with campaign props: long poles affixed to box-shaped placards bearing 'Vote for O' and 'Vote for Adam Zero' on all sides. Adam returns with his Wife in Victorian costume, descending the stairs to meet the crowd. The men stack their three placards to create a tiered podium upon which Adam stands proudly. By now, two additional characters have appeared on stage – the Understudies, his Son and Daughter (Alexis Rassine and Gillian Lynne) – dressed in earlier versions of Adam's and his Wife's costumes to indicate the emergence of a younger generation. The siblings flank Adam on the podium as he mimes an impassioned election speech. It is worth noting here that the Character Dancers (Pauline Clayden and Gordon Hamilton), costumed

Fig. 10.4: Adam Achieves Power: Adam, Robert Helpmann, and his Wife, June Brae, attend the election. Sadler's Wells Ballet, Royal Opera House, 1947. Photo: Merlyn Severn (Royal Ballet School/ArenaPAL).

Fig. 10.5: Dance of Summer: Robert Helpmann and June Brae are joined by the corps de ballet. Sadler's Wells Ballet, Royal Opera House, 1946. Photo: Edward Mandinian © Victoria and Albert Museum, London (Royal Ballet and Opera/ArenaPAL).

Fig. 10.6: Dance of Summer: Adam, Robert Helpmann, and his Wife, June Brae. Sadler's Wells Ballet, Royal Opera House, 1946. Photo: Baron (Royal Ballet School Special Collections /ArenaPal).

humorously as a Cat and Dog, join the action and provide moments of levity – lingering on the staircase, sitting with the Son and Daughter on a sofa and interacting amiably with Adam. They are the only characters to offer him consistent friendship.

Meanwhile, the corps de ballet appears in classical ballet attire to mark the Dance of Summer, with Adam and his Wife reappearing in similar, more ornate costuming. The couple begins a grand *pas de deux* during which, as Audrey Williamson notes, 'contrapuntal timing gives a new effect to Petipa-like dives and pirouettes'.[14] At the conclusion of the scene, the Fates remove Adam's blue jacket and bestow it upon his young successor to signify the next generation inheriting the gains of the previous. The Stage Director ages Adam further by inscribing additional lines on his face with make-up received from the Dresser, who places a white wig upon his head and gives him a black velvet jacket. The corps de ballet – now helmed by Adam's Son and Daughter – returns in new costumes and horn-rimmed glasses to begin the Night Club Scene, featuring a vibrant jazz-fuelled routine.[15] Adam's Wife reappears in a shoulder-length tan wig to connote her transformation into his Mistress, and the pair partake in the merriment.

Once more, the celebratory tone is disrupted. The Fates and the Stage Director strip Adam of his black jacket, replace his white shirt with a tattered equivalent, add further markings of age to his face and substitute his wig with straggling white strands. Out of despair, Adam assaults the Spiritual Adviser, prompting the scenery to dismantle around them and appear ablaze – the symbolic Destruction of Adam's World begins.[16] Through soft lighting the corps de ballet emerges onstage in torn costumes, crawling about in a disturbing, Belsen-inspired scene that would have resonated viscerally with post-war audiences.[17] Adam's Son and Daughter, in outfits that allude to some form of uniform, adopt roles as the refugees' jailers and tormentors. The Spiritual Adviser is attacked by the oppressed refugees, who turn their ire upon the Son and Daughter too, dragging them from the stage. As they exit, the remaining pieces of scenery are cleared, revealing the imposing figure of Death – the Destroyer. Amid the commotion, Adam appeals one final time to the Spiritual Adviser, who can do little but gesture heavenwards. With the stage denuded, Adam is abandoned in a wide, solitary expanse – a dying old man in red tights and clutching the rags of his white shirt. June Brae, who has transmuted several times throughout the ballet (from Adam's

Fig. 10.7: Approach of Autumn: Adam's Son, Alexis Rassine, inherits his father's clothes with the aid of the Fates – Julia Farron, Jean Bedells and Palma Nye – and Stage Director, David Paltenghi. Sadlers's Wells Ballet, Royal Opera House, 1946. Photo: Edward Mandinian © Victoria and Albert Museum, London (Royal Ballet and Opera/ArenaPAL).

Fig. 10.8: Night Club Scene: Stage Director, David Paltenghi, with Adam, Robert Helpmann. Sadler's Wells Ballet, Royal Opera House, 1947. Photo: Merlyn Severn (Royal Ballet and Opera/ArenaPAL).

Fig. 10.9: The Spiritual Adviser, Leslie Edwards, laments the disintegration of Adam's world. Sadler's Wells Ballet, Royal Opera House, 1948. Photo: Roger Wood (Royal Ballet and Opera/ArenaPAL).

First Love to his Wife and then Mistress), assumes saintly omnipotence in her final role as 'Lovely and Soothing Death, serenely arriving'.[18] Covered by an enormous red cloak, she advances from the back of the stage towards Adam with gentle grandeur. As Williamson comments, 'The cyclorama is nowhere more impressive than when it stretches, an endless wintry wasteland, behind the scarlet-cloaked figure of Death, and Helpmann's dance arrangement fully exploits the pity and the majesty, as well as the visual beauty, of this scene in which Death enfolds the dying man in arms like wings of an enveloping flame.'[19] Death guides Adam to the centre of the stage where – billowing her vermilion cloak like a sail to mask him from the audience – he disappears through a trapdoor. The cloak drops to reveal that Adam has vanished, and Death departs from the stage as the cyclorama folds back.

For the Finale, as described in Bliss's score, '[t]he stage is reset for the next life-cycle'.[20] The Fates return to remove the discarded scarlet cloak, exposing beneath it the same tights and white shirt seen at the ballet's start. The Stage Director attends, once more, to cleaning the blackboard as he did when the curtain rose, wiping away the collection of chalked pluses and minuses before him. Three plus signs are awarded to Adam during the ballet to mark his ascendency: the marriage, the successful election, and his appearance as chief dancer during the Dance of Summer. His decline is represented by three corresponding minuses in a parallel column, with a ruled line beneath totalling 'zero'. Wearing blue and brown uniforms, the corps de ballet resumes its position as the ballet barres return – rehearsing and preparing once more – and the Choreographer reappears in yellow to begin the creative agony of (re)conceiving her latest work. The curtain descends swiftly: '[T]he cycle of creation begins again with the birth of a new ballet'.[21]

Fig. 10.10: Destruction of Adam's World: Robert Helpmann, Adam, is surrounded by anguished members of the corps de ballet, while his Spiritual Adviser, Leslie Edwards, laments. Sadler's Wells Ballet, Royal Opera House, 1946. Photo: Edward Mandinian © Victoria and Albert Museum, London (Royal Ballet and Opera/ArenaPAL).

Critical reflections

In a 1947 edition of *Dance Magazine*, Bliss revealed that *Adam Zero*'s convoluted plot was devised before the music was completed, with the final dramaturgical structure coalescing due to the cohesion between the composer and his creative counterparts.[22] 'This is the only way to produce music that is really balletic,' asserted Bliss. 'For *Adam Zero*, I wrote a symphony of the four seasons: Spring takes Adam's pilgrimage from birth to courtship; Summer brings marriage and success; but in Autumn there is a falling away, fears and doubts obsess him, until, with the coming of Winter, he loses everything he has, and only the dark figure of [D]eath is kind.'[23] Katherine Sorley Walker argued more broadly that many critics viewed the ballet's scenario as 'a declaration of despair, but this was not a Helpmann characteristic'. She noted his temperament included a balanced mixture of vision and practicality, evinced by his own reflections about the ballet's genesis during an interview in 1971:[24]

> *Adam Zero* was a title meaning Man and Nothing. […] It came about in a curious way, because all the other ballets, *Hamlet*, *Comus*, *Birds*, *Miracle in the Gorbals*, had been conceived for smaller theatres, and I was due to do one for the Royal Opera House. Michael Benthall – who had written the scenario for *Miracle in the Gorbals* – said 'Well, why don't you do something that will show the vastness of the Opera House?' […] I wanted to start with an empty stage, and finish with an empty stage. We took the 'technique of ballet' as a means of expression: the creation of a ballet, which was the creation of a Man. As he was created, the

Fig. 10.11: Dance with Death: The Destroyer, June Brae, confronts Adam, Robert Helpmann. Sadler's Wells Ballet, Royal Opera House, 1947. Photo: Merlyn Severn (Royal Ballet School/ArenaPAL).

Fig. 10.12: The Destroyer, June Brae, is poised to envelop Adam, Robert Helpmann, in the Dance with Death. Sadler's Wells Ballet, Royal Opera House, 1948. Photo: Roger Wood (Royal Ballet and Opera/ArenaPAL).

stagehands started to build the set; and as he progressed, so did they build the set. The height of the time when the set was built also reflected the height of the Man's career. Then, he started to get older, and the [stagehands] gradually took the set away.[25]

Such a conceptually dense scenario involving multifaceted characters, costume changes, mechanistic staging and symphonic orchestrations made *Adam Zero* a challenging production to mount, with the dress rehearsals necessitating important scenic and choreographic alterations at the last minute. 'It would be true to say that no two performances of this work have ever been the same,' Benthall declared, 'but because the contributions of its four creators are complementary to each other, it does retain a certain unity.'[26] Embracing the 'pluses' and 'minuses' metaphor to assess the critical reception of the ballet, much positivity was received for the production's immersive sense of spectacle and drama: 'marvellously danced by Helpmann as Adam and June Brae as the woman'.[27]

Whatever we may think of Michael Benthall's depressing Essay on Man, it provides splendid opportunities for the designer and is a superb vehicle for the art of Robert Helpmann. The score is brilliant, the handling of crowds masterly and the eye remembers unforgettable moments of rare beauty. Roger Furse has used scenery and lack of scenery with imagination, as he did in *The Skin of Our Teeth*, but with far greater effect.[28]

The *New English Weekly* insisted that the 'unsympathetic might call *Adam Zero* an overpacked box of tricks, nevertheless they would be wrong, because the means are justified to convey in a peculiar idiom the forms which time imposes upon man's ever-young spirit'.[29] From the audience's perspective, dancer Margaret Dale felt that Helpmann's choreography was unable to match the philosophical scope of the ballet – 'he was overreaching himself' – but she was struck by the production's technological inventiveness, describing how 'things happened on the stage with lights that had never happened in ballets before'.[30] Ironically, the very staging innovations that Helpmann, Benthall and Furse engineered to reflect the rise and fall of Adam contributed to the work's limited life. Helpmann stated:

> [*Adam Zero*] was very much before its time: it was the first time I choreographed and let a producer produce it. And, as he had thought of the idea – Michael Benthall – he produced it. [...] He used things which are now used practically all the time, the lights being visible, suddenly coming down, people swinging on ropes – all this I did in *Adam Zero*. [It] showed all the tricks that the Opera House had – the lifts, the huge cyclorama that opened ... This was why it was impossible to do it anywhere else – it was conceived for that particular stage.[31]

Revisions to *Adam Zero* in 1947 were unable to address the site-specific technical demands of the production or simplify the complex scenario sufficiently to improve its mixed audience reception, resulting in the ballet vanishing after its final performance on 18 February 1948. Bliss suggested the ballet's disappearance was partly due to Helpmann's injury on stage, while Anna Bremrose hypothesised more broadly that '[w]hether Helpmann's works in the 1940s were praised or criticised, a change in venue from smaller theatres to the Royal Opera House in 1946 appears to have contributed to a noticeable absence of his dance-dramas in the Sadler's Wells Ballet repertoire'.[32] Compounding matters further, Frederick Ashton's involvement during the war had given Helpmann and Benthall the opportunity to imprint upon the Company a heightened sense of theatricality – best exemplified by the three dance-dramas, *Hamlet*, *Miracle in the Gorbals* and *Adam Zero* – which, for many critics, steered the art form 'as far as ballet will dare in dramatic pretension'.[33] Ashton's return from military service allowed for a realignment of the Company's creative trajectory: precisely two weeks after the opening of *Adam Zero* he debuted his minimalist masterpiece, *Symphonic Variations* – a 'sudden dive into pure, interpretation-of-music abstraction, a field foreign to British choreographers'.[34]

In contrast, Bliss's vivid composition received collective praise and has continued to exist independently as a concert suite,[35] serving as the basis for two choreographic vignettes by Andrew McNicol at The Royal Ballet School.[36] *Dance Magazine* commented affectionately on Bliss's creative life beyond *Adam Zero*, noting that 'one day he will surely write the music for another ballet – if only to please his fourteen-year-old daughter, who has studied at the Sadler's Wells Ballet School since she was eight'.[37] Almost seventy years later, Bliss's daughter Karen Sellick found herself in Bremerhaven at the opening night of Sergei Vanaev's neoclassical reimagining of *Adam Zero*, bearing no stylistic resemblance to the 1946 original, but proudly animating her father's expressive score.[38] The metaphor of a ballet company rehearsing and performing a new work strengthens the foundation upon which the post-war dance-drama *Adam Zero* was first predicated – a recursive blend of spectacle, stagecraft and rich characterisation. More symbolically, Sellick's attendance at the premiere in Germany felt an affirming nod to the cyclical allegory – every ending is an invitation for renewal and regeneration – that Bliss, Helpmann, Benthall and Furse strove so ambitiously to create in 1946.[39]

11.
Bliss in Bremerhaven: Sergei Vanaev Reawakens *Adam Zero*

MICHAEL BYRNE

'David Drew tells me you are also planning to fly from Stansted to see *Adam Zero* in Bremerhaven,' wrote Karen Sellick to me ahead of the ballet's premiere in Germany on 11 April 2015. Had Sellick's father, Arthur Bliss, been alive today, he would have revelled in the discovery that not only had his daughter experienced the production first-hand, but also his finest ballet score had been enlivened by Sergei Vanaev – almost seven decades after Bliss first collaborated with dancer-choreographer Robert Helpmann, librettist Michael Benthall and designer Roger Furse at the Royal Opera House in London. Vanaev's reconceptualisation of *Adam Zero* at the Stadttheater Bremerhaven warrants renewed critical attention, highlighting the dramatic action and choreographic impulses that brought Bliss's long-overlooked composition back to the stage:

> The creation of man serves as the model for my story. What interests me in *Adam Zero* is not so much the life journey of a man, but rather the complex and multifaceted relationship between the Creator and his work. For this reason, my choreography incorporates motifs from the original libretto and connects them with the biblical story of Adam and Eve. In my view, this is the first reworking of the libretto since the world premiere in 1946.[1]

Bolshoi-trained Vanaev chose to simplify Benthall and Helpmann's original scenario – a convoluted allegory about 'the relationships between human existence, its capacity for artistic expression, and its connection to nature' – by centring *Adam Zero* on the creation of the world. The ballet was framed as a 'metaphysical construction site', an artistic laboratory in which God could imprint his ideals upon the universe and mankind.[2] Unlike the shifting scenery designed by Furse in the 1940s, Kimie Nakano and Matt Dely furnished the updated reworking with a striking metal assemblage that allowed for a minimalistic yet highly effective division of space: grey scaffolding, configured like a stack of industrial bamboo, occupied the centre of the stage, while silver orbs were lowered to symbolise the arrival of the planets. The ballet opened with an imperious Constructor (Shang-Jen Yuan) seated atop a suspended platform, which slowly descended to allow the omnipotent architect an opportunity to survey the work of his angels (Jessica De Fanti Teoli, Maria Hoshi, Lidia Melnikova and Louisa Poletti). These four assistants – costumed in abstracted nurses' outfits – hurried about in preparation for the creation of Adam (Volodymyr Fomenko), who soon emerged, somewhat bewildered, from a translucent egg-shaped incubator. Such visual metaphors and abstractions resonated with the Theatre of the Absurd; however, the dramatic unity of Vanaev's

Fig. 11.1: Cristina Commisso, Eve, and Shang-Yen Yuan, Constructor, and Oleksandr Shyryayev, Deconstructor. Photo: Heiko Sandelmann (Courtesy of Stadttheater Bremerhaven).

choreography and Bliss's evocative score ensured the narrative maintained a suspense-filled logic.[3]

Just as Adam began the tentative exploration of his new surroundings, the Deconstructor (Oleksandr Shyryayev) surfaced through a trapdoor, creeping through the lattices of scaffolding with Mephistophelian intent. The ballet suffered a momentary lull in action before regaining momentum with the creation of Eve (Cristina Commisso) and a revised 'prototype' in the form of Adam II (Joshua Limmer). The Deconstructor continued to roam the stage, intervening with gestural taunts and temptations – including an apple suspended on a single cable – to reflect the timeless tensions between good and evil. During a moment of stillness, the cunning provocateur revealed a laptop, appearing to upload a virus as if to corrupt the 'system' of his saintly opponent. Frustrated by his human experiments, the Constructor – nested once again in the scaffolding – littered the stage with discarded pages as evidence that his ambitions had failed. The lights dimmed and it became apparent that his utopic ideals, no matter how well intended or systematised, were ultimately undermined by the corruptibility of man.

Vanaev's production was lauded as a triumph of (re)imagination, evidenced by the standing ovation that greeted the cast following the presentation of both *Adam Zero* and his second new ballet, *Die Vier Jahreszeiten*, that same evening. I had the privilege of attending the premiere with Karen Sellick and Andrew Burn (Chair of The Bliss Trust), and – despite the bleak philosophy depicted on stage – we were in agreement that a repeat viewing of Bliss's affecting, multifaceted work was desired. Admittedly, the expulsion of Adam and Eve from Eden is an overtraded trope, but Vanaev's anachronistic subversion of the parable proved captivating. It is worth noting here that Helpmann's 1946 staging of *Adam Zero* drew censure for prioritising dramatic spectacle over choreographic innovation, favouring theatricality at the expense of expressive dance.[4] Such criticisms, however, did not apply to Vanaev's dynamic forty-minute offering: the angularity and animalistic richness of his movements evoked the stylistic traces of Mats Ek, while the patterning systems were layered with an erratic gestural vocabulary that appeared incongruous, yet remained legible within a broader theatrical coherence.

Bremerhaven Ballet's international cast – hailing from Australia, New Zealand, Taiwan, Japan, Russia, Ukraine and Canada – impressed with dizzying displays of dance that negotiated the tensions between technicality and theatricality with supreme skill. Fomenko invoked the perfect degree of anxiety as an ill-fated Adam, while Yuan and Shyryayev – in the respective roles of Constructor and Deconstructor – fuelled their combative performances with wit and athleticism. In fact, their feats of virtuosity were so impressive that it was a shock to discover the dancers were not of Goliath-sized stature during the ballet's opening night reception. Having been fortunate to view the Company in class earlier that day, I noticed

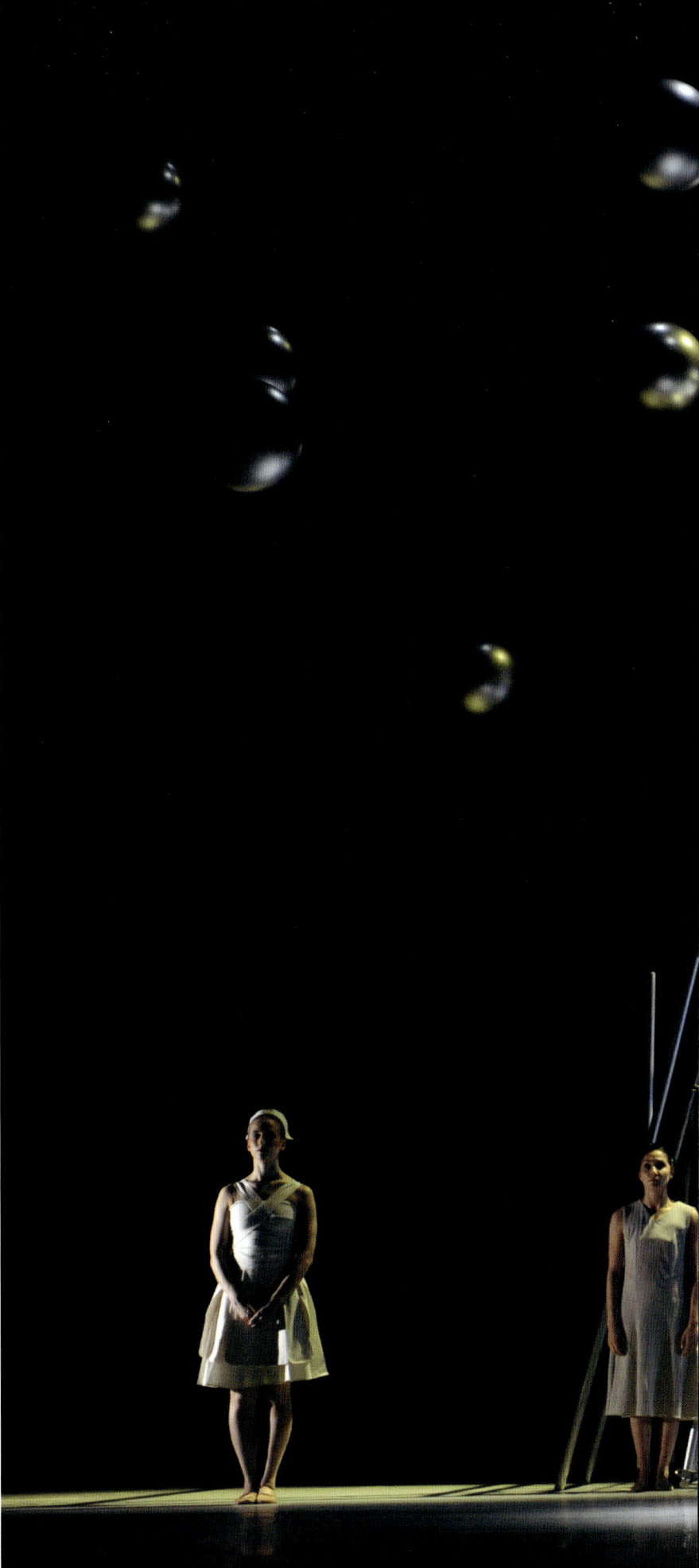

Fig. 11.2: The Constructor, Shang-Jen Yuan, towers over Adam, Volodymyr Fomenko, surrounded by Ballet Bremerhaven's dancers: Louisa Poletti, Cristina Commisso, Jessica De Fanti Teoli, Shang-Jen Yuan, Oleksandr Shyryayev, Volodymyr Fomenko, Lidia Melnikova, Joshua Limmer, and Maria Hoshi. Photo: Heiko Sandelmann (Courtesy of Stadttheater Bremerhaven).

Shyryayev remained motionless in the far corner of the studio, stretching his back gently against the wall to accommodate an injury – an ironic echo of Helpmann's own affliction during the 1940s production. Later that evening, however, there was no hint of restraint or temperance: the Ukrainian dancer commanded attention from the first chord to the last, bending and contorting fluidly to meet the demands of Vanaev's choreographic envisioning.

Under the baton of Marc Niemann, the Philharmonisches Orchester Bremerhaven filled the theatre with a musical crispness and vibrancy that is absent in some of the composer's denser orchestrations. While it was lamentable that such an evocative score had remained 'inactive' as a ballet for almost seventy years, Vanaev's choreography demonstrated the versatility of Bliss's music in accommodating multiple interpretations of *Adam Zero*. Furthermore, it is important to recognise that David Drew – a widely respected and long-serving member of The Royal Ballet – championed the reworking of *Adam Zero* in England for a number of years, encouraging the prodigious Andrew McNicol to choreograph scenes for the Helpmann Symposium in 2013. Although Vanaev and McNicol boast different movement lexicons, there exist opportunities for both creators to present individual responses that are unique but still faithful to the theatrical fundamentals of the ballet's score.

It is apparent that the 2015 'reawakening' of *Adam Zero* succeeded in addressing the dramaturgical imbalances that had haunted Helpmann and Benthall's 1946 production, demonstrating how Bliss's original composition remains relevant, vital and rich with creative affordances for contemporary choreographers to explore.[5] As Sellick remarked during the post-performance gathering in Germany, 'My father would have been delighted by what was displayed on stage this evening.'[6] In my view, there could have been no higher praise for Vanaev, his creative team and the accomplished dancers of Bremerhaven Ballet.

This essay has been adapted from a review of Adam Zero, *originally published for Oxford DanceWriters.*[7]

Fig. 11.3: Opening night ephemera: Andrew Burn, Karen Sellick and Michael Byrne at the premiere of *Adam Zero* in Bremerhaven, 2013. Photo: Michael Byrne.

Fig. 11.4 (opposite, top): Andrew McNicol choreographing vignettes based on Arthur Bliss's *Adam Zero* with Central School of Ballet students Tom Arnold and Harriet Marden at The Royal Ballet Upper School, 2013. Photo: Nigel Hodgson (Courtesy of the photographer).

Fig. 11.5 (opposite, bottom): Andrew McNicol leads a choreographic workshop exploring Arthur Bliss's *Adam Zero* with Central School of Ballet students (left to right): David Smale, Luna Othnin-Girard, Jessica West, McNicol, Cara Downes, Reece Hudson at The Royal Ballet Upper School, 2013. Photo: Nigel Hodgson (Courtesy of the photographer).

PART FOUR

The Lady of Shalott

1958

12.
Early and Late:
Bliss's Attraction to Dance and *The Lady of Shalott*

LEWIS FOREMAN

The reappearance of Sergei Diaghilev and the Ballets Russes on the London musical scene immediately after the First World War was an important and widely felt influence for modernism (and indeed escapism from the horrors of the recent war) that was deeply felt by Arthur Bliss, who had lost his brother, Kennard, and was twice wounded while at the Western Front. When he returned to musical life he bore a significant shadow of grief. But he was determined to embrace the new and could do so enjoying the freedom given by a private income. He championed the musical avant garde with considerable energy, promoting performances and writing radical new works; and, finding himself on the fringe of the society circles around Diaghilev, this included the ballet. It is clear that his music had a rhythmic impulse from the first, so that much, much later, for example, his *Colour Symphony* of 1922 could become a suitable score for ballet.

There were many straws in the wind. Bliss's most substantial was *Rout*, originally written for a musical party at the Piccadilly home of Baroness d'Erlanger in which he evoked 'the sound of a carnival overheard at a distance'.[1] Here, a soprano is given a medley of made-up words, 'A string of syllables corresponding to the scraps of song that might reach a listener watching a carnival from an open window,'[2] said the composer. 'One hardly knows whether to describe it as chamber music or programme music, street music or "Jazz". It has elements of them all,' wrote one critic after this performance.[3]

Fig. 12.1: The front cover of *Bliss: One-Step* (1923) is typical of the prevailing aesthetic of the time. Artist unattributed (Private Collection).

Fig. 12.2: The cover of the score for *Rout* (1920). Artist unattributed (Private Collection).

Fig. 12.3: Diversions was premiered on 15 September 1961 by The Royal Ballet at the Royal Opera House, with choreography by Kenneth MacMillan, design by Philip Prowse and lighting by William Bundy. Pictured (left to right): Petrus Bosman, Georgina Parkinson, Derek Rencher, Christine Beckley, Bryan Lawrence, Monica Mason, Keith Rosson, Deanne Bergsma and Principal dancers: Donald Macleary and Svetlana Beriosova.[4] Photo: Zoë Dominic (ArenaPAL).

While Bliss did not embrace any kind of fame writing popular dance music at the time, the 1920s saw the appearance of a succession of new dances such as the flapper walk, charleston, soft-shoe shuffle, black bottom, trot or one-step. Bliss was sympathetic to these and wrote two for piano solo. His *One-Step* dates from 1923; it was later orchestrated by Leighton Lucas, when he was the Markova-Dolin Ballet Company touring conductor, for use as an interlude between ballets. Subsequently, dance band leader Victor Fleming expanded it to play during wartime performances with his own larger orchestra and first performed it in a broadcast from BBC Midlands on 19 March 1940. When recorded by Martin Yates and the BBC Concert Orchestra in 2020, it was clearly seen as a really catchy number.[5]

Although we usually do not associate Bliss with the piano as a solo instrument, he wrote a substantial catalogue of music for it, notably in the 1920s. The Suite for Piano, written in 1925, was performed and published in 1926. The Polonaise is the second of the four movements (the others are Overture, Elegy and Finale). It was orchestrated by Bliss for his friend, the conductor Eugene Goossens, who must have realised that when heard with orchestra it

Fig. 12.4: Arthur Bliss with dancers Elaine MacDonald and Kenn Wells backstage at Sadler's Wells Theatre at the premiere of *Frontier* by John Neumeier for Scottish Dance Theatre, 24 November 1969. Photographer unknown © *The Times*/News Licensing (Bliss Archive Cambridge University).

quite transcends its origin and is in fact but another engaging short orchestral piece, suitable not only for concert but also for the ballet stage.

As far as *Rout* was concerned, when orchestrated the forces were larger than its chamber music predecessors and in the later portions of the score the texture he creates is quasi-orchestral. So, it was not surprising that when Diaghilev asked the critic Edwin Evans to help him commission British composers to write orchestral 'interludes' for performance during the London seasons of the Ballets Russes in the early 1920s, it was natural that Bliss's brilliant score should be an early candidate for full orchestral treatment. It was announced in June 1921 and was subsequently choreographed by Ninette de Valois in 1927, and played on two pianos. It was probably Bliss's first ballet to be seen in the theatre. While Bliss did not compose a piece specially for the Ballets Russes interludes, he did orchestrate Christian Sinding's *Fire Dance* (unfortunately now lost) for Tamara Karsavina's 1921 summer season at the London Coliseum.[6] Later came de Valois' *Narcissus and Echo* (1932), conducted by Constant Lambert, at which Bliss's vocalise *Rhapsody* of 1919 was danced.[7]

Bliss's music includes scores in most conventional forms, notably orchestral works, major choral works, chamber music and film music. But probably his greatest claim to fame in his lifetime were his ballets, with *Checkmate* (1937) becoming a familiar score not only on the ballet stage but also in the concert hall. In addition to the other commissioned ballets – *Miracle in the Gorbals* (1944), *Adam Zero* (1946) and *The Lady of Shalott* (1958) – it is worth taking note of the various works that were considered for dance.

Viewed chronologically, there were three late ballets, all danced to existing scores: *Diversions*

(1961) by Kenneth MacMillan, choreographing *Music for Strings*; *Frontier* by John Neumeier (1969), a danced version of the Oboe Quintet seen not only in London and Perth, but also in Germany as *Die Sperre*; after Bliss's death, *A Royal Offering* was danced in 1977 to *A Colour Symphony*, in a production by Robert de Warren, Director of Northern Ballet Theatre at the Royal Northern College of Music. The short orchestral Mêlée Fantasque from 1921 was described by Bliss himself as being in effect his first ballet score, although no staging has been traced. And if any further evidence is needed of Bliss's feeling for dance, his aborted film music for the Independent Production Film *Caesar and Cleopatra* (1944) contains a dance interlude consisting of three dances all followed by a barcarolle; and among his early piano music we find the printed but withdrawn Valses Fantastiques of 1913.

Artistic friendship with Christopher Hassall

Christopher Hassall, some twenty years Bliss's junior, had 'become a close friend' and musical collaborator late in Bliss's career.[8] His own career flourished through a fortunate early association with Ivor Novello. Hassall's ability to take an original view combined with an enviably wide literary knowledge enabled him to write lyrics for Novello's musical ideas and sketches at very short notice, and he came to have a material role in 1930s musical shows at Drury Lane and elsewhere, such as *Glamorous Night*, which opened in May 1935. Other familiar productions included *The Dancing Years* (1939) and *King's Rhapsody* (1949). He was poetry editor for the Third Programme and also wrote opera libretti for various younger

Fig. 12.5: Alexandra Worrall and Herman Jiesamfoek in *A Royal Offering* choreographed by Robert de Warren for Northern Ballet Theatre. Premiered on 19 May 1977 at the Opera Theatre, Royal College of Music, Manchester, the ballet depicted three periods in English history dominated by notable queens and marked the celebrations for Queen Elizabeth II's Silver Jubilee. Photographer unknown (Courtesy of Northern Ballet).

composers, among them Antony Hopkins and Franz Reizenstein; his first, much celebrated, libretto was for William Walton's *Troilus and Cressida* (1954). Bliss jokingly noted how 'he often referred to himself as "the composers' moll!"'.[9]

In his autobiography Bliss writes enthusiastically about his collaboration with Hassall: 'We used to have what we termed "inspirational evenings" together when we would shoot ideas into the air until one hit a target that interested us both.'[10] They worked on four substantial works together before Hassall's unexpected early death at the age of fifty-one. After *The Lady of Shalott*, there came the television opera *Tobias and the Angel* (1960), the selection of texts for the Coventry Festival commission *The Beatitudes* (1961) and what became Bliss's least known large-scale choral work, the sacred cantata *Mary of Magdala*, first performed in 1963 at the Three Choirs Festival in Worcester and which Bliss dedicated to Hassall's memory.

The Lady of Shalott

The Lady of Shalott was the first of Bliss and Hassall's collaborations. The ballet takes Alfred Tennyson's poem as its 'book'. This was a work of the poet's youth, first appearing in 1833, but the much-revised version that was widely accepted dates to 1842 and was the one used by Bliss and all the composers making musical settings. The young Tennyson's sources and imagery look back to a medieval world, notably the thirteenth-century Italian novelette *Donna di Scarlotta*, and a fascination with the minutiae of the dress and manners of the period. It was almost a footnote to his obsession with Arthurian legend and his sequence of poems *Idylls of the King*, one of which is 'Lancelot and Elaine', in fact the lily maid of Astolat.

In a sense Tennyson anticipated many of the concerns of the Pre-Raphaelite Brotherhood; the evocative images they created in their paintings echoed the themes of Tennyson's poetry. Among the principal Victorian artists who provided such images was John William Waterhouse, who painted three, in 1888, 1894 and 1915. The third features some of the issues explored in the poem.[11]

Tennyson, with his careful balance of poetic description and narration, provided the perfect

Fig. 12.6: As with the other covers for Arthur Bliss's scores, this striking design for *Mêlée Fantasque* (1921) is of its time. Artist unattributed (Private Collection).

combination of costume and action for it to be danced as a ballet. In the dance context, it is worth noting Frederick Ashton's twelve-minute version of *The Lady of Shalott*, for which he devised the scenario using a selection of piano pieces by Jean Sibelius. It was created for the Ballet Club's winter season and first performed on 12 November 1931.[12]

Previous musical settings of Tennyson's poem

Before Bliss there had been other musical settings of Tennyson's poem, but all underline the originality of Bliss's treatment. We know little of Amy Horrocks's approach of 1899 except that it had an accompaniment for a piano trio. The first choral setting with orchestral accompaniment appears to have been by Cyril Rootham in 1909. The fact that Tennyson structured the poem in four parts is reflected in all the musical settings except that by Bliss. Rootham created structure by having a choral first part, verse by verse introducing different

Fig. 12.7: John William Waterhouse, *I Am Half-Sick of Shadows, Said the Lady of Shalott*, 1915. The painting depicts some of the characters and scenes from Alfred Tennyson's poem. Art Gallery of Ontario (Alamy).

voices, followed by a mezzo soprano soloist in part two, then the chorus returning for the entry of Sir Lancelot and the remainder of the narrative. Unperformed in its time, it was researched and chosen by Robert Tucker for his 1999 Broadheath Singers concert at Eton College.[13]

Similarly, Armstrong Gibbs in 1926 adopted a straightforward narrative approach, opening with the chorus singing in unison over a marching ostinato falling Holstian bassline.[14] Originally intended for performance by a school choir, it was revived on BBC Radio Children's Hour in January 1949. These and another early setting by W.H. Reed (for female voices and orchestra, 1934) would have been completely unknown to Bliss. Later settings of which he might have been aware are by Maurice Jacobson (1940) and Phyllis Tate (1956), but, thanks to his collaboration with Hassall, Bliss had a strong treatment in terms of its staging as a ballet and did not set any words to music. Jacobson's setting for chorus and orchestra with a tenor soloist dates from the early years of the Second World War,[15] while Tate turned to Tennyson's poem in 1956 to fulfil a BBC commission, composing a cantata in four movements for tenor, viola, percussion, pianos and celesta. Although well received, it has not been heard since.

Bliss's *The Lady of Shalott*

Bliss's ballet *The Lady of Shalott* was written in response to a commission from the University of California for the May T. Morrison Music Festival at Berkeley and first performed on 2 May 1958.[16] The British premiere came in a remarkable production by a ballet group from New Parks Girls' School in collaboration with the Leicestershire Schools Symphony Orchestra. First seen on 13 May 1975, it was the subject of a fascinating Thames Television documentary, *Girl in a Broken Mirror*.[17]

In summary, Tennyson's poem, in an Arthurian setting, tells of the Lady confined in a tower on the island of Shalott in the river that flows down to Camelot. Bliss underlined the theme when he wrote that '"The Lady", living her emotional life vicariously and unable to survive when at last compelled to face reality (a true Henry James heroine, in fact) appealed to me'.[18] Her only contact with the outside world is what she can view in 'a mirror clear that hangs before her all the year, [where] Shadows of the world appear'.[19] She sees the reapers, the villagers dancing, a page and his knight, tumblers, the abbot, young lovers, a funeral cortège. All populate the ballet. Eventually, Sir Lancelot appears and tempts her from her isolation. She is freed but, cursed, she

Fig. 12.8: 'The mirror crack'd' and Jocelyn Vollmar as the Lady falls dying before Roderick Drew as Lancelot in San Francisco Ballet's 1958 production. Photo: Henrietta McDowell (Henrietta McDowell Memorial Photography Collection/Museum of Performance and Design, San Francisco).

Fig. 12.9: The same scene in the 1975 production by New Parks Girls' School with the Leicestershire Schools Symphony Orchestra, retitled *Girl in a Broken Mirror*. Photographer unknown (Courtesy of John Whitmore, volunteer archivist, former member of LSSO).

The Lady of Shalott: A ballet in one act after the Poem by Tennyson

I. Prelude
II. The Lady at her Tapestry Frame
III. The Reapers
IV. Dance of the Villagers – Dance of the Village Belle
V. Entry of the Page
VI. The Page and the Lady
VII. Entry of the Knight
VIII. The Tumblers
IX. Re-entry of the Page
X. The Abbot
XI. The Young Lovers
XII. The Funeral Cortège
XIII. Lancelot: Lancelot Enters and the Lady Rises to Her Feet
XIV. The Fatal Dance: the Lady Dances with Delight
XV. The Lady in Love with Lancelot
XVI. Epilogue

dies. As an allegory of the problem of choice facing all young people, torn between inexperience of life and concern for the experiences to come, it is telling.

Bliss and Hassall, in their adaptation, tell the story in sixteen musical scenes, with detailed instructions in the rehearsal piano score, which expand on Tennyson and are quoted here at length as the score is unpublished;[20] double quotation marks are used to indicate where Tennyson's words are included within the Bliss/Hassall text.

The opening Prelude (I) evokes the atmosphere in twenty-eight mysterious bars – the pianissimo dissonance of the flute's Eb against the oboe's D perhaps a musical 'once upon a time'. The curtain rises on a tower room. The rest of the stage shows "the river flowing down to Camelot".

> It is early dawn with a red streak in the sky. In the tower the Lady droops with sleep over a tapestry frame. A huge mirror hangs before her. At the foot of the tower sits an old crone dressed in black, symbolic of inexorable fate and the curse which she is held by. The Lady stirs and wakes, with the spell on her.

The music plays straight on into the brief first scene, The Lady at her Tapestry Frame (II) and as the music moves into 6/8 she "begins to weave her magic web with colours gay".

The third scene introduces The Reapers (III). 'It has grown light, and the reapers set forth for the day's work. They glance up at the Tower struck by the sound of music, and look at each other in bewilderment before continuing on their way.' This continues into scene IV, the Dance of the Villagers. This is a 'lively' dance in the awkward time signature of 8/8, Bliss alternating 3+3+2 with 2+3+3 and using 7/8 when he needs a link. 'A group of villagers, "surly village-churls, and the red cloaks of market girls" come in.' Moving into 3/8 we now have the Dance of the Village Belle, who is characterised as 'The handsomest of the village girls [and who] calls special attention to herself. She plainly will allow her favours to anyone.' Eventually, the time signature reverts to 8/8 (3+3+2) and soon the music fades to the quiet closing episode: 'The Lady longs to make contact with the dancers, but the spell warns her against looking out of the casement window. She often strays to it but puts her hand to her eyes and mournfully turns back to the mirror for her only knowledge of the outside world. The villagers listen spell-bound to the music from the tower.'

Here, the sound of harp and celesta over tremolando strings evokes a moment of magic before moving straight into the Entry of the Page (V), a key change to D major in 3/4, which starts gently and elegantly. In the extended slower sections of the ballet the woodwind plays an important role and so when the brass is heard in vigorous writing, such as for The Tumblers (VIII), Bliss instructs 'In lively march time'. The delightful slow music for The Abbot (X) is followed by the lyrical flow of The Young Lovers (XI) complete with octave strings and harp arpeggios. When Bliss's score is vigorous, it is loud with brass in evidence, but much of this music is quiet and thoughtful.

The central action of the ballet comes with the Entry of the Page and then his Knight, in scenes V, VI and VII. Here, Bliss takes a succession of characters all of whom receive but a brief mention in the poem and finds some action for them. Quoting Tennyson, Bliss describes a "long-hair'd page in crimson clad" who appears bearing a token of flowers. 'He has been sent half in sport, half in earnest, by the Knight to whom he is Squire, and whose curiosity has been aroused by the Lady of Shalott. He is notably disdainful and affected as the rustics gather round to finger his fine clothes.' In a brief scherzando, 'he mounts the steps of the tower, guarded by the old crone, and enters the room'. The music slows and runs on into The Page and the Lady (VI). 'The Lady is startled and uneasy', Bliss communicating her discomfort by changes from 5/8 (2+3) to 7/8 (2+2+3, later changing to 2+3+2). 'She cannot believe the significance of the token, though the Page tries to reassure her.'

Eventually, 'the Page bows himself out ceremoniously, giving his hand to the old crone to kiss'. Ten lightly scored bars of staccato semiquavers on flute, then oboe, then bassoon, take us to VII, the Entry of the Knight, who crashes onto the scene, side drum driving the narrative forward. The Knight and his doings are an invention of Bliss and Hassall. They tell us that:

> He carries no sword, as he comes courting.
> He is an aristocrat, perfumed, insincere
> exquisite – a good counterpart of his Page.
> He plainly shows that he thinks the rustics
> scum. He is seen in the mirror of the Lady,
> who holds his token clutched in her hand.
> The Knight abetted by his Page, imperiously
> waves the villagers away, flinging them
> money. Three of the older ones manage to
> remain out of curiosity, and settle down to a
> game of dice. The Knight dismisses his Page.
> The Knight addresses himself in courtly
> fashion to the Lady.

At this stage the Knight is still on the riverbank, and the Lady before her mirror in the tower; yet they dance a *pas de deux* over 48 bars and widely separated on the stage. 'They never touch and yet their movements complement each other.'

'The Village Belle strolls past. The Knight, seeing her as easy prey, turns from the Lady to watch her. He draws the Village Belle into the dance. During this the Lady, disillusioned, lets the token drop from her hand.' The dance of the Knight and the Village Belle develops at some length before she eventually 'tears herself from his arms and runs off'. The Knight immediately turns again to the Lady but she repulses his overtures and weeps. 'The Knight leaves the scene, discomforted, much to the scorn and amusement of the dice players.'

There follow five scenes featuring aspects of the medieval times portrayed. First, The Tumblers (VIII), announced by trumpet and side drum – effectively pipe and tabor. Bliss notes: 'They might be three in number, with a fourth to lay down the mats and go round with the hat. The tumblers perform. The three old villagers mockingly tell the crowd that has assembled what they have seen of the Knight and his Page.' Eventually, the crowd applauds and the tumblers move off.

With the Re-entry of the Page (IX), who is looking for his master and bears his helmet and sword, the crowd jeers and surrounds him. They 'use the Page roughly, seize the helmet and sword and mockingly play with them'. The knockabout is brought to an end by the entry of The Abbot (X), who has only a passing mention in Tennyson's poem, in a brief interlude: 'The crowd respect his authority. As the Abbot leaves, telling his beads,[21] the crowd quietly disperse, and "two young lovers lately wed" remain behind' (XI). 'During the crowd scenes, the Lady has remained like a statue at her tapestry frame, but on seeing in the mirror the lovers she picks up the token again, and gazes at it sadly. She is troubled and moved by the dance of the two lovers.'

At the end, the mournful tone of a church bell 'sounds across the water'; it heralds The Funeral

Cortège (XII). Bliss quotes Tennyson's brief mention of this episode '"A funeral, with plumes and lights and music, went to Camelot". The Lady is grieved by the juxtaposition of young love and death', whereupon, we hear 'afar off the trumpet of Lancelot' – a sustained timpani roll on F-sharp with low cellos and basses builds to a crescendo and the contrasting energy of Lancelot (XIII), all brassy confidence.

Thus far, many of the episodes that have been danced receive but a passing mention in Part II of Tennyson's poem. But Lancelot is the subject of Part III and the next three scenes in the ballet (XIII–XV) are devoted to him and the Lady.

> Lancelot enters, and the Lady rises to her feet. She watches with agitation, and admiration his dance of gaiety. He is a magnificent creature, in love with life, as Tennyson describes him in Part III of the poem. Drawn irresistibly, the Lady disobeys the spell's commands. She gazes straight at Lancelot. She opens the tower door, and runs down the steps to meet him. The old crone tries to stop her, but in vain.

The Lady Dances with Delight (XIV) and the music runs on into The Lady in Love with Lancelot (XV): a vigorous score revealing a new extrovert character and Bliss's remarkably persuasive – if brief – love music. The music dims with the appearance of the funeral barge, but the Lady throws caution to the wind, and she and Lancelot kiss. With a great crash on the gong '"The mirror crack'd from side to side". The Lady droops and falls at Lancelot's feet.'

There is a general pause before the Epilogue (XIV), the final scene.

> Two black 'figures of legend' enter at the back of the funeral barge. They uncover the prow on which is emblazoned '*The Lady of Shalott*'. Sir Lancelot crosses himself: he "mused a little space; He said, 'She has a lovely face; God in his mercy lend her grace'". The villagers have tiptoed in. It has grown dark, and, as at the beginning, only a red streak in the sky relieves the half gloom.

Bliss's ballet has never had a professional staging in the UK. There have been only a few performances of the music, all under the aegis of the BBC. The complete score, played by the BBC Symphony Orchestra under Bliss's baton, was broadcast in December 1968. Then in 1991, after more than twenty years of silence, conductor Barry Wordsworth broadcast a series of programmes during which all the Bliss ballets were performed with the BBC Concert Orchestra.[22] Another thirty years on, *The Lady of Shalott* was recorded by Dutton Epoch and conducted by Martin Yates with the BBC Concert Orchestra.[23] The mixed programme of music by Bliss included several world premiere recordings; in a session that ran over three days, 20–22 January 2020, the ballet was recorded first.

The Lady of Shalott is clearly revealed as a candidate for stage revival, if only upstaged by the even more pressing demands from three celebrated Bliss ballets from the period of his high maturity: *Checkmate*, *Miracle in the Gorbals* and *Adam Zero*.

13.
From Fragments a Portrait: Lew Christensen's *Lady of Shalott*

JENNIFER JACKSON

The premiere of *Lady of Shalott*,[1] Arthur Bliss's last commissioned ballet, took place on 2 May 1958 in a concert hall setting on the Berkeley campus of the University of California. Commissioned by the Music Department, the ballet was the headline event in a music festival celebrating the opening of a new building complex and featured commissions by other renowned composers, including Darius Milhaud, Ernest Bloch and Roger Sessions.

Lady reflects both Bliss's standing as a composer and his close personal and professional associations with California. He was a member of the Music Faculty in Berkeley early in the Second World War and he had met his future wife, Trudy (née Hoffman), the daughter of a prominent botanist, in Santa Barbara, where she was born and raised. In February 1957 Professor David Boyden, then Director of Music at the university, wrote to Bliss proposing the creation of a new ballet in collaboration with Lew Christensen, San Francisco Ballet's resident choreographer, and regarded as 'one of the three best in America'.[2] With sets and costumes by Hollywood designer Tony Duquette, it was an ambitious venture. As plans were developing, prohibitive costs threatened its successful completion. But critics and audience declared the first performance at the Alfred Hertz Memorial Hall a 'robust success',[3] and later that month when *Lady* transferred to San Francisco's War Memorial Opera House, its 'bewitching beauty' would be fully realised. On seeing the first performance of the ballet on 24 May under 'full-dress theatrical conditions', dance critic Alfred Frankenstein declared: 'it has a distinctive, decided character of its own and resembles nothing else in anybody's repertoire'.[4]

Lady was widely performed on tour to South America[5] later that year and during the 1959 international tour to the Middle East and North Africa. It made 'a highly distinguished contribution to the San Francisco Ballet company's resources'[6] and remained in the repertoire until 1967, revived every year except 1966 during the spring seasons at the Opera House, Alcazar and Geary theatres. In October 1969 the ballet was remounted with the original sets and costumes for Ballet West, in Salt Lake City.[7]

Bliss and his wife had planned to attend the premiere of *Lady* and both looked forward to reconnecting with colleagues and friends in Berkeley. For Trudy, it would have been a return visit to her homeland and to the scene of their younger daughter's ballet lessons in 1943, at San Francisco Ballet School. But the invitation from Dmitri Shostakovich for Bliss to attend the International Piano Competition in Moscow as one of the judges had to take precedence, and although they never saw the original production of *Lady*, they would have been cheered by the reports they received.

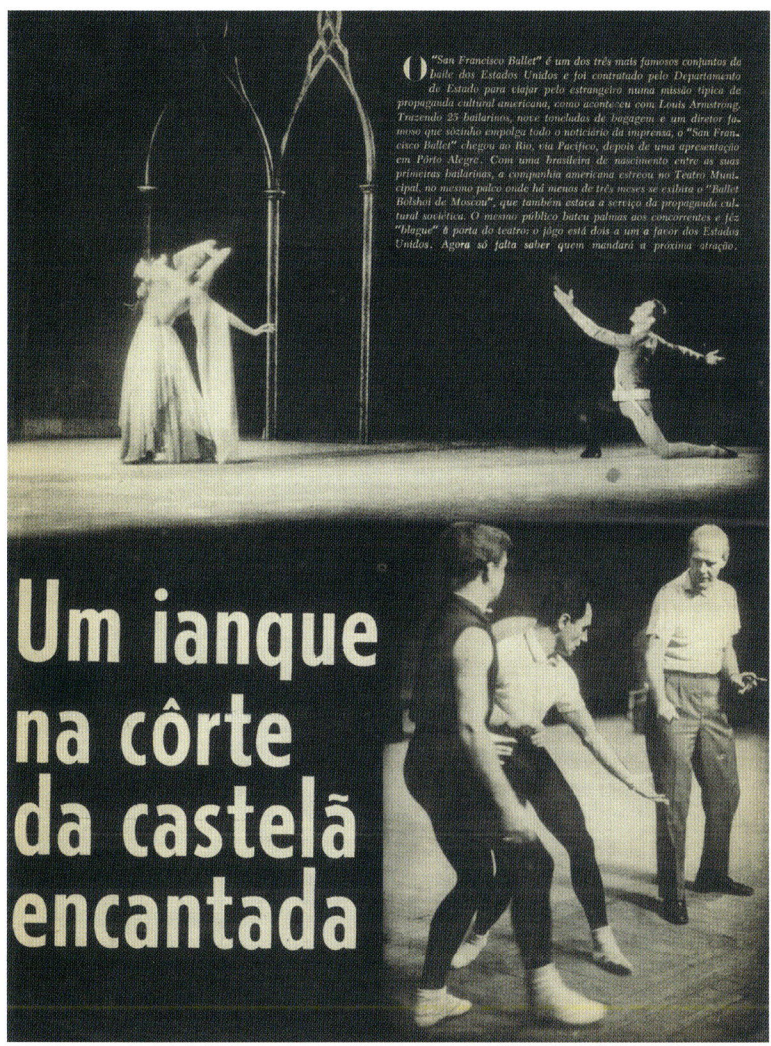

Um ianque na côrte da castelã encantada

O "San Francisco Ballet" é um dos três mais famosos conjuntos de baile dos Estados Unidos e foi contratado pelo Departamento de Estado para viajar pelo estrangeiro numa missão típica de propaganda cultural americana, como aconteceu com Louis Armstrong. Trazendo 25 bailarinos, nove toneladas de bagagem e um diretor famoso que sozinho empolga todo o noticiário da imprensa, o "San Francisco Ballet" chegou ao Rio, via Pacífico, depois de uma apresentação em Pôrto Alegre. Com uma brasileira de nascimento entre as suas primeiras bailarinas, a companhia americana estreou no Teatro Municipal, no mesmo palco onde há menos de três meses se exibira o "Ballet Bolshoi de Moscou", que também estava a serviço da propaganda cultural soviética. O mesmo público bateu palmas aos concorrentes e fêz "blague" à porta do teatro: o jôgo está dois a um a favor dos Estados Unidos. Agora só falta saber quem mandará a próxima atração.

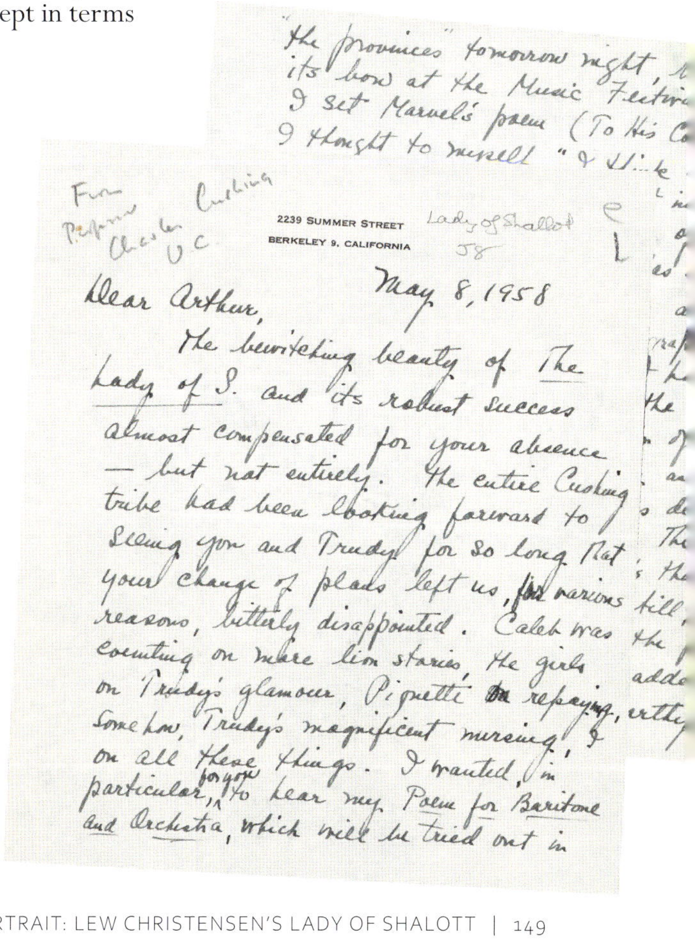

Fig. 13.1: 'A yankee in the court of the enchanted castle':[8] Lew Christensen and his latest work, *Lady of Shalott*, attracted much interest during the South American tour. The Brazilian magazine *Mundo Ilustrado*, 27 August 1958, featured Jocelyn Vollmar as the Lady with Kent Stowell as the Red Knight, and the choreographer in rehearsal with two dancers. (Museum of Performance and Design, San Francisco).

Charles Cushing, a fellow composer and Professor of Music at Berkeley, had read the score, attended two full rehearsals of the ballet, and the opening night with his own family. Although, 'bitterly disappointed' not to see Bliss and Trudy in person, he wrote enthusiastically about the work:

> The Lady is superb and Christensen's imaginative choreography is a match for it. For months I had wondered how he would treat the aquatic journey, whether the realisation of the 'Complement dance' of the Lady with that foul Red Knight would be as delightful as I pictured it, et cetera, et cetera. The answer is – yes! And for many other bits that were completely captivating. Best of all – the work preserved the poetry and mystery of the Tennyson, and added, I felt for the better, the earthy and exuberant qualities (you mentioned Breughel [*sic*]) which served as a foil both for the delicacy of the allegory – and as a true Arthurian touch – in both senses ... The choreographer saw all of this and he caused the dancers to convey it with a conviction which was, by times, foreboding, tender, humorous, and exceedingly moving.[9]

Critics noted the immediate success of the ballet as a piece of theatre that seamlessly integrated the music, dance and scenic elements. When he wrote to thank Bliss for 'such a good score and scenario' and to express his hope that there would be another opportunity to collaborate, Lew bemoaned conditions that were 'no credit to the art of ballet' under which *Lady* 'made its debut'.[10] Yet, despite the mere 'hints of scenery',[11] Frankenstein's review points to the way all the visual elements combined to communicate the narrative: 'the invention of designer and choreographer are inseparable. The ballet's numerous sharply individualised characters are unimaginable except in terms

2239 SUMMER STREET
BERKELEY 9, CALIFORNIA

May 8, 1958

Dear Arthur,

The bewitching beauty of The Lady of S. and its robust success almost compensated for your absence – but not entirely. The entire Cushing tribe had been looking forward to seeing you and Trudy for so long that your change of plans left us, for various reasons, bitterly disappointed. Caleb was counting on more lion stories, the girls on Trudy's glamour, Pignetti on repaying, somehow, Trudy's magnificent nursing, & on all these things. I wanted, in particular, for you to hear my Poem for Baritone and Orchestra, which will be tried out in

Fig. 13.2: Letter from Charles Cushing to Arthur Bliss from California, written 8 May 1958 after the premiere at Hertz Hall of *Lady of Shalott* (Bliss Archive, Cambridge University Library).

of their costumes and their action is unimaginable except in terms of the shrewdly handled lighting.'[12]

> But who hath seen her wave her hand?
> Or at the casement seen her stand?
> Or is she known in all the land,
>   The Lady of Shalott?

Like the poem by Alfred Tennyson that was its starting point, what more can we know of the enigma that is this *Lady* on stage? There are no known film recordings. The account in this chapter of what an audience may have seen is pieced together from letters, reviews, photographs, programmes, scenario, the score and interviews. Fragments remembered by members of the original cast and tiny black-and-white dress rehearsal photographs reveal some of its secrets. The literature about the creative artists involved, their situation, influences and tastes, is also vital context for a closer look at Lew Christensen's *Lady*.

San Francisco Ballet – the Christensen brothers

In the history of twentieth-century ballet in America the stripped-down abstract aesthetic that George Balanchine forged on the East Coast overshadows significant choreographic endeavour elsewhere. *Lady of Shalott* throws light on another narrative: the pioneering work of the remarkable Christensen brothers who were developing their brand of classic and theatrical dance on the West Coast. The three boys grew up in a tight community understanding the value of tradition. Raised in a Mormon family whose business was the selling, performing and teaching of music and dance, the brothers played musical instruments and learnt ballet from their 'Uncle Pete' L.P. Christensen, who had studied with Stefano Mascagno.[13] In 1958 (when *Lady* premiered) the oldest, Willam, was then Professor of Dance at the University of Utah, where the performing group he established would become the professional Company, Ballet West. Known as 'The Boss', he was ambitious, entrepreneurial and 'undaunted by reality'.[14] Harold, known as Mr Christensen or 'The General', was the steady and stern Director of San Francisco Ballet School. The youngest, Lewellyn, reserved and noted for his ironic wit, was San Francisco Ballet's director and choreographer – known to everyone as 'Lew'. When the brothers received the prestigious Dance Magazine Award alongside Rudolf Nureyev in 1973, Lew wryly commented on being 'the only family with two ballet companies and two deficits'.[15]

San Francisco Ballet Company is the oldest in the USA. It was initially tied to the opera, and Willam was first a dancer there in 1937, becoming ballet master and choreographer in 1938. He and Harold bought the opera ballet school during the Second World War and established the Company as independent of the opera, financed by a guild and subscription series. The school was the lifeblood of the whole enterprise, subsidising the cost of performances and productions as well as finding and nurturing new talent. Lew's star had risen under Balanchine and Lincoln Kirstein in New York, and for many years he served as dancer, ballet master and choreographer on both sides of the continent. But he was drawn to the opportunities 'back home' for developing his own choreographic world and his brothers welcomed the cachet his impressive pedigree brought to the organisation. When Willam moved to Utah in 1951, Lew took over the

Fig. 13.3: Lew Christensen, Willam Christensen and Harold Christensen, *c.* 1940s © Cristof Studio (Christensen-Caccialanza Collection/Museum of Performance and Design, San Francisco).

Fig. 13.4: San Francisco Ballet dancers Suki Schorer and Tilly Abbe photographed at the equator in Ecuador, during the 1958 tour that took in nineteen South American cities and lasted four months. Photographer unknown (Courtesy of Suki Schorer: Private Collection).

Company: instead of crediting all three brothers as personnel, letters were thereafter simply headed 'San Francisco Ballet'.

Former dancer and ballet mistress Betsy Erickson now restages Lew Christensen's works for San Francisco Ballet School and professional ballet companies. She regards the late 1950s as exciting times that brought new opportunities for the Company. Its first performances at Jacob's Pillow Dance festival in 1956 led to international tours, funded by the State Department as part of the cultural effort to 'spread American influence and goodwill'. In 1957, while New York City Ballet and American Ballet Theatre were touring Europe and the Middle East, San Francisco Ballet became the first American Company to tour Southeast Asia under the aegis of the State Department's 'International Exchange Program'.[16] These tours were a significant boost to the Company's financial growth and profile, raising awareness at home and

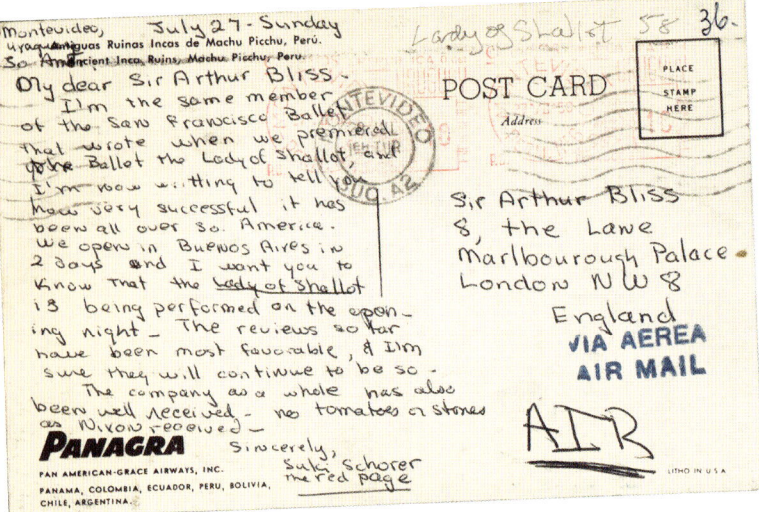

Fig 13.5: In Suki Schorer's postcard to Arthur Bliss from Montevideo she writes of 'most favourable reviews' for *Lady of Shalott* and that his ballet is being performed on opening night in Buenos Aires. (Bliss Archive, Cambridge University Library).

abroad, not only of San Francisco Ballet, but also of the art form – as cultural and political capital in the Cold War era.[17] Kent Stowell, former Director of Pacific Northwest Ballet and an original member of the cast of *Lady*, remarks on how, with its rich variety of forms, 'dance is the art form of America … It encapsulates the energy of the restless American spirit.'

Studio practice

The Christensen brothers' schooling was highly respected and foundational for many generations of dancers. In her comprehensive history of the brothers' careers in dance, Debra Sowell writes that Willam was passionate about 'the physical challenge of ballet'.[18] And although a naturally gifted dancer, Lew's fascination was primarily with 'theatre' in general – as a teenager, he would build models and experiment with rigging, lighting and stage effects.[19] The two brothers' aspirations and tastes in repertoire also differed. While Willam, who danced with Mikhail Fokine, had made a name for creating the first productions in the USA of the 'Russian' classics – *Swan Lake*, *The Nutcracker*, *Coppélia* and *Cinderella* – Lew focused on new works. He 'wanted to create his own style'.[20]

As a choreographer, Lew began with movement and his own embodied knowledge and experience, rather than dramatic intention. Erickson recalled his physical and mental agility in the studio: 'We looked up to Lew, he was like a Greek God. He knew what he wanted and could show any part: men, women, any age'.[21] His training ground as a jobbing dancer in vaudeville and on Broadway honed skills in partnering,[22] acrobatics and technical prowess in ballet (he was known as one of ballet's greatest turners).[23] Pre- and post-war at the Metropolitan Opera and Ballet Society, his craft and artistry grew. 'Working with a choreographer as experienced as Balanchine,' he said 'was a schooling for my own choreography,'[24] and in dancing the title role in *Apollo Musagète* at the 1937 Stravinsky Festival, his reputation as America's first *danseur noble* became firmly established.[25]

It was Lincoln Kirstein who befriended and championed him throughout his life. Kirstein regarded Lew as the first American classicist and Lew shared Kirstein's commitment to building a repertoire made by Americans and rooted in American themes and life. Many of his early choreographies, for example *Pocahontas* (1936) and *Filling Station* (1937, the year Bliss's *Checkmate* premiered in Paris), contributed to this project. The latter, initiated by Kirstein for Ballet Caravan, was a collaboration with the composer Virgil Thomson depicting characters from a variety of social backgrounds at a roadside filling station. It became a signature work and the choreography drew on Lew's wide experience of popular and musical theatre, including tumbling, tap, virtuosic ballet and dark comedy. The ballet ended in a similar way to another of Lew's respected works, *Jinx* (1942), with a sombre funeral procession and then a lone figure on stage. Set in the closed community of circus folk, the central character is a clown who, isolated in his unrequited love for a tightrope walker, becomes associated with everyone's misfortunes and is murdered. In both works, Lew danced the central roles: in the one he was a good-humoured attendant and in the other the jinxed, sinister clown. Critics commented on the complex emotional territory that *Jinx* explored, in the dramatic contrast between the intensity of the fear that steadily built and the 'seemingly joyous lives' of the circus performers.[26]

For the musically trained Lew, music was a refuge. He would retreat into playing his cello alone as a way of offloading anxiety, and his imaginative use of the music for the development of the choreography for *Jinx* – Benjamin Britten's *Variations*

Fig. 13.6: Lew Christensen and Daphne Vane in George Balanchine's *Apollo Musagète* at the 1937 Stravinsky Festival, conducted by the composer in New York. Photo: Richard Tucker (Christensen-Caccialanza Collection/Museum of Performance and Design, San Francisco).

on a Theme of Frank Bridge* (1937) – drew particular praise, as well as the composer's approval. Britten authorised a two-piano reduction of the score, so that the ballet could be performed on tour when a string orchestra was not available.[27]

Collaboration

Given Lew's attributes and interest in exploring psychological territory in dance, the theme of *The Lady of Shalott* — an isolated figure, trapped by fate — would have sparked his creative imagination. Choreographer and composer collaborated by correspondence during 1957. Once Lew had received and agreed the proposed theme and scenario, Bliss composed quickly. Lew worked with an annotated piano reduction of the score, which may then have been recorded on reel-to-reel tape and the dancers did not hear the full orchestral score until the dress rehearsals.

The months leading up to the premiere were busy. Alongside the creation of *Lady*, Duquette was also designing a full evening-length work, *Beauty and the Beast*, for Lew. The Company needed a big ballet with the kind of production values that touring companies, notably Sadler's Wells Ballet, were presenting and audiences flocked to see. But *Lady* was the first in the series of works on which the choreographer and designer collaborated to explore elaborate scenography. They made an

unusual team. Unlike his brother Willam, Lew resisted invitations for the Company to perform at society gatherings and his quiet, measured style was in stark contrast to that of Duquette, who was seen as chic and influential in social circles and amid moneyed patrons.[28] The flamboyant Duquette was a costume, stage and film designer and also designed interiors and jewellery for royalty and Hollywood celebrities. Stowell, who as a nineteen-year-old danced in *Lady*, says that 'they got on famously'.[29] Lew delighted in experimenting with the visual elements and theatrical illusion,[30] and critics remarked on Duquette's 'mature artistic method and sensitivity for organic integrated creativity'.[31] Both were 'meticulous and totally committed to the work'. And with the 'unbelievably opulent' *Lady*, Stowell remembers thinking that they 'had arrived as a major ballet company.'[32]

The scenario developed by Bliss and Christopher Hassall invents characters and action that expand on the Tennyson poem and describe the setting on stage. It envisages the river flowing on either side of a Tower Room centre stage, where the Lady sits at her tapestry, and beside her a set of stairs, at the bottom of which sits the 'old crone'. Both budget constraints and the practicality of touring sets and costumes would have played into the choreographic and design concepts. Without a theatre base and chasing performance opportunities, San Francisco Ballet spent more time on tour than at home, and Lew made significant departures from the scenario with both staging and his own cast of characters. There is minimal scenery, no elevated tower and rather than representing the curse in the form of the 'old crone' (reminiscent of Carabosse's disguise at Aurora's sixteenth birthday party in *The Sleeping Beauty*), he moves the story away from fairy tale into a more symbolic allegorical space that draws on

Fig. 13.7: Costume designs for the Lady and a Figure of Legend by Tony Duquette. Courtesy of the Anthony and Elizabeth Duquette Foundation (Museum of Performance and Design, San Francisco).

his exposure to Japanese kabuki theatre.[33] Figures of Legend dressed in black cloaks and gloves with plumed headpieces suggest an otherness, not of this time or place – they are the 'dark unconscious workings of fate'.[34] They are listed twice on the programme and make clear interventions into the drama. Thus, the emphasis may not only be on the strict narrative elements in the ballet. Bringing these figures into the dance arena, an open flat stage, evokes the interior psychological space of the Lady's experience, the world of the Lady's mind.

The question posed by Bliss and quoted in the programme – 'Is Tennyson's poem, "The Lady of Shalott", an allegory of the dilemma of youth, trapped between its desire and dread of experience?' – offers a key to the choreographic treatment and the focus on aspects of romantic love through the character of the Lady. Framed within the sixteen scenes[35] are a series of duets, each evoking a different facet of the rituals of courtship and experience of romantic love: fear, confusion, longing, duplicity, danger, abandon, joy, surrender.

Into the theatre

Bliss's music evokes action and atmosphere in each scene with characteristic intensity of feeling for dramatic expression.[36] As a piece of theatre, the ballet's 'strangeness and enchanted lyricism … is altogether of its own'.[37] Duquette's front cloth rises on a space that gestures towards its medieval source: a backcloth with a painted staircase, and upstage right, tall free-standing Gothic arches positioned so they appear to straddle a staircase, and at the base of the stairs a tapestry frame. Upstage right is the tower room, the world of the imagination, and downstage left the characters from the 'real' world pass by on the road to Camelot. The Lady, wearing an elaborate headdress and long flowing robes, is present throughout. The glamorous Jocelyn Vollmar danced the title role in every performance by San Francisco Ballet and was perhaps central to its mysterious effect. She adored Lew,[38] and having toured internationally as leading ballerina of the Marquis de Cuervas and Borovansky Ballet, her

Fig. 13.8: Designed by Tony Duquette, the front cloth evokes a distant medieval world. Courtesy of the Anthony and Elizabeth Duquette Foundation (Museum of Performance and Design, San Francisco).

SATURDAY EVENING, MAY 24, 1958

LADY OF SHALOTT

Libretto and Music – ARTHUR BLISS
Choreography – LEW CHRISTENSEN
Décor and Costumes – TONY DUQUETTE

CAST (in order of appearance)

Lady of Shalott	Jocelyn Vollmar
Reapers	Roderick Drew, Michael Smuin
Villagers	Bene Arnold, Constance Coler, Sue Loyd, Maurine Simoneau, Eugenia Van Horn
Village Belle	Fiona Fuerstner
Reflection	Louise Lawler
Page of the Red Knight	Suki Schorer
Red Knight	Kent Stowell
Two figures of legend	Christine Bering, Glen Chadwick
Tumblers	Roderick Drew, Michael Smuin
Abbot	Glen Chadwick
Couple Lately Wed	Louise Lawler, Kent Stowell
Cortege	Bene Arnold, Christine Bering, Fiona Fuerstner, Maurine Simoneau, Eugenia Van Horn, Julien Herrin
Page of Sir Lancelot	Tilly Abbe
Sir Lancelot	Richard Carter
Figures of Legend	Christine Bering, Gerrie Bucher, Paula Tracy, Glen Chadwick, Roderick Drew, Maurice Lemus, Kent Stowell

Is Tennyson's poem, "The Lady of Shalott", an allegory of the dilemma of youth, trapped between its desire and its dread of experience? The Lady of Shalott is imprisoned in her tower by the threat of a mysterious curse that denies her the privilege of looking directly towards Camelot through her window. She can observe reality only as the shadowy reflections of the world outside appear in her mirror – reapers in the fields, villagers, an abbot, tumblers, knights, lovers, stately processions – all of which she weaves into her tapestry; and further, through the ministrations of the imaginary "figures of legend," clothed in black, who are the inevitable embodiments of the curse, her fate. The Red Knight sends his page to present his compliments to her and then he comes himself to offer a proposal, but he, who does not meet her ideal, is rejected, and the page is routed by the villagers. The Lady, at first only "half sick of shadows", grows desperate after she observes the idyl of two young lovers, a "couple lately wed", and when the reflection of Sir Lancelot appears in her mirror, she defies the curse and springs toward him and Camelot. The curse descends: the tapestry disintegrates, the mirror shatters, and she moves through the breach to the reality of death.... Mark Shorer.

return to San Francisco Ballet in 1956 gave him a ballerina with international status. *Lady* was a vehicle for her particular gifts and range. Although mostly in the background, her strong facial features, clarity of hand and arm movements, and beauty of the gestural dance language carried to the back of any theatre.

> She knows not what the curse may be,
> And so she weaveth steadily,
> And little other care hath she,
>   The Lady of Shalott.

The first four scenes of the ballet reflect the opening verses from the Tennyson poem; they describe community life and the potential for human connection that for the Lady is forbidden. Passages of dancing for the courtiers and villagers provide contrast and the ground for developing narrative action alongside reflection on the inner emotional life of the Lady. Choreographing for a cast of characters would have played into Lew's skill and knowledge of a variety of styles. The whole Company of dancers is involved, with academic ballet classicism and popular acrobatic dancing juxtaposed to indicate character and status. The resulting 'crowded tapestry of village people, tumblers, ecclesiastics, and black garbed servants of death is wonderfully effective'.[39]

Frankenstein notes the strength of the interweaving of pantomime and dance and the contrast between 'deathly doings in the tower' with 'lively doings on the green outside'. Towards the end of scene IV, the robust bucolic dance for the villagers gives way to a mournful yearning theme, for which Lew created an 'eerie mirror sequence'.[40] A dancer named in the programme as Reflection, a role invented by the choreographer, is seen framed as a mirror image of the Lady. As the Lady moves, reaching out to touch the image with her hand, the Reflection moves, mimicking each gesture; the frame then revolves and, as Erickson recalls, 'someone walks out of the mirror'.[41] The Lady longs to be part of the life outside her tower, and this theatrical device – the reflection of herself merged with the way she is cursed to observe the world – symbolises the nature of the curse that imprisons her, casting a shadow over the episodes of courtship and promise of romantic love that follow and which are the heart of the ballet.

In scenes V and VI a 'pert'[42] page enters "crimson clad"; danced by Suki Schorer, now a renowned teacher in the Balanchine style, she is not unlike a red pawn from *Checkmate*. She bears a bunch of flowers as a token of intent on behalf of her Knight – a 'worthless wooer'.[43] The Lady is unsure of its meaning; in the words of the poem, "she hath no loyal knight and true". When in scene VII the

Fig. 13.9: Jocelyn Vollmar as the Lady, 1961. Photo: Henrietta McDowell (Henrietta McDowell Memorial Photography Collection/Museum of Performance and Design, San Francisco).

158 | PART FOUR – THE LADY OF SHALOTT

Fig. 13.10 (opposite): San Francisco Ballet dancers as villagers, 1958. Photo: Chester Kessler (Chester Kessler Dance Photography Collection/Museum of Performance and Design, San Francisco).

Fig. 13.11: Suki Schorer as the Red Page in 1958, her headdress reminiscent of a Red Pawn in *Checkmate*. Photographer unknown (Courtesy of Suki Schorer: Private Collection).

Knight is introduced loudly and with full orchestral swagger,[44] Bliss's music signals his brash approach as a potential suitor. This was 'an era of story ballets'.[45] Cast both as the Knight and in the Couple Lately Wed, Stowell recalls how his natural acting ability helped him as a new Company member perform with the feeling for characterisation alongside the technical acumen that Lew's choreography demanded.

Lew enjoyed partnering and in the forty minutes of the ballet, Bliss wrote three different *pas de deux*, each with its own context and importance in the narrative thread. The first is for the Lady imprisoned in her tower and the Knight on the riverbank. The scenario indicates that their complementary moves are played out at a distance. This presents an interesting choreographic challenge. Lew responded by drawing on a theatrical convention from Japan, the Bunraku-like puppeteers who manipulate actors and objects onstage. Two black-clad Figures of Legend are introduced: upstage a male Figure who partners the Lady, and downstage a female Figure who is partnered by the Knight, dancing exactly the same choreography. The effect of this double duet is to underline the duplicitous nature of the Knight, who then proceeds to besmirch his suit in a brief dalliance with the Village Belle. The Lady, distraught, drops his token and he leaves the stage, rejected.

The focus in scenes VIII–XI shifts to the road to Camelot, bringing on the colourful mix of medieval characters: acrobatic tumblers, the supercilious page, no-nonsense villagers and an abbot, who restores a kind of equilibrium. The Couple Lately Wed remain on stage for the next *pas de deux*, set to music evoking 'not merely their love-sighs, but the Lady's own love-sickness'.[46] At one point the man reclining on the floor looks up at his new wife, her gaze caressing him as she holds his head between her hands. Their tender duet darkens the Lady's thoughts – she turns from her mirror, her body arching away from their physical presence as she raises her arms to shield her eyes from the sight of their bliss.

> Came two young lovers lately wed;
> 'I am half sick of shadows,' said
> The Lady of Shalott.

The duet itself may be a lost gem, described by Cushing after the first performance as 'a page of music and a dance as lovely as I have ever met'.[47] Erickson recalls Lew's note to move expansively and that the choreography, while being '*en pointe*, was carefree and loose'.[48] Roderic Dunnett contends that the music is 'a classic instance – there are many in the earlier ballets – where Bliss's balletic inspiration

Fig. 13.12: Jocelyn Vollmar as the Lady and Tina Bernal as the Red Page, 1962. Photo: Henrietta McDowell (Henrietta McDowell Memorial Photography Collection/Museum of Performance and Design, San Francisco).

Fig. 13.13: Jocelyn Vollmar as the Lady with the Red Knight, each partnered by a Figure of Legend, 1961. They dance a *pas de deux* but never touch. Photo: Henrietta McDowell (Henrietta McDowell Memorial Photography Collection/Museum of Performance and Design, San Francisco).

Fig. 13.14 (opposite): Overwhelmed, the Lady, Jocelyn Vollmar, abandons her tapestry and looks directly towards Lancelot, Roderick Drew, 1961. Photo: Henrietta McDowell (Henrietta McDowell Memorial Photography Collection/Museum of Performance and Design, San Francisco).

easily stands comparison with passages' from the ballets of Prokofiev, his near contemporary.[49]

In scene XII, with the entry of a funeral cortège and the intensity of Bliss's deeply felt score, the implicit danger of the curse is given form. By this point in the ballet, the Lady has been exposed, albeit through the mirror, to profane and sacred love; now she is confronted with the juxtaposition of love and death, that leads inexorably to the final section. A pageant of standard bearers heralds the appearance of Lancelot, splendidly costumed in white and gold – a classic *danseur noble* in the mould of the choreographer himself – tall, with elegant lines and finely honed shapes in the air. Indeed, it was watching Lew onstage performing powerful leaps that had inspired the first Lancelot, Richard Carter, to pursue a career in ballet.[50]

> The gemmy bridle glitter'd free,
> Like to some branch of stars we see
> Hung in the golden Galaxy.
> The bridle bells range merrily
>   As he rode down to Camelot:

The poetic image is compelling: the Lady leaves her weaving to look directly at Lancelot – in Tennyson's words as "The mirror crack'd from side to side". An invisible barrier that has held the upstage space apart from the downstage space is broken and the third *pas de deux* – uniting the doomed heroine with her Arthurian knight – explores the entire stage with released freedom. Tiny photographs suggest a classic romantic duet, the couple held in dynamic tension through the ballet forms: supported adagio, long arabesques with the Lady pitched forward against Lancelot's firm hold, deep arching back bends to evoke ecstatic abandon and close touch, the Lady swept into attitude *en pointe*, her arm wrapped around his neck, his around her waist. The music pulls towards the inevitable denouement; with their embrace, her fate is sealed. Two male Figures of Legend carry the Lady away from Lancelot in a high lift, their arms at full stretch, her spirit hovering in the air like a bird of prey, suspended in the moment. Other Figures of Legend manipulate the free-standing elements of scenery – the frame of the mirror now cracked from side to side – and in 'a highly spectacular moment reminiscent of Balanchine's *L'Errante*'[51] sheets of white silk marking the filmy boundary between life and death fall from above.

> Lying, robed in snowy white
> That loosely flew to left and right–
> The leaves upon her falling light–

In the final scene 'solemn bells sound out … sad echoes of the Lady's six-note motif hover in brass and woodwind over the gloomy repeating funeral chords'.[52] Seven Figures of Legend assemble, and as a living set piece, the broken mirror becomes the Lady's funeral bier. Two truncated poles, once the sloping supports of the mirror's apex, rest on the shoulders of the black-garbed Figure at the front of the structure. Another Figure holds the rear, and two more support the centre of the processional barge that bears the Lady's body, her drapes falling either side. Three interlinked Figures are in the wake of the craft. They touch the shoulders of the dancer in front, and the lines across their bodies, reaching from the tips of plumed headdresses and outstretched hands to their extended legs, suggest the flow of the river and the whole image of the "gleaming shape she floated by".

Lady – donnée

We cannot be certain exactly how the choreographer and designer effected the poetic drama on the stage. Lew was commuting between San Francisco and New York, as ballet master for Ballet Society, until 1951. He may have been influenced by Balanchine's use of the silk curtain in *Orpheus* (1948); Pavel Tchelitchew had designed something similar for *L'Errante* (1933) – about a woman living out the last ten seconds of her life – which had premiered in Paris. Answering those journalists who focused on the similarity between his and Balanchine's choreographic works, Lew insisted that no one could match the master's genius. Sowell writes that rather than reinvent classical vocabulary, Lew had learnt about approach and intent: he 'absorbed Balanchine's innovations, … employing them according to his own musical training, his native wit and his frequent interest in narrative structures'.[53]

Fig. 13.15: The Lady's aquatic journey to Camelot. Her funeral bier is constructed from the wooden frame of the mirror 'crack'd from side to side', and carried by Figures of Legend, 1958. Photographer unknown (Museum of Performance and Design, San Francisco).

Although Alexander Fried in the *San Francisco Examiner* considered Bliss's music 'routine theatre stuff',[54] other critical response recognised its quality. As Bliss would have intended, the music serves its theatrical purpose, having 'no complete or logical life apart from its association with dancing'.[55] Delving into the fragments of the choreographic setting, my impression is that it is the Lady in Tennyson's poem as the starting point, the *donnée* that Bliss always waited for, which brings the work together. It drew out of the creative team a ballet described as 'enigmatic', 'mysterious', 'strange', and which evoked 'dark colours that contrast with bright vivid ones'.[56] Cushing, whose letter written after the first performance is quoted earlier, mused that the ballet added new dimensions to the poem. Others concurred. In 1960, Dean Wallace wrote:

> *Lady of Shalott* is one of the few examples in the history of the dance where choreography improves upon, analyses and clarifies a great work of literature. Its mosaic of moods — mystery, horror, gaiety, flirtation, noble love and frustration — makes it unique. Lew Christensen's tasteful choreography, Tony Duquette's exciting décor and costumes and Arthur Bliss's superbly woven musical texture make it a masterpiece.[57]

Stowell, with his wife Francia Russell, transformed the Pacific Northwest Ballet in Seattle into one of the big five ballet companies in the USA today. Their work in dance on the West Coast is part of the Christensen brothers' living dance legacy in America. Like Stowell, the first Red Knight, who so generously shared his memories of working with Lew, I wish that I could have seen *Lady* — in performance, from the front.

14.
Girl in a Broken Mirror: Ballet and Music in Education

SUSIE CROW

Unexpected surprises in one's musical life are always welcome and most of all in old age.[1]

This chapter traces a remarkable project that culminated in the only European performances of Arthur Bliss's final ballet, *The Lady of Shalott*, in May 1975. Rather than entering the repertoire of a major classical company, this ballet was brought to life to be performed by schoolchildren through the collaboration of music and dance educators with the committed support of Local Education Authority officers and a visionary headteacher. Tragically, Bliss never saw the final outcome, although he gave warm support throughout to this ambitious and impressive endeavour. A Thames Television documentary recorded sections of the work in performance and followed the young dancer who took the leading role, bringing the work to wider attention.

Bliss demonstrated through his own positive engagement a public-spirited approach to classical music, and a desire to make it available and accessible to a wider public, in particular children and young people. An assignment in 1935 to write a series of articles on 'Musical Britain' for *The Listener* was embraced wholeheartedly as he travelled 2,500 miles the length and breadth of the country in 'musical exploration'. Aiming 'to discover the lesser-known activities in English musical life…, and not primarily to visit those that are already famous',[2] he unearthed and delighted in a broad range of musical activity, from school orchestras and music festivals to brass bands and community choirs.

When the Second World War broke out in 1939 Bliss agonised over how to contribute to wartime efforts, offering his services to the BBC. In 1941 he accepted the invitation of Kenneth Wright, the BBC's Director of Overseas Music, and returned to the UK to help in Wright's department. Bliss contributed to overseas broadcasting to North America and Canada, introduced concerts, participated in discussions, hosted request programmes, and became the BBC's Director of Music in 1942 before resigning from the BBC in 1943. In 1953, when Arnold Bax died, Bliss was appointed Master of the Queen's Music and filled this public-facing role with commitment and distinction until his death in 1975.

Informed by this spirit of support for adventurous endeavour and educational outreach, Bliss developed a warm relationship with the internationally renowned Leicestershire Schools Symphony Orchestra (LSSO) over the years leading up to the Leicestershire production of *The Lady of Shalott*. Policy developments stemming from the 1944 Education Act had encouraged Local Education Authorities (LEAs) to initiate or support out-of-school activities and programmes. Thus, 'access to initial, in-service and post-graduate teacher training was essential'.[3] Leicestershire's plan was drawn up by its Director of Education Stuart Mason, who

Fig. 14.1: Arthur Bliss rehearsing the Leicestershire Schools Symphony Orchestra. John Whitmore (in glasses on the left), volunteer archivist, former member of LSSO, leads the second violins. Photographer unknown (Bliss Archive, Cambridge University Library).

had in 1948 appointed Eric Pinkett to work as principal music adviser, supporting music teaching in schools, managing peripatetic music teachers and subsequently establishing the Leicestershire School of Music and the Leicestershire Schools Symphony Orchestra. The senior orchestra became widely respected for its high standards, touring not only nationally but also internationally in Europe, and making recordings.[4] Its repertoire included contemporary works by British composers, among them Sir Michael Tippett, who became its patron, conducting and composing for them. The orchestra had shown itself as more than capable of playing the suite from Bliss's *Checkmate* (1937) at the 1967 Leicestershire Schools Festival of Music, and it accompanied soloist Frank Wibaut in a performance of Bliss's Piano Concerto in Oxford at Easter 1970. That July, Bliss again conducted LSSO for a performance of the Piano Concerto with Wibaut at the Cheltenham Festival. In a radio interview, Bliss was full of admiration, promoting the orchestra as a highlight of the Festival, impressed at what such youthful players (aged between fourteen and eighteen) were able to achieve:

This is a very difficult work, written for the New York Philharmonic, one doesn't expect youngsters to be able to tackle it properly. I think they are extremely good … very well-disciplined orchestra … their rhythm is good … they are remarkable … I think it will be great fun, that's the whole point, we shall enjoy ourselves and I think the audience will enjoy seeing these youngsters play.[5]

In her supplement to the composer's memoirs *As I Remember*, Bliss's wife Trudy recalls how in the following year, 1971, Bliss was commissioned by the Isle of Man Arts Council to write a work 'for the April Arts Festival at Douglas, in which LSSO was to take part with six hundred Manx schoolchildren'. Bliss chose to set two ballads, a Manx folk poem and one by Edith Sitwell, which were later performed as part of the County School of Music's pageant at Leicester's De Montfort Hall. The performance in Douglas, which the Blisses attended, left Trudy 'with a magical memory of someone very old in harmonious accord with the very young'.[6]

In 1972 Maurice Gilmour became adviser for drama and dance for Leicestershire LEA. Gilmour's substantial experience in schools and establishing youth theatre in Northumberland had brought him national recognition. His extensive remit included building teams 'of drama, dance, design and other specialist staff to widen provision across schools in the area', and in the community colleges that 'served 11–18-year-old school pupils and youth and adult/community education outside school'. Over the years he forged links and partnerships with universities, but also Leicester's theatres, the Haymarket and the smaller Phoenix.[7] Gilmour backed an unusual and innovative initiative introducing ballet into a state school, which from modest beginnings developed into something much bigger, similar to the trajectory of the LSSO.

Having trained professionally, ballet teacher Mary Hockney, originally from Leicester, had returned there to live in her father's home with her young daughter Tracie. In 1968 she began providing weekly informal ballet sessions at lunchtime, initially with three pupils, at New Parks Girls' School, a secondary modern on a housing estate built after the war. Headmistress Grace Eldridge observed that, 'within a term it became apparent that its appeal was widespread'. Ballet training was mostly available only through private dancing schools. There was consequently interest in general school provision and a demand from parents who were unable to afford such lessons for their children. As a result, 'thought had to be given to the introduction of ballet as a subject within the curriculum'.[8]

Ballet as a 'special skill' was introduced as an option in addition to the girls' general physical education in swimming, gymnastics, athletics, games and 'general dance'. All pupils in the first year did one class a week, increasing to two classes a week in the second year. It became an option in the third year; those who wished to continue studied ballet for three periods of the twenty-five-period school week, with a view to taking ballet as an O level subject. In the fourth and fifth years, as for other O level subjects, ballet was scheduled for four periods a week.

New Park Girls' School was in the vanguard. In January 1967 the Royal Academy of Dancing (RAD) had announced the acceptance of ballet as an O level subject by the Associated Examining Board for the Certificate of General Education. This had taken years of preparation and fractious negotiation with other ballet teaching organisations such as the Imperial Society of Teachers of Dancing, concerned that an examination initiated and devised by the RAD would put students trained in other methods at a disadvantage.[9] The four-part examination was to include written papers on the historical development of ballet, and 'Stage Ballet and Theory', a project file, and a practical test, set at a level equivalent to the RAD's Grade 4.

In line with the wider educational agenda of the ballet O level curriculum, provision at New Parks was not simply of classes but also opportunities to perform and to see performances. Up to 1966 The Royal Ballet Touring Company had intermittently visited Leicester, performing in the large De Montfort Hall. Early in 1974, in its smaller manifestation as the New Group, the Company visited Leicester's Haymarket Theatre; its repertoire at that time comprised both classical and more contemporary works by Hans Van Manen and George Balanchine, alongside those by British choreographers, Frederick Ashton, John Cranko

Fig. 14.2: Ballet class in the hall at New Parks Girls' School, *Leicester Mercury*, 1969. Photographer unknown (Mirrorpix).

and Ninette de Valois. The Royal Ballet Company's Ballet for All offshoot was founded in 1964, and by 1970 was offering 200 performances a year all round the country, including visits to Leicester's smaller Phoenix Theatre. Its popular combination of ballet education and entertainment was supported by lectures, paperback publications and television programmes. New Parks student Tanya Cope, in her second year in 1975, remembers Hockney taking students to the Phoenix to see a ballet – this was the first she had ever seen.[10] Students were also taken to London and elsewhere where they had the opportunity to be inspired by great dancers such as Margot Fonteyn. As a headteacher, Eldridge wholeheartedly endorsed the exposure of her pupils to excellence: 'it is clear that when high standards are placed before our young people, they respond in like manner'.[11]

This wider viewing and exposure must have contributed to a perception of ballet as a varied theatrical form with capacity not just for virtuosic dance but for dramatic storytelling – as Arnold Haskell had argued, a composite form bringing together dance, drama, music and design.[12] Students were not only encouraged by Hockney to participate in lunchtime drama classes led by the New Parks English teacher Mr Watkins, but also to learn a musical instrument.[13] Hockney was soon mounting ambitious works for her students and the emerging New Parks Ballet Group. Its first performances at the school included versions of *The Sleeping Beauty*, *Coppélia*, *Giselle* (1841), *The Firebird* (1910) and *Perséphone* (1961), and of John Cranko's *Pineapple Poll* (1951). One can perhaps see here a philosophical parallel with the development of the LSSO. From the start, Pinkett had believed in the importance of performance as the motivation that would keep young people involved. When advised early on that his nascent Saturday morning orchestra should rehearse for five years before giving performances, he rejected this suggestion: 'I had the unshakeable belief that what I was about to do could only be achieved by enthusiasm, and enthusiasm would only be created by doing and performing.'[14]

Hockney seems to have been a charismatic and characterful teacher with high professional standards. Caroline Salem[15] started learning ballet at the Leicester Academy of Dance with Alva Buck, but at the age of ten her mother removed her to attend classes on Saturday mornings with Hockney. Caroline remembers these classes as 'a notch up' – big classes with girls of a good standard and live piano accompaniment.[16] Jonathan Gray[17] was also sent to Hockney for classes. He remembers Hockney as 'quite shouty and strict',[18] corroborated by Tanya Cope: 'She [Mrs Hockney] would always speak her mind and never put up with any nonsense.'[19]

Classes were rigorous, with concern for posture, walking and barre work, but also lots of enjoyable jumping.[20] Caroline remembers jumps and beats, but also Hockney talking about internal sensation and 'knowing where the body is'.[21] She did not teach examination work, and instead of syllabus music she sometimes used recorded music, which Caroline found inspiring. Already a young musician herself, she later played with the LSSO, as did her siblings.[22]

Gilmour's briefing paper for the Deputy Director of Education for Leicestershire County Council in the summer of 1974 gives an idea of how quickly ballet became established at New Parks, and its perceived benefits. Gilmour saw it as a route for some students to 'a secure and satisfying career', for which the county should make provision. He praised the high level of performance achieved over the five years under Hockney's teaching, and singled out wider transferable benefits such as 'self confidence, discipline and poise'.[23] He made a case for extending provision to children in other schools through the establishment of two area centres in Leicester and Loughborough. As well as creating opportunities for progression to vocational training, Gilmour also envisaged founding a Leicester Ballet Company, to be directed by Hockney, aimed at enabling those who did not go on to professional training to continue study and enjoyment and have opportunities for performance. Thus came into being the Leicestershire County School of Dance, which similarly to the School of Music offered Saturday classes free of charge to selected students identified through schools.

Fig. 14.3: Rehearsals for *The Lady of Shalott* at New Parks Girls' School, *Artefact*, Spring issue, May 1975 (Freemantle/DE10594/Box3F folder development of ballet in Leicestershire, 1974–1993/By kind permission of Leicester Record Office).

Fig. 14.4: Leicestershire Schools Symphony Orchestra and New Parks Ballet Group in rehearsals as featured in 'Eye on TV: Ladies of the Dance', *TVTimes*, 25 September 1975, pages 24–5 (Future Publishing Ltd/ Leicester Record Office).

Making the new ballet

In 1974 'the boundaries of Local Education Authorities across the country were re-defined most often bringing large towns or cities within a wider county compass. In Leicestershire, this brought Leicester City and the small county of Rutland into its LEA'.[24] New Parks Girls' School, previously under city control, and LSSO (a county initiative) now came together under one local government educational roof.

In October that year Bliss was approached by Pinkett and Jack Richards of the Leicestershire School of Music 'to discuss the possibility of a new ballet, as they were keen on opening a ballet school in the department'.[25] David Hodgson of Thames Television accompanied them, with the idea of filming a documentary about the making of the new ballet. Bliss was able to offer them *The Lady of Shalott*, hitherto unseen in Europe. He had in fact written to de Valois in 1958 just before its premiere, sending her the piano score and scenario with a view to a possible collaboration with The Royal Ballet's emerging choreographic star: 'I should be delighted to work with Kenneth MacMillan if he likes the idea of the Lady.'[26] It would appear that de Valois intended to do a version of *The Lady of Shalott* herself in 1959, but sacrificed it in order to let MacMillan make *The Invitation*, which premiered in 1960. MacMillan did, however, use Bliss's Music for Strings in 1961 to make a neoclassical plotless work, *Diversions*.[27]

The Leicestershire project got underway immediately, and in November 1974 Eldridge, Hockney and Pinkett took a group of seven dancers to London to meet the Blisses at their home. This encounter was filmed for the documentary. Bliss talked about the narrative of the work and played extracts of the score to them on the piano. He was impressed by the young dancers and convinced by brunette Karen Hutton who had been selected for the role of the Lady: 'I always imagined the lady to be fair but it doesn't matter, you're just right.'[28]

Work began immediately on the ballet, with rehearsals in the lunch hour or after school, to enable dancers from outside the school such as Caroline Salem to join. Male performers for the roles of the Knight, the Lover and Lancelot as well as the ensemble (as in San Francisco Ballet's production, the Page was played by a girl) were recruited from Wreake Valley Community College, a local boys' school that had opened in 1971. Its Department of Sound and Movement covered music, drama and PE including some Laban-style movement. Drama teacher Simon Taylor observes that 'joined up activities, including musicals, were frequent and important'.[29] In the documentary, Hockney comments on the challenge that their participation initially presented them with: 'I think the first problem for them was shyness; they were very tense and uptight. They were afraid! Of making fools of themselves. Because, you know, I think the other boys at school would probably make fun of them; and there's a preconceived idea that to be a ballet dancer is sissy.'[30]

In addition to some group dance material, the boys, only one of whom had any ballet training, had to acquire classical ballet partnering skills, supporting the girls *en pointe* and in simple lifts. Perhaps most challenging was the scene for the Lady and the Knight,[31] as Hockney explains:

> In the *pas de deux* that the Lady of Shalott does with the Knight where she is in the tower and he is on the bank, Sir Arthur wants their movements to synchronise: and even though they are not together, it must appear that they are actually dancing together. So this is going to take quite a lot of thinking out. For me there are limitations because obviously Karen Hutton's technique is much stronger than Neil's.[32]

This section is shown complete in performance in the documentary footage, but frustratingly, apart from starting in long shot, focuses almost exclusively on the Lady in the tower, so it is hard to know how effectively Hockney was able to meet Bliss's wish.[33] However, it is a fine example of Bliss's ability to conceive of the ballet as more than just his music, showing his interest in its design and visual references as well as in the way the dance might portray the narrative. His refined scenario marked over relevant passages in the score provides the choreographer with a clear guide to his musical intentions.[34]

From the start, rehearsals were accompanied with live music, the school's much-loved music teacher Muriel Wells playing from Bliss's piano score. However, at Easter an intensive residential gave the opportunity for dancers and orchestra to rehearse together. Bliss was to have rehearsed with the orchestra in March, but his failing health made this impossible. Touching letters were sent from

Fig. 14.5: Poster for *Dance Mosaic* performances at Leicester Haymarket Theatre, May 1975 (By kind permission of Leicester Record Office).

Fig. 14.6: M.J. Laxton's striking minimalist tower and sloping ramp, with the Lady at her mirror and the Village Belle below. Photographer unknown (Bliss Archive, Cambridge University Library).

both the New Parks Ballet Group and LSSO wishing him well.[35]

The Lady of Shalott was the major work in a series of performances at the Leicester Haymarket Theatre entitled *Dance Mosaic* in May 1975, which showed off the range and ability of the New Parks Ballet Group, performing for the first time with the Leicestershire Schools Senior Orchestra conducted by Pinkett. Despite his illness, Bliss found time and energy to write about the project for *Artefact*, the recently established broadsheet of East Midlands Arts Association. Its edition appearing in advance of *Dance Mosaic 75* included the article by Eldridge about ballet at New Parks and photographs of the work in rehearsal.[36] Sadly, Bliss's generous article had to be prefaced by the notice of his death on 27 March.

Get-in and technical rehearsals began on Friday 9 May, continuing over the weekend until the opening night of Tuesday 13 May. Tanya Cope remembers the thrilling experience of preparing and performing in a proper theatre:

> Our dressing rooms were just how I had pictured them to be with lights around the mirrors and the path to the stage was longer than I could have imagined. We would rehearse during the morning there and have a

Fig. 14.7: The Lady torn between her love for Lancelot and the crone. Photographer unknown (Courtesy of John Whitmore, volunteer archivist, former member of LSSO).

little nap on the seats in the auditorium in the afternoon before getting ready for the evening performance … Performing on the stage was both exciting and scary. Once I was on the stage, I didn't want to come off! Loved it.[37]

In 1975 the school offered two programmes of works choreographed by Hockney, some new and some from the Group's existing repertoire. The first comprised a classical interpretation of Erik Satie's *Gymnopédies* and an exuberant piece set to Camille Saint-Saëns's *Danse Macabre*, with two premieres to more contemporary music. *The Listeners*, based on Walter de la Mare's 1912 poem, had an innovative score for narrator, voices, strings and tuned percussion by Douglas Young; and *New Orleans Suite* was set to Bryan Kelly's *Cuban Suite*, a popular staple of the orchestra's repertoire. Following a brief interval, *The Lady of Shalott* filled the second half of the evening. Penny Taylor read *The Listeners* and Simon Taylor *The Lady of Shalott* before the respective choreographic works.[38] The second programme included *Masquerade* with music by Aram Khachaturian, a ballet to Pyotr Ilyich Tchaikovsky's Violin Concerto, a reprise of *New Orleans Suite* and Hockney's own abbreviated version of *Pineapple Poll*. This programme seems to have been performed to recorded music.

The Lady of Shalott featured a striking but minimal construction designed by M.J. Laxton: situated upstage left and set against blacks, it represented the Lady's tower, with a mirror through which she observed the happenings onstage in the real world, and a curving ramp down which she finally ran to meet Lancelot. Wardrobe was by Mrs J. Hammond, a school parent. Simple costumes evoked the medieval imagery that had influenced Bliss's original vision for the ballet, with children in skirts of yellow and brown, villagers in dark green dresses and wimples, tumblers in tunics of red and white, and the Lady in a long, deep crimson gown. At the base of the tower a limping crone in dark flowing robes embodied the ever-present fateful curse, clinging to a supporting pillar with expressively reaching arms. Caroline Salem remembers this figure as very impactful.[39]

The Lady, older dancers playing the country girls and the young woman in love wore *pointe* shoes, the villagers and tumblers flat ballet slippers, and the Village Belle heeled shoes, allowing for a range of dance styles, mime gestures and characteristic movement, including some acrobatic tumbles and cartwheels to Bliss's jaunty dance. In the documentary, Hockney talks of being inspired by Pieter Bruegel the Elder, drawing on his depiction of peasants in clogs with arms linked, to make a 'robust' stamping dance to Bliss's irregular 1-2-3, 1-2-3, 1-2 rhythm for a group number involving all the dancers.[40]

Reviewing the opening night, the *Leicester Mercury*'s critic Ralph Pugsley complimented Hockney on her creation of 'a ballet of excellent quality': 'Mary Hockney's choreography, in turn, was intelligently alert to the diverse variety of moods and fancies in which the score abounds and combines with the music in evoking quite wonderfully the mystery, the joy, the youthfulness, the romance and the ultimate tragedy of the poem.' He observed that the standard of the choreography was all the more remarkable as she had created it 'for a group of schoolgirls with a wide range in age and dance attainment and has trained them to perform before a theatre audience with all the poise, assurance, concentration and discipline of a mature company'. He also praised other choreography for the *Dance Mosaic* programme: Hockney's 'clever use … in modern idiom of a full company of dancers incorporating solo counterpoint and some tellingly simple mass effects' in *The Listeners*.[41] This work made a strong impression on the young Caroline, an early exposure to a more contemporary movement idiom.[42]

The critics remarked on the ability and grasp of a range of styles by the young dancers and musicians. *New Orleans Suite* 'was swaggeringly presented in cabaret style – band on stage and the girls and boys playing up sleazily and hip-swayingly to Latin-American rhythms'.[43] Tantalising snippets from national dance critic Fernau Hall's review of the evening for the *Daily Telegraph*, which never appeared publicly because of a strike, compliment the dancing of the New Parks girls in Hockney's version of Satie's *Gymnopédies*: 'clear how devotedly the girls had worked … points were excellent … their line was clear … danced with cool assurance'.[44]

The documentary *Girl in a Broken Mirror* was finally shown on Thames Television on 1 October 1975, attracting significant publicity. Reviewing it

Fig. 14.8: Villagers waiting in the wings for their entrance. Photographer unknown (Courtesy of John Whitmore).

Fig. 14.9: Karen Hutton as the Lady. Photographer unknown (Bliss Archive, Cambridge University Library).

for *Dancing Times*, Michael Bayston commented on Hodgson's sensitive direction of the double story line: 'the rehearsing and performance of the ballet, and its effect on Karen Hutton, a sixteen-year-old student who danced the title role'.[45] He admired Hockney's success against the odds, and found Karen's story heart-warming, impressed by her will to succeed, and suggested that the film should go out as a programme to schools to show what can be achieved.

Caroline describes Hockney as 'not a warm character', but possessing 'a fieriness that was creative',[46] with magnetism and a dream; perhaps it was ultimately the art form that was her great love. The girls did not feel oppressed by her discipline and demands, but excited by her apparent connection with the wider ballet world, her professionalism and artistry. It seems that she treated them more as grown-ups and potential professionals and took seriously her responsibility to help some towards careers in dance. *Girl in a Broken Mirror* shows her escorting a small group of pupils to an audition for the Rambert School in London; Karen gained a place there. Other students from the school later went into vocational training at The Royal Ballet School and the Arts Educational Trust as well as Rambert.[47] A conversational letter from Hockney to Lady Bliss in the autumn of 1975, after the documentary went on air, reports on another emerging talent featured in *The Lady of Shalott*, 'a very strong classical dancer', fourteen-year-old Alison Clay, who aspires to study in London, and reveals that Karen had written to her to say that she was 'very happy and working hard' at Rambert.[48]

There was evidently more creative work to come. Hockney's letter to Lady Bliss refers to plans for further choreography for performance at the Haymarket in May 1976, a ballet with a new score by Douglas Young, as well as a work to Giuseppe Verdi's *I Vespri Siciliani*, at the time also being used for a new ballet at Covent Garden by MacMillan. Lady Bliss had thought highly enough of Hockney's choreography for *The Lady of Shalott* to mention her to composer John McCabe in connection with his *Dance-Movements* (1967), and Hockney had plans to follow up this connection.

Yet a year later, Hockney suddenly resigned from her position at New Parks, and two years after that she disappeared to America. Her role teaching and leading the New Parks Ballet Group was taken over by Valerie Egri; performances continued in the ensuing years and further young dancing talents from the area went on to successful professional careers. *The Lady of Shalott* was not performed again, but dance activity in Leicestershire flourished and expanded, embracing other genres and directions beyond ballet, with Peter Kyle employed from the summer of 1975 by the County School of Dance, working closely with Egri and choreographing works in a more contemporary idiom for the Group. The pioneering arts educational practice of Leicestershire's LEA was recognised in the seminal report *The Arts in Schools*, with Gilmour and Director of Education Andrew Fairbairn both on the Advisory Committee.[49] An impressive number of the young LSSO players went on to distinguished professional careers in music, not least Caroline's brother Peter Salem, who played in the orchestra for *The Lady of Shalott* as a fourteen-year-old cellist and is now an internationally recognised composer of successful ballets for major companies.

The impact of *The Lady of Shalott*, however, reached far wider than simply those who chose to make music or dance their life, as Gilmour and Eldridge had intended and intuited:

> all who are members of the school have been made aware, at some level, of ballet as an art form … the effect though perhaps not immediate, will become clearer in the years to come … this ballet … has been an instrument of change. It has changed the quality of thinking and the direction of lives. It has brought together in a spectacular and acceptable way the inner and outer worlds of personality. Ballet as a dance form, if left free to develop, will emerge as a splendid and individual art, capable of providing a visible and compassionate link between idea and reality.[50]

Thanks to the documentary *Girl in a Broken Mirror*, we are able to trace the realisation of Bliss's last ballet through inspired young performers, and see substantial excerpts of the finished work. Hockney faithfully followed the composer's refined vision, making resourceful use of the dancers at her disposal to choreograph a coherent and moving dramatic ballet. Both dancers and orchestra showed the high professional standards of which young people are capable, given opportunity, challenge and encouragement. Bliss, had he seen the finished performance, would have been proud of them.

14.
Epilogue
Remembering Karen Bliss

SUSAN JONES

This book came into being at the suggestion of Arthur Bliss's younger daughter Karen (Sellick). Before her death in 2020, Karen expressed her ambition that celebrations of her father's distinguished musical career should give a special place to his outstanding contribution to dance. The chapters in this book are carefully curated to explore Bliss's ballet music and his engagement with dance from a wide range of perspectives, thus honouring Karen's wishes. The conclusion rightfully belongs to Karen herself, whose life and career in dance in many ways complete the arc of the book. We might easily forget that Karen's gifts as a dancer and dance teacher were inherited from both her parents and followed on naturally from Bliss's musical life and talents. While the book begins with Ninette de Valois' important collaboration with the composer, Bliss's legacy as a ballet composer was also expressed through his daughter's love of dance, teaching dance and *her* knowledge of his music and ballets, as well as her own engagement with de Valois and the Sadler's Wells Ballet before she married, and became a remarkable ballet teacher in Oxford. I did not meet Karen until 1989, long after she had established her life in Oxford, but with the help of friends' testimony this chapter explores Karen's extensive contribution to dance in Oxford and the Bliss legacy she brought with her.

First, a few words about Karen's life and upbringing. Karen was Arthur's second daughter, born to his wife Trudy Hoffmann in 1932. Bliss had moved back to England after a period from April 1923 to June 1925 in the USA, where he had met Trudy. As his compositional work developed, they were simultaneously establishing a family. Bliss's memoir and letters are full of the intense importance to him of his family, and following his eldest daughter Barbara's birth in 1926, Karen's arrival was anticipated with great joy. Bliss remarked that while Barbara seemed most like him, 'Karen was to be an obvious Hoffmann in appearance and character.'[1] Yet Karen's early interest in dance also showed her inheritance of Bliss's musical talents.

Karen's was a colourful childhood, with some of her early years spent in America when Bliss took academic appointments in California. Of course, Karen would have been exposed to the innovative musical and cultural life of her father's profession, at that time centred on the West Coast of the USA, and her upbringing was populated by eminent figures from music and the theatre as her father rose to prominence. During the period of separation when Bliss was contributing to the war effort in England and the family remained in America, Bliss kept up their close contact right from the beginning. In 1941, before leaving the USA via Canada, Bliss wrote about the importance of their correspondence in alleviating the pain of separation. 'During the month I was delayed in Canada before sailing many letters went to Trudy and my two daughters, Barbara

Fig. 15.1: Carlos Sancha, *Portrait of Karen Sellick*, 1957 (Private commission). Photo: Branca Ilic (Courtesy of the Sellick/Bliss family).

and Karen, and once in England a weekly letter went to California, and a weekly letter came to London.'[2]

Bliss was always interested in his daughters' activities. In 1941 he wrote to Trudy, 'I can imagine the Greek theatre the centre of B[arbara]'s life these days … I long to know of my Karen's doings. I am writing to each of them this evening.'[3] Bliss's memoirs and quotations from the family's letters are full of how the girls were throwing themselves into their preferred occupations: Barbara followed an interest in drama, while Karen devoted herself to dance. In 1942 Bliss expressed total support for their choices: 'I had told [my daughters] that when they had finally made up their minds what career they wished to pursue, I would be one hundred per cent behind them. Barbara had chosen the stage as her first wish, and Karen was already taking ballet lessons.' He elaborated on his support for Karen's dancing in America: 'Two years before in the San Francisco Opera House I had introduced Karen to [Léonide] Massine, who was dancing there, telling him that she wished to study ballet. "How old is she?" he asked; "Seven," I said. "*Too* old," he replied. "I started at five!"' Bliss continued to note Karen's determination to dance: 'In spite of this depressing drawback of old age, Karen persisted, and in eight years' time could be seen dancing at Covent Garden in the second act of my Opera, *The Olympians*.'[4] This

REMEMBERING KAREN BLISS | 177

moment in Bliss's memoir records his perception of Karen's fierce attachment to dance, his pride in her, as well as giving us a fascinating insight into the way she rubbed shoulders early on with eminent figures from the dance world while she lived in America. In a letter to Karen of 1942 from London, Bliss thanked her for her latest letter, which 'is a lesson in ballet with all the important positions clearly marked'. He tells her that he had shown a photo of her to Arnold Haskell, the ballet writer, who observed, 'she has very good points indeed'. Bliss goes on to tell Karen, 'I felt very proud.'[5] In 1943 she studied dance with the Christensen brothers in San Francisco, as well as in 'the ballet school founded by Ruth St Denis and Ted Shawn at Jacob's Pillow in the Berkshires'.[6]

When Trudy and the girls returned to London in November 1943, Karen continued to pursue dance with great seriousness. Bliss recorded that 'While we were living in the flat in Cavendish Square for the remainder of the war, Karen went three mornings a week to the ballet class at Sadler's Wells.' After the war, Bliss tells us that Karen 'was to enter the disciplined training of the Sadler's Wells Theatre Ballet',[7] joining the Company in January 1947.

In conversation with Karen in 2019 I was privileged to hear first-hand her account of these years as she spoke excitedly about her Sadler's Wells' training and about performing and touring abroad briefly with the Company (in difficult ballets like Frederick Ashton's *Les Patineurs*, 1937). She related her first forays into independent life away from the family home when she was flat-sharing in London with Annette Page.[8] She talked of the thrill and camaraderie of touring, and then she remarked on one of the most formative experiences of her life at the end of this period – one that signalled a change of direction for her, when she first considered a career in teaching. She said that after receiving advice from de Valois (delivered to her, as Karen described it, in de Valois' characteristically forthright fashion on the boat returning from the North American tour), she decided not to pursue a career as a performer in ballet. She recounted the way in which the initial disappointment of this decision was followed swiftly by an opening up of other avenues, a determination to 'get on with life' with great positivity. She was extremely intelligent, she taught French for a period and she did not abandon the art form of ballet. Instead, she developed into a dance teacher of rare charisma and ability with an extraordinary gift for communicating with, and choreographing for, children. She also found happiness and fulfilment in family. After meeting and marrying Christopher Sellick (1956), they raised a loving family and eventually settled in Oxford in 1984, where Karen simultaneously sustained a successful career as a prominent teacher and contributor to the vibrant dance community in the city.

Karen always spoke warmly and proudly of her father's achievements. During that conversation in 2019, Karen gestured to the eminent figures who visited the family in her childhood. She also revealed that Bliss sometimes occupied a somewhat distanced role in family life while she and her sister were growing up. By contrast, she recalled with glee the visits of Robert Helpmann to the family home when he arrived principally to discuss the progress of *Miracle* with her father. Helpmann was a hit with the children, entertaining Karen and her sister as they frolicked together in the garden creating wonderful games of make-believe involving dancing and wearing masks and improvised costumes. This was the kind of play that her father, with his intensely busy musical career, was unable to provide. Yet Karen showed no resentment of her father's immersion in work. And she expressed a deep love and devotion to both her mother (a broadcaster and writer who gave her confidence and inspired her beyond a conventional maternal role) and to her father. Their fondness for each other was apparent in Karen's conversations, and from the evidence of letters and Bliss's memories.

To conclude the volume I turn to the recollections of those of us who knew Karen in Oxford during that second, major period of her life. All remarked on her joyful countenance and those who saw her dance observed how even at a considerable age she retained an ability to spring vibrantly in the air, spin and to 'travel' effortlessly across the floor. She was still taking class and teaching ballet well into her eighties, and friends of Karen agree on her distinctive style. My own memories of Karen's dancing come from the late 1980s and 1990s, when I first arrived at the

University of Oxford as a 'mature' undergraduate and, having danced for many years with Scottish Ballet, continued to take classes with the Oxford Dance Society. My literature classes in 1989 focused on modernist poetry, and Karen's dance style immediately struck me as a great example of T.S. Eliot's claim for the 'impersonality' of the poet. Far from lacking personality in the literal sense, when she was dancing Karen nevertheless encapsulated this very idea of 'impersonality', in Eliot's parlance – referring to a technical term for the role of the poet. Stéphane Mallarmé, W.B. Yeats and Eliot had all written of the poet as vehicle or vessel of the poetic material without the interference of the author's personal subjectivity. Karen seemed to achieve that very poetic ideal when she moved. There were no histrionics in her performative style – what mattered was the dance itself; she simply became the conduit of the movement, whether in class or demonstrating for her pupils. Her overriding hallmark was musicality and understanding of the centrifugal force of the body in motion. My enduring image of her is gliding across the floor smoothly and almost imperceptibly maintaining the direction of travel while gracefully turning. Never simply executing a series of steps, she was always *dancing*, often joyfully, accenting the *épaulement* of the upper back, shoulders and arms as they spiralled around the central core of the body.[9] I imagine her pupils found her style both tantalising and liberating. Karen was just as enthusiastic about studying dance as an art form with a rich history, and was a loyal attendee and interlocutor of Dance Scholarship Oxford (DANSOX), a research group that focuses on dance at a university that has no official dance faculty.

But Karen's work as a brilliant and ballet teacher generates the most striking memories from colleagues and friends who worked with her. We also get a glimpse from them of her interest in choreographing for children's productions.

Penny Cullerne-Bown, now Principal of the East Oxford School of Ballet, captures Karen's contribution to Oxford dance teaching where she set up a ballet school in the Grandpont area: 'Many families in that neighbourhood and far beyond will have very happy memories of their association with her school. She had tireless enthusiasm, and an unforced warmth and love for her young pupils which clearly drew in whole families.'[10] Penny, who took over Karen's school when she retired, had met Karen in 1984 when they both attended the same ballet classes,[11] and remarked that her 'Sadler's Wells training was evident in the beauty of her arm lines and the elegant carriage of her head'. Having spoken to Karen about her early dance training in America, I also wondered whether something of the freedom of her dance quality derived in part from those US influences as much as from the rigour of the Sadler's Wells training.

Susie Crow, Oxford-based dance artist, teacher and scholar recalls that she choreographed some dances for Karen's production of *Perséphone* (2004), and her chapter in this book (on the 1975 Leicester production of *The Lady of Shalott* danced by school pupils) is a reminder that Karen also followed her father's ballet scores closely. Karen told me in conversation that she had later contemplated taking on a reworking of *The Lady of Shalott* herself for young dancers. I also have vivid memories of Karen's understanding of *Miracle*. I attended Gillian Lynne's recreation of *Miracle* at Sadler's Wells in 2014, and meeting Karen in the audience with her sister, her kind but discerning critique focused on the distinguished quality of the score rather than the new choreography. She said that her keen memories of the original ballet by Helpmann made it difficult for her to enjoy fully the reworking by another, but she nevertheless praised the attempt to keep Bliss's ballet work alive.

One of the most fascinating memories of Karen comes from Peter McMullin, who was Karen's class pianist and musical collaborator in Oxford for many years. His eloquent recollections of her methods and temperament and as a contributor to community arts deserve extensive quotation.[12]

> I first met Karen in about 1999 when my eldest daughter, then five, decided she would like to try dancing. Karen ran a class for small beginners in St Matthew's church hall in Marlborough Road, not five minutes' walk from St Ebbe's School. As the classes were short, either I or my wife Janet would stay to observe. In front of a class of six or seven young girls (plus the occasional boy) Karen

would then weave a gentle spell of dance. She had a pattern that would subtly introduce those who might be caught up by its magic, to the long-term discipline that would be required of any dancer keen to improve. But her method also seemed like play and fun to those for whom it would forever simply be that. Exercises that taught you to take control of your body and make shapes that could be seen as beautiful, an awareness of the aesthetic potential in movement and the excellent discipline of having to move in unison with other people. What struck me then was Karen's implacability, her seemingly angelic ability to ignore the one or two difficult children with tiny attention spans and shorter tempers, her way of knowing exactly what was enough and when to stop. As my daughter (and subsequently my younger daughter joined as well) grew and the classes became more sophisticated, my own interest grew. I felt I could be of use in a dance class because, as well as being able to read music, I could improvise on the spot … I would play regularly both for classes of all standards plus the examinations of the Royal Academy of Dance into which she would enter anyone dedicated enough to step up.

One of Karen's abiding achievements was the ballet productions she put on. Her primary concern was inclusivity, so practically every person who wanted to have a role was accommodated. Rehearsals would be rigorous and plentiful, but that meant that every performance was assured as could be. Over the years I witnessed a wonderful *Coppélia* (performed with full orchestra!) and a sparkling *Sleeping Beauty* that simply dazzled the audience with its charm and wit. My favourite of all was *Persephone*, an original ballet by Karen using music she gleaned from a wide variety of sources including the little-known Harp Concerto by the Ukrainian composer Reinhold Glière. One of the features of this production, given at the theatre in Headington School, was that parents were included in the dance. While several of the parents were extremely

Fig. 15.2: Karen Bliss with her father on her wedding day in 1956. Photographer unknown (Bliss Archive, University of Cambridge Library).

confident movers I, despite any musical skill I might have, was not. Yet I found myself in full flowing costume, golden lyre in hand, as a Greek God dancing a choreographed minuet with others. While appreciating dance from the sidelines, this remains the only time I have danced in public, and the only person who could ever have got me to do it was Karen.

Peters's account shows the degree to which Karen inherited her father's musical abilities as well as his sense of responsibility to community music-making, and to passing on the traditions of art in the community.

As to Karen's final words, both Peter and Susie have provided poignant evidence. Peter wrote that:

> Our last conversation was on the telephone about three weeks before she died. 'Ah, I'm so glad you rang as I have a whole list of musical questions I want to ask you.' Although seriously unwell by then, what still came across was her unique radiance, by which I mean the almost magical presence she would bring with her into a room. Some people seem to bump into the world as they walk through it as though, in Dickens's words, it were full of invisible furniture they were trying to avoid. Karen sailed through the world as a proud barque, dancing through the atmosphere and turning mundane lives special.

And in her last email to Susie, Karen, writing from the hospice, expressed her sustaining spirit and ever generous and thoughtful attitude to others, as well as her love for the way creativity in dance for her emanated from music. Susie had recently completed a PhD, and Karen wrote in response on 12 September 2020: 'Sometime ago I started to read your thesis and so enjoyed the first chapter about whether a ballet class allows for creativity. I have always enjoyed being trained in a craft and letting interpreting the music fulfil any need for being creative.'

Most touchingly, Karen mentions in this email her grandson's help with the upkeep of the garden in Fairacres Road, where she had spent so many happy years with Chris and the family: 'I had always wanted a pond in my garden. [My grandson] came and dug a very pretty one. In only a few days a frog took up residence.' Something of the sunny tone of her words in this email suggests Karen's continuously joyous spirit, attachment to family, to dance and music right up to the end.

These concluding remarks have been gathered from the people who knew and loved Bliss's daughter Karen during the period of her life in Oxford, where she spent so much of her time as a dear friend to many and as a gifted communicator of the art of dance. For a book focusing on the distinguished contribution of Arthur Bliss to the dance world, it seems fitting to close by remembering that his daughter nurtured in a new generation the love of music and dance for many years to come.

Endnotes

Introduction

1. Spicer 2023, 6.
2. *Ibid.*, 9.
3. Bliss 1938; reprinted in Roscow 1991, 160.
4. The ballet was named *Lady of Shalott*. San Francisco Ballet dropped '*The*' from the title.

Chapter 1

1. Haskell 1951, 257.
2. De Valois 1926; reprinted in Cave and Worth 2012, 150.
3. See Chapters 3, 4 and 5.
4. Sadler's Wells School Governors' Meetings, from 1947 (Royal Ballet School Special Collections).
5. Spicer 2023, 166.
6. Bliss, 23 April 1921, 523; reprinted in Roscow 1991, 8.
7. De Valois 1926; reprinted in Cave and Worth 2012, 152.
8. See Sorley Walker 1987, 333–6.
9. Cited in Bliss 1970 (1989 rev. edn), 64.
10. Spicer 2023, 63. This event reappears from different perspectives in Chapters 2, 3, 6 and 12.
11. Macdonald 1975, 262.
12. Sorley Walker 1987, 77.
13. 'Marcato' is a musical term indicating an accented, or marked, emphasis.
14. Marcato. 'The Rise of Arthur Bliss', feature in 'Musicians and Their Ways'. *The Weekly Dispatch*, 10 July 1921, 6.
15. Spicer 2023, 159.
16. Marcato. 'The Rise of Arthur Bliss', feature in 'Musicians and Their Ways'. *The Weekly Dispatch*, 10 July 1921, 6.
17. Stravinsky wrote two other major ballet scores for Diaghilev's Company: *Les Noces* (1923) and *Apollon musagète* (1928), later known as *Apollo*.
18. Spicer 2023, 63.
19. *Ibid.*, 60.
20. Bliss 1970 (1989 rev. edn), 28.
21. *Ibid.*
22. Bliss, 2 July 1921; reprinted in Roscow 1991, 17.
23. *Ibid.*, 23.
24. See Hussey 1947, 183–6, 184.
25. Cited in Spicer 1923, 72–3.
26. De Valois 1947, 7.
27. *Ibid.* Perhaps because de Valois was writing this twenty years later in 1947, she overlooked her 1925 choreographic debut, *The Arts of the Theatre*, which remained in the Vic-Wells repertoire until 1932.
28. De Valois 1957, 49.
29. Tudor's comment (originally made in *Ballet Review*, Spring 1983, 62) is cited in Chazin-Bennahum 1994, 27.
30. Although the word 'Ballet' was originally included in its title, the Society was known and is generally referred to as the Camargo Society.
31. Edwin Evans. 'The Interregnum: The Camargo Society'. *Dancing Times*, October 1935, 24.
32. Lloyd 2014, 159.
33. *Ibid.*, 126.
34. Spicer 2023, 57.
35. Sorley Walker 1987, 76–7.
36. Joy Newton, letter to Audrey Harman, 6 June 1980 (Royal Ballet School Special Collections).
37. *Ibid.*
38. Beatrice Appleyard, letter to Audrey Harman, 19 March 1981 (Royal Ballet School Special Collections).
39. See O'Brien 2012, 58–64.
40. See Sorley Walker 1987, 77, 91, 341–2.
41. Unattributed. *The Era*, Wednesday 22 January 1930, 8.
42. Spicer 2023, 60.
43. Cited in Sorley Walker 1987, 77. Also see Chapter 2.
44. Kane and Pritchard 1994, 42.
45. Sorley Walker 1987, 102. Another source lists twelve dancers: eight women and four men. See Kane and Prichard 1994, 42.
46. Lloyd 2014, 135.
47. Clarke 1955, 45.
48. Sorley Walker 1987, 77.
49. *Ibid.* Clarke erroneously reverses this order.
50. Clarke 1955, 45–6.
51. Sorley Walker 1987, 77.
52. Clarke 1955, 45–6.
53. Unattributed. *The Times*, 17 December 1920; reprinted in Bliss 1970 (1989 rev. edn), 59–60.
54. Also see *Rout* in Chapter 12.
55. Cited in Kane and Pritchard 1994, 42.
56. *Ibid.*
57. Sorley Walker cites the 'Sitter Out' review of *Rout* in *Dancing Times*, February 1928, which referred to its 'futuristic' movement.
58. Marshall's *The Other Theatre* (1947), cited in Sorley Walker 1987, 78.
59. Review in the Cambridge undergraduate journal *Granta* (4 February 1927), cited in Sorley Walker 1987, 78.
60. Rudolf von Laban (1879–1958) was influential primarily through his work as movement theorist and teacher; Mary Wigman (1886–1973), who was a pupil of Laban, was renowned as a choreographer and dancer. Both were pioneers of Expressionism in European modern dance.
61. See Beth Genné cited in Jones 2013, 84. Also Cave 2011, plate 22.
62. Arnold L. Haskell. 'The Ballet in England', the *New English Weekly*, June 1932, 47–8.
63. De Valois 1926; reprinted in Cave and Worth 2012, 149–52.
64. Also see Chapter 5 for the relationship of de Valois' choreographic style with academic ballet.
65. Haskell 1943, 48.
66. De Valois 1937, 248–9.
67. Beatrice Appleyard, letter to Audrey Harman, 19 March 1981 (Royal Ballet School Special Collections); Joy Newton, letter to Audrey Harman, 6 June 1980 (Royal Ballet School Special Collections).
68. Beatrice Appleyard, letter to Audrey Harman, 19 March 1981 (Royal Ballet School Special Collections) (original underscore).
69. See Sorley Walker 1987, 119, 350. Also see Chapter 2.
70. Lloyd 2014, 124.
71. Spicer 2023, 55.
72. Bliss 1970 (1989 rev. edn), 55. Also Spicer 2023, 55.
73. Bliss 1970 (1989 rev. edn), 55.
74. Spicer 2023, 55.
75. Cited in Spicer 2023, 56.
76. Sorley Walker 1987, 119. A footnote on p. 326 gives her source as an interview with Dame Alicia Markova.
77. *Ibid.*, 119.
78. Markova 1986, 44.
79. Dolin 1953, 156.

80 Markova 1986, 44.
81 Scholl 1994, 50.
82 Aeschylus's *The Oresteia* was the first and most influential of these productions, premiered on 22 November 1926. Co-directed by Gray and Herbert Prentice, movement direction was by de Valois.
83 From *The Times*, 21 March 1932; reprinted in Spicer 2023, 166.
84 Bliss 1970 (1989 rev. edn), 13.
85 Hopkins 1947, 102, 107.
86 Evans 1947, 111.
87 De Valois 1947, 7–8.
88 Roscow 1991, 4.

Chapter 2

1 Diaghilev began to present ballets in 1909. The Ballet Russes as a company was established in 1911.
2 Playfair 1925, 59.
3 Macfall 1923; reprinted 2015.
4 Fraser 1970, 276–8.
5 Harley Granville-Barker's production of Shakespeare's *Twelfth Night* designed by Norman Wilkinson was first presented at the Savoy, London, on 15 November 1912. Léonide Massine's *The Good-Humoured Ladies* designed by Léon Bakst was created for the Ballets Russes on 12 April 1917 in Rome and first danced at the London Coliseum on 5 September 1918.
6 Fraser 1970, 260.
7 Ibid., 272–3.
8 See Chapters 1 and 12.
9 Bliss 1970 (1989 rev. edn), 59.
10 Paul Spicer 2023, 159, erroneously writes that Sinding's *Fire Dance* was arranged for Karsavina to perform with Diaghilev's Ballets Russes.
11 'Karsavina Dances. Lovat Fraser's Last Designs', the *Observer*, 17 July 1921, 5.
12 Frank Rutter. 'Art in Movement. The Last Designs of Lovat Fraser', the *Sunday Times*, 17 July 1921, 4.
13 For more on Karsavina's role, see Chapters 1 and 3.
14 Also see Chapter 1.
15 Hopkins 1947, 107.
16 Stevenson 2007, 283.
17 While Bliss was a chess player, de Valois picked up any knowledge she had of the game from him. The famous photograph of the three collaborators studying a chessboard was surely set up for publicity, not a lesson in how to play chess.
18 De Valois in her notes on *Checkmate* sent to Martin Lewis in 1983. Manuscript available in the Royal Opera House Archive.
19 *Checkmate* predated Hepworth's stringed sculptures, which she began in 1939.
20 See the images in Chapter 3.
21 See the photograph by Zoë Dominic in Chapter 12.
22 Ayrton 1947, 79.
23 See Fig. 6.5.
24 A version of the design on paper reproduced in Clarke and Crisp 1978 (page 190, plate 138) shows far more of the docks and factories painted on the backdrop beyond the tenements than the surviving set model held at the Victoria and Albert Museum, London. This may have been planned for use on the wider stage of the Royal Opera House or may have been Burra's original intention, but it would not fit on the stage of the Prince's Theatre. The production photographs show a narrow passage through the multistorey buildings.
25 Buckle 1955, 36.
26 A built set is a three-dimensional set of wood or metal enabling performers to appear on a number of levels rather than a flat painted canvas to give the illusion of a place.
27 Bliss 1970 (1989 rev. edn), 169.
28 Beaumont 1955, 53.
29 See Chapter 10 for a full description of the onstage action.
30 Clarke 1955, 206.
31 Ayrton 1947, 80.
32 Pavel Tchelitchew (1898–1957) was a fine artist and theatre designer. His designs focused on light, space, colour and fabrics; his ballet *L'Errante* (1933), choreographed by George Balanchine featuring cloaked figures in greens and reds, ended with a fall of silk cloth leaving the audience with a sense of emptiness, an effect used by subsequent designers. Chapter 13 also references Tchelitchew's influence on stage design.

Checkmate

Chapter 3

1 Unattributed. *The Bystander*, 6 October 1937, 15.
2 Bliss 1970 (1989 rev. edn), 113.
3 Ibid., 71.
4 See Chapter 1 for a detailed account of *Rout* and *Narcissus and Echo*.
5 See Chapter 2 for further details of Sinding's *Fire Dance*.
6 Bliss, *Mêlée Fantasque* (1921). Programme note. See https://www.wisemusicclassical.com/publishers/novello/ (accessed 15 January 2026).
7 Bliss 1938; reprinted in Roscow 1991, 161.
8 Ibid., 162.
9 Ibid., 163.
10 Ibid.
11 Bliss 1970 (1989 rev. edn), 114.
12 Ibid., 113.
13 Bliss 1938; reprinted in Roscow 1991, 163.
14 Bliss 1970 (1989 rev. edn), 114.
15 Arthur Bliss. 'Checkmate', *Record Review*, June 1960, 5.
16 Bliss 1970 (1989 rev. edn), 115.
17 Constant Lambert. 'Checkmate', *Radio Times*, 8 October 1937, 17.
18 Adolf Aber. 'Checkmate. Arthur Bliss's Ballet in Paris', *The Musical Times*, 38 (1133), July 1937, 648–9.
19 Bliss 1938; reprinted in Roscow 1991, 162.
20 Bliss, Prologue – The Players, Stage Directions, *Checkmate* Study Score, Novello, 2007.
21 Bliss, Dance of the Red Pawns, in *ibid*.
22 Bliss, Dramatis Personae/Scenario, in *ibid*.
23 Bliss, Dance of the Four Knights, Stage Directions, in *ibid*.
24 Spicer 2023, 163.
25 Bliss, Dance of the Four Knights, Stage Directions, 2007, in *Checkmate* Study Score, Novello, 2007.
26 Bliss, Entry of the Black Queen, in *ibid*.
27 Bliss, The Red Knight's Mazurka, in *ibid*.
28 Bliss, Ceremony of the Red Bishops, in *ibid*.
29 Bliss, Entry of the Red Castles, in *ibid*.
30 Bliss, Dramatis Personae/Scenario, in *ibid*.
31 Bliss, Entry of the Red Castles, Stage Directions, in *ibid*.
32 Bliss, Entry of the Red King and Queen, in *ibid*.
33 Bliss, The Attack, in *ibid*.
34 Bliss, The Duel, in *ibid*.
35 Bliss, The Black Queen Dances, in *ibid*.
36 Bliss, Finale – Checkmate, in *ibid*.
37 Bliss 1938; reprinted in Roscow 1991, 163.

Chapter 4

1 *Masterpieces of British Ballet: Checkmate/The Rake's Progress*. Sadler's Wells Royal Ballet, filmed at Sadler's Wells Theatre. Dir. Jolyon Wimhurst, Jaras Entertainments Ltd, 1982. Reissued on DVD, Video Artists International 2006.

Chapter 5

1 Bliss 1938, 163; reprinted in Roscow 1991.
2 Stephen Lloyd. 'Every Word He Said Lifted You Up', the *Guardian*, Saturday Review, 5 July 2014, 7.
3 Stephen Jeffries, interview with Jennifer Jackson, 16 August 2024, recalling a conversation with Madam when she was in her eighties. Jeffries, Royal Ballet Principal, danced the Red Knight in 1977.
4 Beryl Grey in *Call Me Madam: The Life and Achievements of Dame Ninette de Valois*, Broadcast BBC2, 6 June 1998; Exec. Prod. Bob Lockyer, Dir. Ross MacGibbon.
5 Graham Lustig, email to Jennifer Jackson, 14 October 2024.
6 All interviewees comment on how 'hard' the ballet is, referring to the stamina and strength needed to perform the choreography.
7 Barry Wordsworth, interview with Jennifer Jackson, 15 August 2024.
8. See Chapter 4.
9 Margaret Barbieri, interview with Jennifer Jackson, 9 July 2024.
10 Durà-Vilà 2019, 160.
11 Darcey Bussell, interview with Jennifer Jackson, 10 January 2024.
12 Mark Silver, interview with Jennifer Jackson, 16 August 2024. Silver was known for his unusual ability to reproduce choreography accurately having seen but not danced it.
13 De Valois 1926, 589–93; reprinted in Cave and Worth 2012, 150.
14 Jacquie Hollander, interview with Jennifer Jackson, 2 January 2025.

15 Ninette de Valois in *Masterpieces of British Ballet: Checkmate/The Rake's Progress*. Sadler's Wells Royal Ballet, filmed at Sadler's Wells Theatre. Dir. Jolyon Wimhurst, Jaras Entertainments Ltd, 1982. Reissued on DVD, Video Artists International 2006; Jacquie Hollander, interview with Jennifer Jackson, 2 January 2025.
16 Lynne Wake, film-maker and former dancer, in conversation with Jennifer Jackson, 2 April 2025, recalls how meaningful the choreography for the Red Pawns felt to dance and how these gestures fed the emotional power of the ballet.
17 Michael Corder, interview with Jennifer Jackson, 15 August 2024.
18 Margaret Barbieri, interview with Jennifer Jackson, 9 July 2024.
19 As described in the photographic feature on *Checkmate* in Anon. 1964, 46–51.
20 Monica Mason, interview with Jennifer Jackson, 26 September 2023.
21 Clement Crisp. 'An Appreciation', the *Financial Times*, 7 March 1963, quoted in Dowler 2021, 139.
22 Beryl Grey in *Call Me Madam: The Life and Achievements of Dame Ninette de Valois*, Broadcast BBC2, 6 June 1998; Exec. Prod. Bob Lockyer, Dir. Ross MacGibbon.
23 Margaret Barbieri, interview with Jennifer Jackson, 9 July 2024.
24 Maina Gielgud, interview with Jennifer Jackson, 3 September 2024.
25 Fernau Hall. 'Power in Checkmate', *Daily Telegraph*, 7 October 1975.
26 Margaret Barbieri, interview with Jennifer Jackson, 9 July 2024.
27 *Ibid.*
28 Darcey Bussell, interview with Jennifer Jackson, 10 January 2024.
29 Zenaida Yanowsky, interview with Jennifer Jackson, 27 September 2024.
30 Linton 2012, 77.
31 Ninette de Valois in *Masterpieces of British Ballet: Checkmate/The Rake's Progress*. Sadler's Wells Royal Ballet, filmed at Sadler's Wells Theatre. Dir. Jolyon Wimhurst, Jaras Entertainments Ltd, 1982. Reissued on DVD, Video Artists International 2006.
32 Margaret Barbieri, interview with Jennifer Jackson, 9 July 2024.
33 *Ibid.*
34 The dance notation system devised by Rudolf and Joan Benesh is widely used for writing ballet scores. The Royal Ballet was the first ballet company to hire a professional choreologist in 1960.
35 *Épaulement* is a ballet term referencing the use of the upper torso for expressive and technical function in the dance.
36 Mark Silver, interview with Jennifer Jackson, 16 August 2024.
37 Jacquie Hollander, interview with Jennifer Jackson, 2 January 2025.
38 *Ibid.*
39 *Ibid.*
40 Stephen Jeffries, interview with Jennifer Jackson, 16 August 2024.
41 Jacquie Hollander, interview with Jennifer Jackson, 2 January 2025.
42 Mark Silver, interview with Jennifer Jackson, 16 August 2024. Silver danced the Red Knight aged thirty-six with Kobayashi Ballet, Japan.
43 Michael Corder, interview with Jennifer Jackson, 15 August 2024.
44 Ninette de Valois in *Masterpieces of British Ballet: Checkmate/The Rake's Progress*. Sadler's Wells Royal Ballet, filmed at Sadler's Wells Theatre. Dir. Jolyon Wimhurst, Jaras Entertainments Ltd, 1982. Reissued on DVD, Video Artists International 2006.
45 *Ibid.*
46 Darcey Bussell, interview with Jennifer Jackson, 10 January 2024.
47 Genné 2012, 27.

Miracle in the Gorbals
Chapter 6

1 Haskell, *Miracle in the Gorbals*, 1946, 12.
2 *Ibid.*, 13.
3 See Chapter 7 for further discussion of the themes explored in the ballet.
4 Haskell, *Miracle in the Gorbals*, 1946, 9.
5 *Ibid.*, 17.
6 Salter 1978, 215.
7 A page from Helpmann's notebook, reprinted in Haskell, *Miracle in the Gorbals*, 1946, shows his first ideas for the ballet and lists the character of The Official as The Priest, and scored out. The 2014 Birmingham Royal Ballet production names this character as The Minister.
8 Cited in Byrne 2018, 132.

Chapter 7

1 Arnold's reforms notably promoted moral character, Christian duty and intellectual rigour. During Bliss's years at Rugby, he also excelled at fencing and field sports – physical disciplines that echo classical ideals of bodily grace and control, and which may have shaped his appreciation for choreographic movement.
2 Hynes 1990, 386.
3 As recalled by Arthur Benjamin, quoted in Adams 2013, 39.
4 T.S. Eliot, another Anglo-Catholic artistic figure, expressed relevant spiritual themes in his poetry – for example, the use of dance in 'Burnt Norton' (1935) – as a representation of timelessness: 'at the still point, there the dance is'.
5 Basil Nicolls, quoted in Foreman 2002, 253.
6 Bliss gave a speech to the Society of Women Musicians on 2 July 1921, which was published soon after in three instalments in the *Musical News and Herald*. Bliss, 2 July 1921; reprinted in Roscow 1991, 15–24.
7 These two positions, and the continuum between them, have been explored in a twenty-first-century context in Goodhart 2017.
8 Indeed, Haskell reveals that Bliss composed the score with the scenario and Burra's designs 'spread out before him'. See Haskell, *Miracle in the Gorbals*, 1946, 19.
9 *The Shepherds of the Delectable Mountains* was later incorporated by Vaughan Williams into his four-act 'morality' opera, *The Pilgrim's Progress* (1951).
10 Saylor 2017, 87.
11 Marinelli 1971, 6.
12 Saylor 2017, 26.
13 *Ibid.*, 95.
14 For a discussion of Glasgow's post-industrial transformation, and the Clyde Gateway project, see Gray and Mooney 2011, 4–24.
15 *Miracle in the Gorbals* was not universally acclaimed at its 1944 premiere, yet critics widely acknowledged its emotional intensity and striking visual design. Reviews collected by Arnold Haskell (Haskell, *Miracle in the Gorbals*, 1946, 30–31) reflect a mixture of admiration and unease. The *Daily Mail* called the production 'vividly dramatic', while the *Daily Express* praised it as 'a sensational modern allegory, brilliantly executed and staged'. The *Manchester Guardian* cautioned that 'some will view it with discomfort as being too graphic', but added, pointedly, 'let it be disliked, if at all, purely as ballet'. Writing in *Time and Tide*, Edwin Evans captured the work's unsettling boldness: 'A gargoyle in a cathedral is a work of art and that, in sum, is what [Helpmann] has produced.' Together, these responses suggest a work that defied expectation: stylistically confrontational, morally ambiguous and emotionally direct.
16 For a more detailed exploration of the collaboration, see Durà-Vilà 2019, 147–64.
17 Howes 1966, 262.
18 Christopher Butler, the theorist of early modernist aesthetics, has described this kind of negotiation with tradition as a 'compromise with the past'. See Butler 1994, 258.
19 Blake 1997, 54.

Chapter 8

1 See Byrne 2018 for further background to the 2014 production.
2 Haskell, *Miracle in the Gorbals*, 1946.
3 Current roles of the artists interviewed for this chapter: Paul Murphy (Conductor, Birmingham Royal Ballet (BRB)), Jeremy Kerridge (Teacher, Tring Park), William Bracewell (Principal, The Royal Ballet), Ruth Brill (Choreographer, Artistic Director), César Morales Anderson (Director Artístico, Ballet de Santiago), Laura Day (Rehearsal Director, Australian Ballet), Iain Mackay (Artistic Director, The Royal Ballet School), Delia Matthews (retired former BRB Principal), Michael O'Hare (retired former Principal, Ballet Master, BRB), Marion Tait (former Principal, Guest Teacher, BRB).

4 A day with Birmingham Royal Ballet marketing officer Lee Armstrong and volunteer archivist Susan Trucchi led to a vital exchange, by email, phone, Zoom and voice note, with former Company members across the globe. My heartfelt thanks go to them all for generously sharing their reflections.
5 Paul Murphy worked closely with musicologist, Dr Benjamin Earle on the restoration of the handwritten manuscript and to make a conductor's score, parts and printed urtext version.
6 Former dancer and ballet master at Northern Ballet Theatre, Jeremy had met Gillian when she was choreographing *A Simple Man* (based on the life of the painter, L.S .Lowry)
7 Sarah Crompton, 17 December 2014, https://www.telegraph.co.uk/culture/culture-review-of-the-year/11288130/Dance-review-of-2014-what-is-the-purpose-of-this-art-form.html (accessed 24 October 2025).

Adam Zero

Chapter 9

1 Helpmann 1949; reprinted in Cave and Meadmore 2018, 9.
2 *Ibid.*
3 See Chapters 2 and 10 for further details about the design.
4 Robert Helpmann. 'A Choreographer Speaks'. *New Theatre*, March/April 1947, 13.
5 *Ibid.*
6 Bliss 1970 (1989 rev. edn), 169.
7 Also see Chapter 10 for the staging of *Adam Zero* in 1946.
8 The programme note and cast list for *Adam Zero* are included in Chapter 10.
9 McNicol interviewed in 2013, in Cave and Meadmore 2018, 163.
10 Meadmore 2018, 47.
11 The annotation in the score differs slightly from the words in the poem. Quoted from *When Lilacs Last in the Dooryard Bloom'd*: 'Come lovely and soothing death, Undulate round the world, serenely arriving.' See Whitman 2005.
12 Lloyd 2014, 350.
13 *Ibid.*, 349.
14 *Ibid.*, xvii.
15 Also see Chapter 10.

Chapter 10

1 Bliss 1970, 169.
2 Helpmann, Benthall and Bliss collaborated with artist and designer Edward Burra to produce the Sadler's Wells Ballet dance-drama *Miracle in the Gorbals*, which premiered at the Prince's Theatre in London on 26 October 1944.
3 ABC–Australian National Radio 1986.
4 Benthall's reflexivity proved prophetic when a performance-related injury forced Helpmann to withdraw from the lead role. Benthall 1949, 7–12.
5 The revival of *The Sleeping Beauty* took place on 20 February 1946, marking the reopening of the Royal Opera House after its closure during the Second World War, and the return of the Sadler's Wells Ballet to the venue.
6 Ernest Betts. 'Mad, Modern – but Ballet at its Best', *Daily Express*, 11 April 1946 (London).
7 'Ballet', *New Statesman*, 20 April 1946 (London).
8 Lionel Bradley. Ballet Bulletins, 1946–8. Theatre and Performance Collections, manuscript available at the Victoria and Albert Museum, London.
9 Baron refers to the professional name of photographer Stirling Henry Nahum.
10 Bradley acknowledged in his ballet bulletins that – given the density of *Adam Zero*'s dramatic action – it was hard to capture all the narrative constituents.
11 Recreated programme of *Adam Zero* from 1948.
12 This dangerous stunt caused Robert Helpmann to injure himself and retire temporarily during the ballet's 1946 run.
13 'Helpmann's Triumph at Covent Garden', *Sound*, May 1946; *Adam Zero: Ballet by Arthur Bliss* (Piano Score). London: Novello & Company Ltd, 1946.
14 Audrey Williamson. 'Adam Zero: The New Robert Helpmann Ballet', *Theatre World*, May 1946. See press clippings for 1946 for the Sadler's Wells Ballet, Victoria and Albert Museum, London. The 1947 revival of *Adam Zero* saw the removal of the conical hats from the dancers' costumes. See Chapter 9 for more musicological insights into Bliss's score.
15 Described by Lionel Bradley as reminiscent of the foxtrot from Frederick Ashton's *Façade* (1931).
16 *Adam Zero: Ballet by Arthur Bliss* (Piano Score). London: Novello & Company Ltd, 1946. Section title from the score.
17 Bergen-Belsen was a Nazi concentration camp in northern Germany.
18 *Adam Zero: Ballet by Arthur Bliss* (Piano Score). London: Novello & Company Ltd, 1946. The evocative description of Death is quoted from the annotation in the score.
19 Audrey Williamson. 'Adam Zero: The New Robert Helpmann Ballet', *Theatre World*, May 1946. See press clippings for 1946 for the Sadler's Wells Ballet, Victoria and Albert Museum, London.
20 *Adam Zero: Ballet by Arthur Bliss* (Piano Score). London: Novello & Company Ltd, 1946.
21 *Ibid.* It is worth noting that – according to Lionel Bradley – the 1947 revival of *Adam Zero* saw Adam's Son and Daughter reappear for a moment at the back of the stage during the Dance with Death.
22 Joan Littlefield. 'Music for the Ballet: English Composer Arthur Bliss Discusses His Scores for Ballet', *Dance Magazine*, 21, February 1947, 41–4.
23 *Ibid.*
24 Sorley Walker 2009, 78–83.
25 ABC–Australian National Radio 1986.
26 Benthall 1947, 57.
27 'Breathless Ballet', *Star*, 4 November 1946 (London). June Brae was performing as a guest from the Sadler's Wells Opera Ballet.
28 Sadler's Wells Ballet Press Album, Victoria and Albert Museum, London, 1946. Furse received criticism for his *Adam Zero* sets, with reviewers suggesting he recycled his 1945 designs from *The Skin of Our Teeth* in London. It was also purported that this play by Thornton Wilder influenced Helpmann too.
29 'Recent Ballet', *The New English Weekly*, 25 April 1946 (London).
30 Dale 1978.
31 ABC–Australian National Radio 1986.
32 Bremrose 2009, 71–2.
33 'Ballet', *Time & Tide*, 20 April 1946 (London).
34 Ashton's acclaimed *Symphonic Variations* was intended to premiere on 10 March 1946, but was postponed to 24 April 1946 due to dancer Michael Somes sustaining an injury. Bland 1981, 87.
35 Bliss's *Adam Zero* suite was recorded by the English Northern Philharmonia, Royal Liverpool Philharmonic Orchestra and London Symphony Orchestra. See Chapter 9 for greater elucidation on Bliss's score.
36 Choreographer Andrew McNicol was mentored by David Drew, a long-serving and deeply respected member of The Royal Ballet, who also proved the driving force behind the revival of *Miracle in the Gorbals*. See Cave and Meadmore 2018.
37 Joan Littlefield. 'Music for the Ballet: English Composer Arthur Bliss Discusses His Scores for Ballet', *Dance Magazine*, 21, February 1947, 44.
38 For a longer description of Sergei Vanaev's reimagining of *Adam Zero*, see Chapter 11.
39 See Chapter 7 for a discussion of allegory in Bliss's composition.

Chapter 11

1 Sergei Vanaev, quote from the ballet programme for *Adam Zero*, 11 April 2015.
2 Thomas Steiert, translated excerpt from the ballet programme for *Adam Zero*, 11 April 2015.
3 The Theatre of the Absurd is a mid-twentieth-century dramatic movement, identified by Martin Esslin, in which playwrights such as Samuel Beckett and Eugène Ionesco used surreal imagery to express the futility of human existence and the breakdown of meaning.
4 For more insights about the original 1946 production of *Adam Zero*, see Chapter 10.
5 See Chapter 9 for an analysis of the *Adam Zero* score.
6 Karen Sellick, post-performance remarks to the author, Bremerhaven, 11 April 2015.
7 Byrne 2015.

The Lady of Shalott

Chapter 12

1 Bliss 1970 (1989 rev. edn), 59.
2 Bliss, Lyrita, LP SRCS 55, programme note.

3   *The Times*, 17 December 1920; reprinted in Bliss 1970 (1989 rev. edn), 59.
4   Maryon Lane and Graham Usher (not pictured) were the other Principal dancers in *Diversions* (1961).
5   Dutton Epoch, CDLX 7387, released 2020.
6   Christopher St John. 'Music and Public Taste: "Bliss's Orchestration of the Sinding *Fire Dance* is Excellent"', *Time & Tide*, 22 July 1921, 701.
7   See Chapters 1 and 2 for details of the productions.
8   Bliss 1970 (1989 rev. edn), 206.
9   *Ibid.*
10 *Ibid.*
11 Other painters choosing the Lady as their subject include George Edward Robertson (1900), Walter Crane (1862), John Atkinson Grimshaw (1875), William Holman Hunt (1888–1905), Toby Edward Rosenthal (1874), Sophie Gengembre Anderson (1870), Edmund Blair Leighton (1899) and Sidney Harold Meteyard (1913).
12 Kavanagh 1996, 39.
13 Robert Tucker is a music librarian who researches rarely performed and lost works for performance by the Broadheath Singers, an amateur chorus and ad hoc professional orchestra.
14 'Holstian' as an adjective means a repeated pattern in the bass that consists of a falling motif.
15 The surviving private concert recording was made at St George's Church, Stockport, with Alexander Young singing the solo with the Jubilate Choir, 19 March 1983.
16 See Chapter 13 for details of San Francisco Ballet's production.
17 See Chapter 14 for details of the 1975 production as *Girl in a Broken Mirror*.
18 Bliss 1970 (1989 rev. edn), 207.
19 These are words from Tennyson's poem.
20 Extracts from the scenario notes written into Bliss's piano score are included within single quotation marks. Phrases and lines that Bliss included from Tennyson's poem are in double quotation marks. Spelling and punctuation are original as written in the scenario. Tennyson's words, however, were not always accurately reproduced in the score. This was possibly due to a of lack of space – the annotations were written above the stave.
21 'Telling': here Hassall is using an antique expression for reciting the rosary.
22 Barry Wordsworth was Principal Conductor and Music Director for Sadler's Wells Royal Ballet and later for The Royal Ballet between 1973 and 2015.
23 Dutton Epoch, CDLX 7387, 2020.

Chapter 13

1   The ballet was named *Lady of Shalott*, dropping 'The' from the title, and was referred to by the dancers colloquially as '*Lady*', a practice adopted in this chapter.
2   David Boyden, letter to Bliss, 24 February 1957, quoted in Spicer 2023, 264.
3   Charles Cushing, letter to Bliss, 8 May 1958. Bliss Archive, Cambridge University Library.
4   Alfred Frankenstein. 'A Lyric Lady of Shalott by S.F. Ballet', *San Francisco Chronicle*, 26 May 1958.
5   *Mundo Ilustrado*, double-page news spread, 27 August 1958, is indicative of the profile of San Francisco Ballet's international tours.
6   Alfred Frankenstein. 'A Lyric Lady of Shalott by S.F. Ballet', *San Francisco Chronicle*, 26 May 1958.
7   See Sowell 1998, 402–3, for the background to discussions between Willam and Lew Christensen about merging the resources of their two companies, Ballet West and San Francisco Ballet, respectively.
8   The first page of a double-page news spread in the *Mundo Ilustrado*, translated from the Portuguese. 'A yankee in the court of the enchanted castle: 'San Francisco Ballet' is one of the three most famous dance ensembles in the United States and was hired by the State Department to tour abroad on a typical American cultural propaganda mission, as happened with Louis Armstrong. Bringing 25 dancers, nine tons of luggage, and a famous director who alone captivates all the press news, the 'San Francisco Ballet' arrived in Rio, via the Pacific, after a performance in Porto Alegre. With a Brazilian-born dancer among its principal dancers, the American company debuted at the Municipal Theater on the same stage where, less than three months earlier, the Bolshoi Ballet had performed, also at the service of Soviet cultural propaganda. The same audience applauded the competitors and joked at the theatre entrance: the score is two to one in favour of the United States. Now all that remains is to see who will send the next attraction.'
9   Charles Cushing, letter to Bliss, 8 May 1958. Bliss Archive, Cambridge University Library.
10 Lew Christensen, letter to Bliss, 8 May 1958. Bliss Archive, Cambridge University Library.
11 Alexander Fried. 'S.F. Ballet Pleases at UC Festival', *San Francisco Examiner*, week of 5 May 1958.
12 Alfred Frankenstein. 'Lady of Shalott: Premiered at UC', *San Francisco Chronicle*, 8 May 1958.
13 Stefano Mascagno (1877–1950) taught several times in Utah. Originally from San Carlo Theatre in Naples, he established a dance studio in New York and was a leading instructor for the American National Association of Masters of Dancing.
14 Kent Stowell, interview with Jennifer Jackson, 30 October 2024.
15 'Foreign Genius and Native Talent', *Dance Magazine*, July 1973, 63; cited in Sowell 1998, 421.
16 Sowell 1998, 337.
17 See Fig. 13.1 and Chapter 13 Note 8 for commentary on the cultural propaganda associated with the visits of the Bolshoi Ballet and SFB to the same theatre within three months of each other.
18 Sowell 1998, 43.
19 Newman 1982, 41.
20 Erickson, in Betsy Erickson and Anita Paciotti, interview with Jennifer Jackson, 7 November 2024.
21 *Ibid.*
22 Sowell 1998, 53.
23 *Ibid.*, 109. Kirstein described Lew Christensen's pirouettes as 'astonishing': Kirstein 1983, 352.
24 Newman 1982, 41; Sowell 1998, 133.
25 See Sowell 1998, 139, for further evidence of Lew's performance as Apollo.
26 Walter Terry. 'Dance Players present "Jinx" N.Y. Debut', *New York Herald Tribune*, 25 April 1942; cited in Sowell 1998, 206.
27 Sowell 1998, 206.
28 *Ibid.*, 342.
29 Kent Stowell, interview with Jennifer Jackson, 29 October 2024.
30 Sowell 1998, 328.
31 'San Francisco Dance Beat', *Dance Digest*, 1959, 13.
32 Kent Stowell, interview with Jennifer Jackson 29 October 2024.
33 Sowell 1998, 343; Betsy Erickson and Anita Paciotti, interview with Jennifer Jackson, 7 November 2024.
34 Dunnett 2002, 290.
35 Bliss uses Roman numerals to number the scenes in the score.
36 See Chapter 12 for a detailed description of the music. See also Durà-Vilà 2019, 157–60, for Bliss's capacity for developing music for dramatic ballet.
37 Alfred Frankenstein. 'A Lyric Lady of Shalott by S.F. Ballet', *San Francisco Chronicle*, 26 May 1958.
38 Betsy Erickson and Anita Paciotti, interview with Jennifer Jackson, 7 November 2024.
39 Alfred Frankenstein. 'A Lyric Lady of Shalott by S.F. Ballet', *San Francisco Chronicle*, 26 May 1958.
40 Alexander Fried. 'S.F. Ballet Pleases at UC Festival', *San Francisco Examiner*, week of 5 May 1958.
41 Erickson, in Betsy Erickson and Anita Paciotti, interview with Jennifer Jackson, 7 November 2024.
42 Alfred Frankenstein. 'A Lyric Lady of Shalott by S.F. Ballet', *San Francisco Chronicle*, 26 May 1958.
43 Alexander Fried. 'S.F. Ballet Pleases at UC Festival', *San Francisco Examiner*, week of 5 May 1958.
44 Dunnett 2002, 292.
45 Erickson, in Betsy Erickson and Anita Paciotti, interview with Jennifer Jackson, 7 November 2024.
46 Dunnett, 2002, 293.
47 Charles Cushing, letter to Bliss, 8 May 1958. Bliss Archive, Cambridge University Library, 3.
48 Erickson, in Betsy Erickson and Anita Paciotti, interview with Jennifer Jackson, 7 November 2024.
49 Dunnett 2002, 293.
50 Sowell 1998, 273. In his report on San Francisco Ballet's spring season at the Alcazar, *San Francisco Chronicle* critic Dean Wallace firmly asserted the breadth of male talent within the

company, writing on 4 April 1961 that 'Man for man the Royal Ballet would have a hard time matching them'.
51 Nicanor Miranda. 'Bailado: San Francisco Ballet', *Diario de São Paulo*, 17 August 1958.
52 Dunnett 2002, 294.
53 Sowell 1998, 329.
54 Alexander Fried. *San Francisco Examiner*, 23 April 1961. Extract from the review of *Lady of Shalott* at the Alcazar, 15/16 April 1961.
55 Bliss, 'Grace Notes on Ballet' (1949); reprinted in Roscow 1991, 187.
56 Nicanor Miranda. 'Bailado: San Francisco Ballet', *Diario de São Paulo*, 17 August 1958.
57 Dean Wallace. *San Francisco Chronicle*, 21 March 1960, 36. Extract from the review of San Francisco Ballet's performance at the Alcazar, 19 March 1960.

Chapter 14

1 Bliss. 'The Lady of Shalott', *Artefact*, Spring 1975 issue.
2 Bliss 1970 (1989 rev. edn), 109.
3 Simon Taylor, email to Susie Crow, 11 November 2024. Taylor was drama teacher at Wreake Valley Community College, which provided boys to perform in *The Lady of Shalott*.
4 An Argo recording of the orchestra released in 1971 included Bliss's Introduction and Allegro conducted by the composer, as well as works by André Previn, John Ireland, Herbert Chappell, Bryan Kelly and Michael Tippett. Leicestershire Schools Symphony Orchestra (LP, Album, Stereo) Argo (2) ZRG685, 1971.
5 Bliss in a radio interview in 1974, recorded on a LSSO archival compilation CD, Bliss Archive, Cambridge University Library.
6 Bliss 1970 (1989 rev. edn), 280.
7 Simon Taylor, email to Susie Crow, 11 November 2024.
8 Grace Eldridge. 'Dance at New Park', *Artefact*, Spring 1975, 5.
9 'Ballet for O Level', *Times Educational Supplement*, 13 January 1967, 84.
10 Tanya Cope, email to Susie Crow, 11 October 2024. Tanya was a pupil at New Parks who was part of the Ballet Group and performed in *The Lady of Shalott* as a villager at the age of thirteen.
11 Grace Eldridge. 'Dance at New Park', *Artefact*, Spring 1975, 5.
12 Haskell, *The Making of a Dancer*, 1946.
13 Tanya Cope, email to Susie Crow, 11 October 2024.
14 Pinkett 1969, 21.
15 Caroline Salem trained in dance in the UK and New York. Her choreographic career included a nine-month residency with Ballet de Zaragoza and work as a movement director. She now runs the Space Clarence Mews, offering to artists studio space, exchange, work in progress performances, mentoring and dramaturgy.
16 Caroline Salem, telephone conversation with Susie Crow, 25 October 2024.
17 Jonathan Gray studied briefly at The Royal Ballet School, and later stage design at Wimbledon College of Art. He joined *Dancing Times* in 2005, becoming editor in 2008, a role he held until its closure in 2022.
18 Jonathan Gray, interview with Susie Crow, 16 July 2024.
19 Tanya Cope, email to Susie Crow, 11 October 2024.
20 *Ibid*.
21 Caroline Salem, telephone conversation with Susie Crow, 25 October 2024.
22 *Ibid*.
23 Gilmour 1974, 1.
24 Simon Taylor, email to Susie Crow, 11 November 2024.
25 Bliss 1975, 4.
26 Bliss, letter to Ninette de Valois, 21 April 1958, Bliss Archive, Cambridge University Library.
27 Parry 2009, 239–40.
28 *Girl in a Broken Mirror* (1975), Thames Television, 12 mins 11 secs.
29 Simon Taylor, email to Susie Crow, 11 November 2024.
30 *Girl in a Broken Mirror* (1975), Thames Television, 19 mins.
31 See Chapter 13 for a description of this scene in San Francisco Ballet's production.
32 *Girl in a Broken Mirror* (1975), Thames Television, 20 mins 28 secs.
33 *Ibid.*, 21 mins 45 secs.
34 Bliss 1958.
35 LSSO and New Parks Ballet Group, letters to Sir Arthur Bliss wishing him well, March 1975, Bliss Archive, Cambridge University Library.
36 Bliss 1975, 4.
37 Tanya Cope, email to Susie Crow, 11 October 2024.
38 *Dance Mosaic* programme for Leicester Haymarket performances, 13–17 May 1975, Bliss Archive, Cambridge University Library.
39 Caroline Salem, telephone conversation with Susie Crow, 25 October 2024.
40 *Girl in a Broken Mirror* (1975), Thames Television, 15 mins 22 secs.
41 Ralph Pugsley. 'Dramatic Power and Beauty that's Simply Staggering ...', *Leicester Mercury*, May 1975.
42 Caroline Salem, telephone conversation with Susie Crow, 25 October 2024.
43 Ralph Pugsley. 'Dramatic Power and Beauty that's Simply Staggering ...', *Leicester Mercury*, May 1975.
44 Fernau Hall. 'Notes on Fernau Hall's Review of "Dance Mosaic 75"', typed excerpts from Hall's review for the *Daily Telegraph*, which was not published because of a strike, author uncredited, Leicester Records Office.
45 Michael Bayston. 'Girl in a Broken Mirror, Thames Television, October', *Dancing Times*, November 1975, 83.
46 Caroline Salem, telephone conversation with Susie Crow, 25 October 2024.
47 Hockney, letter to Lady Bliss, 17 November 1975, Bliss Archive, Cambridge University Library.
48 *Ibid*.
49 Robinson 1989, iv.
50 Grace Eldridge. 'Dance at New Park', *Artefact*, Spring 1975, 5.

Epilogue

1 Bliss 1970 (1989 rev. edn), 89.
2 *Ibid.*, 130.
3 *Ibid.*, 137.
4 *Ibid.*, 152.
5 *Ibid.*, 156.
6 *Ibid.*, 165.
7 *Ibid*.
8 Annette Page had a highly distinguished career with The Royal Ballet; she was a Principal from 1959 until her retirement in 1967 and danced The Suicide in the 1958 revival of Bliss and Helpmann's *Miracle in the Gorbals* (1944). She and Karen were students together at the Sadler's Wells Ballet School and both performed as pages in the company's inaugural performance of *The Sleeping Beauty* after the war at Covent Garden.
9 *Épaulement* is a ballet term for the use of the upper torso for expressive and technical function in the dance.
10 Thanks to Penelope Cullerne-Bown for her reflections, received on 3 June 2025. Penny also outlined Karen's school productions, as does Peter McMullin in his contribution.
11 Classes were held at the Oxford Fire Station Arts Centre, now a professional theatre space.
12 These memories were sent to Susie Crow on 7 March 2021 but not published at that time.

Contributor Biographies

Sir David Bintley is an internationally renowned choreographer whose ballets have featured in the repertory of many of the world's great companies. His work is highly regarded, in particular his numerous large-scale narrative ballets, many with commissioned scores, and he is well known for his wide knowledge of the early British ballet heritage repertoire. He was The Royal Ballet's resident choreographer before becoming Artistic Director of Birmingham Royal Ballet from 1995 to 2019 and Artistic Director of The National Ballet of Japan from 2010 to 2014. He was knighted for services to dance in 2020.

Andrew Burn is a Trustee of the Finzi and Bliss Trusts, a founder member of the latter and currently its Chair. After reading music at the University of East Anglia, his career embraced theatre and orchestral management, latterly with the Bournemouth Symphony Orchestra. As a writer and speaker, his specialist enthusiasm is twentieth- and twenty-first-century British music, about which he has written extensively in programme and CD liner notes, as well as contributing to publications like *The New Grove Dictionary of Music and Musicians* (2001).

Michael Byrne works at Cornell University's technology campus in New York City, Cornell Tech, researching the collisions between dance, history and immersive applications. Byrne completed his undergraduate design degree in South Africa, before continuing his performance studies at the Royal Academy of Music, King's College London, RADA and the University of Cambridge. For over a decade he appeared within the narrative works of The Royal Ballet, and in several touring productions for the Mariinsky and Bolshoi Ballet companies.

Dr Susie Crow danced with The Royal Ballet and Sadler's Wells Royal Ballet. Her choreography includes works for SWRB, Dance Advance, National Youth Dance and Ballet companies, and Ballet in Small Spaces. Based in Oxford, she teaches ballet to students, professionals and adult learners, runs the Oxford Dance Writers website, and collaborates with other artists in creative research. She holds an MA in Dance Studies from the University of Surrey, a Cert. TLHPE from the Institute of Education, and a PhD from the University of Roehampton.

Dr Sam Ellis leads the Bachelor of Music degree programme at the Royal Conservatoire of Scotland. With two decades of teaching experience including eight years at Bangor University and six years at Glasgow Caledonian University, he has built a wealth of knowledge in music, professional learning and arts pedagogy. He has conducted AHRC-funded research on Bliss's interwar chamber music and is a Senior Fellow of the Higher Education Academy. He represents Scotland on the committee of the Bliss Society.

Lewis Foreman, the biographer of Arnold Bax (3rd edition 2007), has published many books on music, most recently *Recording British Music* (2024). With his late wife Susan he wrote *London: A Musical Gazetteer* (2005). Researching repertoire for many record companies, he is the author of more than 400 CD booklets for Dutton Epoch, Lyrita, Chandos, Hyperion and many others. He is a Trustee of the Bliss Trust.

Jennifer Jackson is a former dancer and choreographer with The Royal Ballet and Sadler's Wells Royal Ballet. She was senior lecturer at the University of Surrey and choreography tutor at The Royal Ballet School prior to joining London Studio Centre, as Artistic Director of Images Ballet Company from 2015 to 2021. Her writing is published in professional journals and books and her edited volume, *Ballet: The Essential Guide to Technique and Creative Practice*, was published in 2021.

Susan Jones is Emeritus Professor of English Literature, University of Oxford. She has published widely on Joseph Conrad, modernism, and the aesthetics and history of dance, including *Literature, Modernism, and Dance* (2013). A former Soloist with Scottish Ballet, she is founding Director of Dance Scholarship Oxford (DANSOX), based at St Hilda's College, Oxford. This interdisciplinary forum for exchange between scholars and practitioners promotes dialogue between core academic disciplines and the history, theory and practice of dance.

Dr Anna Meadmore trained at Elmhurst and The Royal Ballet School (Teachers' Training Course 1988–91). She gained an MA in Dance from Surrey University, joining The Royal Ballet School as archive curator and teacher in 1994. She contributed to *Ninette de Valois: Adventurous Traditionalist* (2012), *Ballet: The Essential Guide to Technique and Creative Practice* (2021) and with Professor Richard Cave, co-edited *Robert Helpmann: The Many Faces of a Theatrical Dynamo* (2018). Her doctoral thesis, funded by an AHRC Techne Scholarship, re-examined Ninette de Valois' work in England, 1925–34 (awarded RHUL, 2024).

Jane Pritchard, MBE, is curator of dance for the Victoria and Albert Museum, London. She has curated exhibitions on dance, design and photography, including *Diaghilev and the Golden Age of the Ballets Russes, 1909–1929* for which she edited the accompanying book. Previously, she was archivist for several British dance companies, including Rambert and English National Ballet, curated seasons of dance films, made radio programmes, and published on dance, including *Anna Pavlova: Twentieth Century Ballerina* (2012).

Paul Spicer is one of the UK's most influential choral conductors. He came to prominence through his work with the Finzi Singers and their numerous recordings for Chandos Records. He conducts the Birmingham Bach Choir, and until 2022 he was conductor of the Royal Birmingham Conservatoire Chamber Choir. He was a Senior Producer for BBC Radio 3 in the Midlands, then Artistic Director of the Lichfield Festival until 2001 and now devotes himself to conducting, teaching, composing and writing. He has written biographies of his composition teacher Herbert Howells (1998), Sir George Dyson (2014) and Sir Arthur Bliss (2023). His most recent book is *Choral Conducting: The Generosity of Gesture* (2026).

Acknowledgements

We first remember Karen, with great affection and heartfelt thanks. Although no longer here, it is as if Karen's presence through her vision for the book has been a constant guide and has imbued us with the confidence to give it shape.

The book is the work of many people. Describing the nature and significance of each contribution would require another book; there is only space for some names and to express our profound gratitude and hope that the book itself will be a fitting token of thanks.

We begin with the Bliss Trust, in particular founder member and current Chair, Andrew Burn, faithfully acting on Karen's wishes to nurture the seed of her idea and assemble a team. Initially comprising Elizabeth Pooley (Bliss Trust Administrator), Anna Meadmore (Manager of Royal Ballet School Special Collections) and myself, and later joined by Jane Pritchard (Curator of Dance, Victoria and Albert Museum), the project has been steered by this small group. I am truly privileged and honoured to have worked with these dedicated Bliss and dance enthusiasts. My heartfelt thanks to the Bliss Trust for inviting and trusting me with the task of editing the volume, especially to Liz for her unswerving commitment, rock-like practical and personal support and encouragement throughout, and to Anna, whose expertise and generosity in gathering images for the book was invaluable. Our collective thanks to all the contributors for their insightful and beautiful essays and for their commitment and stimulating exchanges during the development period.

Karen envisaged a 'coffee table' book, rich in imagery but complicated and expensive to achieve! Our sincere thanks to all the following people and institutions for their generosity in realising this vision:

Biddy Hayward – ArenaPal, for facilitating and co-ordinating images from so many different sources, including the Royal Opera House archives, The Royal Ballet School, Royal Academy of Dance and Victoria and Albert Museum; Anna Pensaert, Music Librarian – Bliss Archive/University of Cambridge; Lee Armstrong, Design Manager and Susan Trucchi, Archivist – Birmingham Royal Ballet; Supriya Wronkiewicz, Rachel Bauer and Kirsten Tanaka – San Francisco Museum of Performance and Design (MP+D); Helen Swainger, Collections Archivist – Royal Ballet School Special Collections; Eleanor Fitzpatrick and Jonathan Gray – Royal Academy of Dance library and archives; Viktoria Helene Ong and Heiko Sandelmann – Stadttheater Bremerhaven; Iain Web and Margaret Barbieri, Directors, Sarasota Ballet; Hutton Wilkinson – Anthony and Elizabeth Duquette Foundation; Chris Christensen – Christensen-Caccialanza Collection; staff of the Dance Division, New York Public Library and Leicester County Records Office; photographers including Frank Arturo, Bill Cooper, Nigel Hodgson, Branka Ilic, Johan Persson and Leslie Spatt; Ian Strathcarron, Felicity Price-Smith, Lucy Duckworth – Unicorn Publishing Group.

And special thanks to Adrian Hobbs for his constant support, advice and practical help preparing images for publication.

We were able to dig deeply into Bliss's last 'lost' ballet, *The Lady of Shalott*, and extend grateful thanks to Tanya Cope, Jonathan Gray, Caroline Salem, Simon Taylor and John Whitmore, who gave so generously of their time and experience in interview and correspondence to inform Susie Crow's research into the Leicestershire production of *Girl in a Broken Mirror*. I am hugely grateful to the Lisa Ullmann Travelling Scholarship Fund and the Bliss Trust for funding research in the USA. It would also not have been possible without the generosity and assistance of cherished dance colleagues: Julia Gleich and Graham Lustig with Bat Abbit, my hosts in New York and San Francisco respectively; Suki Schorer for facilitating contacts with other members of the cast of *Lady*; Kent Stowell and Francia Russell for their hospitality and kindness in Seattle; Suki and Tilly Abbe (affectionately known as 'Tuki and Silly' by Lew Christensen) for sharing their scrapbooks and memories in person with such warmth and humour; Sheila Dietrich, Pacific Northwest Ballet volunteer archivist for donating resources and her knowledge.

My personal thanks to the many distinguished practitioners who contributed their recollections of their involvement with the ballets in interview, on Zoom or in person, by email, telephone, message and voice notes: Tilly Abbe, Margaret Barbieri, Sir David Bintley, William Bracewell, Ruth Brill, Dame Darcey Bussell, Pauline Clayden, Michael Corder, Laura Day, Betsy Erikson, Maina Gielgud, Jacquie Hollander, Ronald Hynd, Stephen Jeffries, Jeremy Kerridge, Graham Lustig, Iain Mackay, Dame Monica Mason, Delia Matthews, César Morales Anderson, Paul Murphy, Michael O'Hare, Anita Paciotti, Suki Schorer, Mark Silver, Kent Stowell, Marion Tait, Lynne Wake, Barry Wordsworth, Alexandra Worrall and Zenaida Yanowsky.

There are countless others to acknowledge and these are a few of them:

David Salter, Chairman of the Bliss Society for allowing us to republish Sir David Bintley's marvellous essays that first appeared in the Society magazine; Donald Scrimegeour for translating reviews from Spanish and Portuguese into English; Nicholas Minns for reviewing the complete manuscript; Judith Amanthis, Betsy Erickson and Kent Stowell for commenting on drafts of chapters; Dame Monica Mason, Rachel Hollings, Patricia Linton, Jann Parry and Paul Jackson for supporting the development in conversations, sharing resources and enabling connections; and Bliss Trustees, in particular Caroline Secombe and Helen Kotz for inspiring exchanges and the loan of precious Bliss scores.

Finally, we would like to thank the Sellick/Bliss family. They have generously given their blessing and donated the photograph of the beautiful painting of Karen by Carlos Sancha.

To everyone involved, thank you for working with us. We fervently hope that the book is an encouragement for many more to listen with enhanced delight and to dance the music of Sir Arthur Bliss.

Select Bibliography

This book includes images reproduced from Merlyn Severn's book, *Sadler's Wells Ballet at Covent Garden*, London: John Lane, The Bodley Head, 1947. The increased grain within theatrical photography, which was ahead of its time, together with the live setting, help to convey the intensity of performance.

Recommended Recordings
Compiled by Andrew Burn

Adam Zero (complete). English Northern Sinfonia, David Lloyd-Jones. Naxos, 8.553460, 1996.

'Bliss Conducts Bliss'. *Checkmate* & *Miracle in the Gorbals* suites. Sinfonia of London, Philharmonia Orchestra, Arthur Bliss. Heritage, HTGCD 220, 2011.

Checkmate (complete), *Mêlée Fantasque*. Royal Scottish National Orchestra, David Lloyd-Jones. Naxos, 8.557641, 2005.

Checkmate (complete). Tribute to Madam. Royal Ballet Sinfonia, Barry Wordsworth. White Line, CDWLS255, 2001.

Checkmate (staged). *Masterpieces of British Ballet*. Dancers of the Royal Ballet, Sadler's Wells Royal Ballet Orchestra, Barry Wordsworth. VAI, DVDVAI14379, 2006.

Miracle in the Gorbals (complete). BBC Philharmonic Orchestra, Michael Seal. Chandos, CHSA 5370, 2025.

The Lady of Shalott (complete), *Rout, Bliss: One Step*. BBC Concert Orchestra, Ilona Domnich, Martin Yates. Dutton Epoch, CDLX 7387, 2021.

Audio, Visual

ABC–Australian National Radio. *Tribute to Sir Robert Helpmann*. New York: New York Public Library for the Performing Arts, 1986 (Call number: LTC-A 1386).

Bliss, Arthur. Radio interview recorded on Leicestershire Symphony Schools Orchestra (LSSO) archival compilation CD, 1974. Bliss Archive, Cambridge University Library.

Checkmate. Royal Ballet. BBC film, Prod. Margaret Dale. Released 21.50, 31 July 1963.

Checkmate, Ballet in One Act. Vic-Wells Ballet. BBC film, Released 21.20, 19 February 1939.

Dale, Margaret. *Interview with Margaret Dale*. Interview by David Vaughan, New York Public Library for the Performing Arts, 1978 (Call number: MGZMT 5-411).

Girl in a Broken Mirror. Thames Television, Documentary, Dir. David Hodgson, Exec. Prod. Jolyon Wimhurst. Broadcast, 1 October 1975.

Grey, Beryl, in *Call Me Madam: The Life and Achievements of Dame Ninette de Valois*, BBC2, Exec. Prod. Bob Lockyer, Dir. Ross MacGibbon. 6 June 1998.

Masterpieces of British Ballet: Checkmate / The Rake's Progress. Sadler's Wells Royal Ballet, Filmed at Sadler's Wells Theatre. Dir. Jolyon Wimhurst, Jaras Entertainments Ltd, 1982. Reissued on DVD, Video Artists International 2006.

The Lady of Shalott, Rout, Bliss: One Step, Polonaise and Other Works. BBC Concert Orchestra, conducted by Martin Yates. BBC/Dutton Epoch, CDLX 7387, 2021.

Scores

Bliss, Arthur. *Adam Zero: Ballet by Arthur Bliss* (Piano Score). London: Novello & Company Ltd, 1946.

Bliss, Arthur. 'Ballet in One Act: The Lady of Shalott, after the poem by Tennyson'. Unpublished piano reduction score, 1958, property of Bliss Trust.

Bliss, Arthur. *Checkmate* (Study Score). London: Novello & Company Ltd, 2007.

Bliss, Arthur. *Miracle in the Gorbals* (Full Score). Critical Edition by Ben Earle. London: Novello & Company Ltd, 2019.

Books and Articles

Adams, Byron. 'Vaughan Williams's Musical Apprenticeship', in Alain Frogley and Aidan Thomson (eds). *The Cambridge Companion to Vaughan Williams*. Cambridge: Cambridge University Press, 2013, 29–55.

Anon. *Princess Ballet Book, No. 3*. London: Fleetway Publications, 1964.

Ayrton, Michael. 'The "Décor" of Sadler's Wells Ballets, 1939–40', in Arnold Haskell (ed.). *The Ballet Annual: A Record and Year Book of the Ballet*. London: Adam & Charles Black, 1947, 74–81.

Beaumont, Cyril W. *Ballets Past & Present: Being a Third Supplement to the Complete Book of Ballets*. London: Putnam, 1955.

Benthall, Michael. 'The Creation of a Ballet', in Anthony Gishford (ed.). *Covent Garden Books – Ballet 1946–1947*. London: Jarrold and Sons Ltd, 1947, 27, 57.

Benthall, Michael. 'The Dance-Drama', in Arnold Haskell (ed.). *Sadler's Wells Ballet Books No. 3: Hamlet and Miracle in the*

Bliss, Arthur. *Miracle in the Gorbals*. London: Bodley Head, 1949, 7–12.

Blake, Andrew. *The Land without Music: Music, Culture and Society in Twentieth-century Britain*. Manchester: Manchester University Press, 1997.

Bland, Alexander. *The Royal Ballet: The First Fifty Years*. New York: Doubleday & Company, 1981.

Bliss, Arthur. 'Unexplained Superstitions: The Cult of the Dead'. *Musical News and Herald*, 23 April 1921, 523. Reprinted in Roscow 1991, 8–9.

Bliss, Arthur. '"What Modern Composition is Aiming At". Lecture to the Society of Women Musicians, 2 July 1921', *Musical News and Herald*, July and August 1921. Reprinted in Roscow 1991, 15–24.

Bliss, Arthur. 'Death on Squares'. *Great Thoughts*, London: Lile and Fawcett, January 1938, 18–22. Reprinted in Roscow 1991, 160–64.

Bliss, Arthur. *As I Remember*. London: Faber and Faber, 1970 (rev. edn, London: Thames Publishing, 1989).

Bliss, Arthur. 'Grace Notes on Ballet' (1949). Reprinted in Roscow 1991, 187–8.

Bremrose, Anna. *Robert Helpmann: A Servant of Art*. Brisbane: University of Queensland Press, 2009.

Buckle, Richard. *Modern Ballet Design*. London: Adam & Charles Black, 1955.

Butler, Christopher. *Early Modernism: Literature, Music, and Painting in Europe, 1900–1916*. Oxford: Clarendon Press, 1994.

Byrne, Michael. 'Reawakening Bliss's *Adam Zero*: New Bremerhaven Staging by Sergei Vanaev', *Oxford Dance Writers*, 19 June 2015, https://oxforddancewriters.wordpress.com/2015/06/19/reawakening-bliss-adam-zero-bremerhaven-sergei-vanaev-michael-byrne-reviews/ (accessed 6 July 2025).

Byrne, Michael. 'The (re)Generation of Miracle in the Gorbals (1944)'. In Cave and Meadmore 2018, 131–51.

Cave, Richard A., and Anna Meadmore (eds). *Robert Helpmann: The Many Faces of a Theatrical Dynamo*. Binstead: Dance Books, 2018.

Cave, Richard A., and Libby Worth (eds). *Ninette de Valois: Adventurous Traditionalist*. Alton: Dance Books, 2012.

Cave, Richard A. *Collaborations: Ninette de Valois and William Butler Yeats*. Alton: Dance Books, 2011.

Chazin-Bennahum, Judith. *The Ballets of Antony Tudor*. New York and Oxford: Oxford University Press, 1994.

Clarke, Mary. *The Sadler's Wells Ballet: A History and An Appreciation*. London: Adam & Charles Black, 1955.

Clarke, Mary, and Clement Crisp. *Design for Ballet*. London: Studio Vista, 1978.

Craggs, Stewart R. *Arthur Bliss: A Source Book*. Aldershot: Scolar Press, 1996.

Craggs, Stewart R. (ed.). *Arthur Bliss: Music and Literature*. Aldershot: Ashgate, 2002.

Crisp, Clement. 'An Appreciation'. *Financial Times*, 7 March 1963. Quoted in Gerald Dowler (ed.). *Clement Crisp Reviews: Six Decades of Dance*. Merthyr Tydfil: International Dance Writing Foundation, 2021, 139.

De Valois, Ninette. 'The Future of the Ballet'. *Dancing Times*, February 1926, 589–93. Reprinted in Cave and Worth 2012, 149–52.

De Valois, Ninette. *Invitation to the Ballet* (1937). London: John Lane, The Bodley Head, 1942 (fourth reprint).

De Valois, Ninette. 'An Appreciation of Edwin Evans'. In Evans 1947, 7–8.

De Valois, Ninette. *Come Dance With Me* (1957). Unabridged republication of first edn, London: Dance Books, 1973.

Dolin, Anton. *Markova: Her Life and Art*. London: W.H. Allen, 1953.

Dunnett, Roderic. '"… If Poets mind thee well …": Bliss and Christopher Hassall'. In Craggs 2002, 281–337.

Durà-Vilà, Victor. 'Arthur Bliss' Scores for Robert Helpmann: Musical Responses to Ambitious Creative Challenges'. *Dance Research*, 2019, 37(2), 147–64.

Evans, Edwin. *Music and the Dance: For Lovers of the Ballet*. London: Herbert Jenkins, 1947.

Foreman, Lewis. *Arthur Bliss Catalogue of the Complete Works, with an Introduction by George Dannatt*, Borough Green: Novello, 1980.

Foreman, Lewis. 'In Search of a Progressive Music Policy: Arthur Bliss at the BBC'. In Craggs 2002, 227–65.

Fraser, Grace Lovat. *In the Days of my Youth*. London: Cassell, 1970.

Genné, Beth. 'Evolution Not Revolution: Ninette de Valois' Philosophy of Dance'. In Cave and Worth 2012, 18–29.

Gilmour, Maurice. *Development of Ballet in Leicestershire*. Briefing paper for Deputy Director, Leicestershire County Council, 1974. Available in Leicester County Records Office.

Goodhart, David. *The Road to Somewhere: The Populist Revolt and the Future of Politics*. London: Hurst and Co., 2017.

Gray, Neil, and Gerry Mooney. 'Glasgow's New Urban Frontier: "Civilising" the Population of "Glasgow East"'. *City*, (15)1, 2011, 4–24.

Haskell, Arnold. *The National Ballet: A History and a Manifesto*. London: Adam & Charles Black, 1943.

Haskell, Arnold. *Miracle in the Gorbals: The Helpmann-Bliss Ballet*, Edinburgh: The Albyn Press, 1946.

Haskell, Arnold. *The Making of a Dancer and Other Papers on the Background to Ballet*. London: Adam & Charles Black, 1946.

Haskell, Arnold. *In His True Centre: An Interim Autobiography*. London: Adam & Charles Black, 1951.

Helpmann, Robert. 'British Choreography and its Critics'. In Peter Noble. *British Ballet*. London: Skelton Robinson, 1949, 27–36. Reprinted in Cave and Meadmore 2018, 6–12.

Hopkins, Antony. 'The Ballet Music of Arthur Bliss'. In Arthur Haskell (ed.). *The Ballet Annual: A Record and Year Book of the Ballet*. London: Adam & Charles Black, 1947, 102–7.

Howes, Frank. *The English Musical Renaissance.* London: Secker and Warburg, 1966.

Hussey, Dyneley. 'A Memoir'. In Evans 1947, 183–6.

Hynes, Samuel. *A War Imagined: The First World War and English Culture.* New York: Collier Books, 1990.

Jones, Susan. *Literature, Modernism & Dance.* Oxford: Oxford University Press, 2013.

Kane, Angela, and Jane Pritchard. 'The Camargo Society Part 1'. *Journal of the Society for Dance Research*, 12(2), Autumn 1994, 21–65.

Kavanagh, Julie. *Secret Muses: The Life of Frederick Ashton.* London: Faber and Faber, 1996 (revd paperback edn, 1997).

Kennedy, Thomas. 'Edward Burra Art on Stage'. In Thomas Kennedy and Eliza Spindel (eds). *Edward Burra,* London: Tate, 2025, 141–180.

Kirstein, Lincoln. 'Ballet Alphabet'. New York: Kamin Publishers, 1939. Reprinted in Nancy Reynolds (ed.). *Ballet: Bias and Belief, Three Pamphlets Collected and Other Writings of Lincoln Kirstein.* New York: Dance Horizons, 1983, 285–363.

Leonard, Maurice. *Markova: The Legend.* London: Hodder & Stoughton, 1995.

Linton, Patricia. 'Fiercely Alone: Personality and Impersonality in de Valois' Poetry and Work'. In Cave and Worth 2012, 73–81.

Lloyd, Stephen. *Constant Lambert: Beyond the Rio Grande.* Woodbridge: The Boydell Press, 2014.

MacDonald, Nesta. *Diaghilev Observed: By Critics in England and the United States 1911–1929.* New York: Dance Horizons; London: Dance Books, 1975.

Macfall, Haldane. *The Book of Lovat Claud Fraser.* London: J.M. Dent and Sons, 1923. Reprinted by Lightning Source Books Inc., 2015.

Marinelli, Peter. *Pastoral.* London: Methuen and Co., 1971.

Markova, Alicia. *Markova Remembers.* Boston and Toronto: Little, Brown and Co., 1986.

Meadmore, Anna. 'The Many Faces of Robert Helpmann: Theatrical Make-up and "make believe"'. In Cave and Meadmore 2018, 33–55.

Newman, Barbara. *Striking a Balance: Dancers Talk about Dancing.* London: Elm Tree Books, 1982.

O'Brien, Victoria. 'The Abbey Theatre School of Ballet'. In Cave and Worth 2012, 58–64.

Parry, Jann. *Different Drummer: The Life of Kenneth MacMillan.* London: Faber and Faber, 2009.

Pinkett, Eric. *Time to Remember.* Northampton: John Dickens and Co., 1969.

Playfair, Nigel. *Story of the Lyric Hammersmith.* London: Chatto & Windus, 1925.

Pritchard, Jane. 'Designs for Robert Helpmann's Wartime Ballets'. In Cave and Meadmore 2018, 113–30.

Robinson, Ken (ed.). *The Arts in Schools: Principles, Practice and Provision.* London: Calouste Gulbenkian Foundation, 1989.

Roscow, Gregory. 'Introduction'. In Roscow 1991, 1–4.

Roscow, Gregory (ed.). *Bliss on Music: Selected Writings of Arthur Bliss 1920–1975.* Oxford and New York: Oxford University Press, 1991.

Salter, Elizabeth. *Helpmann: The Authorised Biography.* Brighton: Angus and Robertson, 1978.

Saylor, Eric. *English Pastoral Music: From Arcadia to Utopia, 1900–1955.* Urbana: University of Illinois Press, 2017.

Scholl, Tim. *From Petipa to Balanchine.* London and New York: Routledge, 1994.

Severn, Merlyn. *Sadler's Wells Ballet at Covent Garden: A Book of Photographs by Merlyn Severn.* London: John Lane, The Bodley Head, 1947.

Sorley Walker, Kathrine, with contributions by Dame Ninette. *Ninette de Valois: Idealist Without Illusions.* London: Hamish Hamilton, 1987.

Sorley Walker, Kathrine. 'The Camargo Society'. *Dance Chronicle*, 18(1), 1995, 1–114.

Sorley Walker, Kathrine. *Robert Helpmann: A Rare Sense of the Theatre.* Alton: Dance Books, 2009.

Sowell, Debra Hickenlooper. *The Christensen Brothers: An American Dance Epic.* Utah: Brigham Young University, 1998.

Spicer, Paul. *Sir Arthur Bliss: Standing Out from the Crowd.* Ramsbury, Wiltshire: Robert Hale, 2023.

Stevenson, Jane. *Edward Burra: Twentieth-Century Eye.* London; Jonathan Cape, 2007.

Tennyson, Alfred Lord. *Idylls of the King and Other Arthurian Poems.* London: The Nonesuch Press, 1968.

Whitman, Walt. *The Complete Poems.* London: Penguin, 2005.

Zeller, Jessica. *Shapes of American Ballet: Teachers and Training before Balanchine.* New York: Oxford University Press, 2016.

Index

A

Abbe, Tilly, *151*
Abbey Theatre, Dublin, 18, 28
Academy of Choreographic Art, 12, *12*, 13, 16, *17*, 18–19, *19*, 20–1, *20*, 28
Adam Zero
   Bliss's score for, 24, 33, 41–5, 85, 109, 111–17, 118, 127, 129, 130, 134, 140
   choreographic action on stage, 120–5
   collaboration on, 29, 33, 128, 129
   costume design, *32*, 33, 114–15, 121, 123 *see also* scenes from
   critical reception, 111, 116, 118–19, 127–9, 132
   dedication to Constant Lambert, *116*, 117
   design, 28, 33, 109, 110, *110*, 118, 120, 127–8, 129, 130
   Furse as designer, 29, 33, 109, 110, *110*, 118, 120, 128, 130
   Helpmann's choreography, 33, 108–9, 111, 118, 129
   as a 'lost' work, 7, 119
   McNicol at the Helpmann Symposium, 111, 134, *135*
   playbill, 118, *119*
   scenario/narrative, 28, 33, 85, 108–9, 111, 117, 118, 119, 127–8, 129
   scenes from, *109*, *110*, *113–14*, *115*, *120*, *121*, *122*, *124*, *125*
   Vanaev's Bremerhaven reconceptualisation, 117, 129, 130–5, *131*, *132–3*, *134*
Ansanelli, Alexandra, *59*
Anthony, Gordon, 30
Appleyard, Beatrice, 18, 21
As You Like It, 26–7, 38, 111
Ashbridge, Bryan, *47*
Ashmole, David, 51, 58
Ashton, Frederick, 24, 108, 166
   as dancer in *Checkmate*, 29, 41
   Dante Sonata, 88
   The Lady of Shalott, 142
   in *Rout*, 19
   Symphonic Variations, 129
Atsuji, Yasuo, *93*

B

Bakst, Léon, 15, *15*, 27
Balanchine, George, 150, 157, 162, 166
   Apollo Musagète, 152, *153*
Ballet Caravan, 152
Ballet Rambert (Club) and School, 16, 142
Ballet West, 150
Ballets Russes, 10, *13*, 14–16, 26, 27–8, 36, 38, 70, 108, 138
   Pulcinella, 27, 28
   Rout as an interlude for, 14–15, 27, 36, 70, 140
   The Sleeping Princess, 27
   see also Diaghilev, Sergei
Barbieri, Margaret, *49*, 51, *54–5*, 58, *58*, 60, 61–2
Barrie, J. M., 28
Bax, Arnold, 14, 28, 164
Baylis, Lilian, 13, 14
Bayston, Michael, 174
Beale, Alan, *47*
Beaumont, Cyril, 20
Bedells, Jean, 88, 120, *121*, *124*
Benesh notation, 64, 65
Benjamin, Arthur, 15
Benthall, Michael
   collaborations with Bliss, 29, 109
   scenario for *Adam Zero*, 33, 108–9, 111, 117, 118, 127–8, 129
   scenario for *Miracle*, 28, 68, 69, 82
Beriosova, Svetlana, 61, *61*, *139*
Bertoni, Ricki, *48–9*, *62*

Bintley, David, 50–5, *50*, *51*, *52–3*, *54*, 58, 94
Birmingham Hippodrome, 92, 94
Birmingham Royal Ballet, 7, 49, 88, *88*, 92, 93
Bliss, Barbara, 68, 176, 177
Bliss, Karen (Sellick), 8, 68, 116, 129, 130, 132, *134*, 136, 176–81, *177*, *180*
Bliss, Kennard, 80, 117, 138
Bliss, Sir Arthur
   admiration for French music, 16, 81, 82
   As You Like It score, 26, 38
   ballet scores, 8–11, 24, 28, 33, 41–5, 55, 73–7, 84, 85, 96, 111–16, 138–41, 155, 160, 162, 176
   at the Ballets Russes, 15–16, 36, 38, 70
   as the BBC's Director of Music, 68, 81, 111, 164
   biography, 8, 68, 73, 80, 148
   career in music, 8, 14–15, 16, 70, 85, 117, 138–40
   as a chessplayer, 36, 38, 39
   Colour Symphony, 70, 138, 141
   Concerto for Piano, Tenor, Strings and Percussion, 70
   Diversions (Music for Strings), *139*, 140–1, 169
   donnée, 36, 69–70, 116, 163
   early social and professional encounters with de Valois, 14, 16–17
   film scores, 70, 73, 141
   Fire Dance, 27, 36, 140
   Frontier (Oboe Qunitet), *139*, 141
   as Governor to Sadler's Wells Ballet School, 13
   Hammersmith Musical Society, 18, 27
   As I Remember (autobiography), 19–20, 24, 36, 47, 110, 118, 142, 166
   and the Leicestershire Schools Symphony Orchestra (LSSO), 164, 165–6, *165*, 171

Mary of Magdala, 142
as Master of the Queen's Music, 78, 81, 112, 164
Mêlée Fantasque, 36–8, 141, *142*
modernism in the music of, 14, 16, 20, 27, 78, 85, 138
Morning Heroes, 83, 117
neoclassicism, 21, 80, 82, 83
The Olympians, 116, 177
One-Step, *138*, 139
outsider status, 78–82, 85
photos of, *9*, *14*, *38*, *116*, *140*
piano music, 139–40
post-war creative innovation in music, 14, 16, 70, 78
relationship with Karen, 176–8, *180*
Rhapsody for Strings and 2 Voices, 13, 16, 21, 23, 24, 28, 70, 140
rhythmic and dramatic scores, 18, 24, 28, 36, 60, 69, 93, 96, 102–4
Rout for Soprano Voice and Orchestra, 13, 138, *138*
Stravinsky's influence on, 15, 26, 27, 70, 82
ties with the USA, 8, 28, 73, 80, 82, 148, 176
World War I's impact on, 78, 80, 109, 117, 138
writings about music and dance, 10, 14, 16, 36, 38, 39, 56, 82, 163
see also *Adam Zero*; *Checkmate*; *Lady of Shalott, The*; *Miracle in the Gorbals*; *Narcissus and Echo*; *Rout*
Bliss, Trudy (née Hoffman), 8, 17, 62, 68, 73, 82, 148, 166, 174–5, 178
Bourne, Matthew, 24
Bracewell, William, 94, 96, 100, *100*, 104, 184 n.3
Bradley, Lionel, 119
Brae, June, *39*, 41, *45*, 61, *113*, *114*, *115*, 120–1, *120*, *121*, 123–6, *123*, *127*, *128*
Bridges-Adams, William, 38, 39
Briggs, Hedley, 18
Brill, Ruth, 94, 95, 96, 98, 99, *103*, 184 n.3
Britten, Benjamin, 152–3
Brown, Danielle, *48–9*, *62*
Bruce, Christopher, 24
Bruce, Henry, 28
Buckle, Richard, 32
Burn, Andrew, 132

Burra, Edward, design for *Miracle*, 28, 29, 30–3, *30–1*, 68, 73, 74, 82, 85
Bussell, Darcey, 6, 7, *56*, 58, 62–3, 65

C

Camargo Society, 17, 21, 28
Carter, Richard, 162
Central School of Ballet, *135*
Chappell, William, 23, 25, 28, 41
Chatterton, Julia, 20
Checkmate
  BBC films, 51, 58, 61
  Black Queen, 28, *39*, *45*, *47*, 52, *54–5*, 55, *56*, 57, *57*, 58, *58*, 59, 60–3, *60*, *61*, 64–5, *65*
  Bliss's score, 24, 28, 36, 39, 41–3, *42*, 52, 55, 56, 58, 70, 85, 140
  costume design, 29, 30, 36, *45*, 64–5
  created for the Vic-Wells Company, 28, 38
  dancers' experiences of, 50–5, 57–9, 60–3, 64
  de Valois at rehearsals for, 51, 58, 61–2, *64*
  de Valois' choreography, 12, 28, 36, 55, 56, 59–60, 62, 63–4, 65
  dedicated to Reginald Owen Morris, 39
  design, 28, 29–30, *41*, *44*, *48–79*, 63
  50th anniversary, *50*
  initial idea for, 28, 38
  international productions, *47*, *49*
  Lambert as conductor, 41, 56–7, 117
  McKnight Kauffer's design, 28–9, 36, 55, 56, 64
  premiere, 39–41, *40*, 52
  productions in Britain, 44–5, *48–9*, *52–3*, *54–5*, 56–7, *57*, 61–3
  Prologue, 29, *41*, 43
  Red King, *46*, *50*, 51–2, *51*, *52–3*, *54–5*, 55, 58, 60
  Red Knight, *39*, 59, 60, 61, 64–5, *65*, 68
  Red Queen, 55, *59*, 60
  role of chess in, 38, *38*
  scenario/narrative, 29–30, 36, 38–9, 41, 43–5, 52–5, 57, 85, 117
  socio-historical contexts, 28, 30, 36, 43, 52, 57
Christensen, Harold, 150, *150*
Christensen, Lew

career as a dancer, 150, 152, *153*, 162
as a choreographer, 148, 152–3
choreography for *The Lady*, 7, 8, 148, 149, *149*, 153, 156–63
collaboration with Duquette, 10, 153–4
Filling Station, 152
with his brothers, *150*
Jinx, 152–3
at the San Francisco Ballet, 148, 150–4
Christensen, William, 150, *150*, 152
Clarke, Mary, 19, 20, 33
Clay, Alison, 174
Clayden, Pauline, *70*, *74*, *76*, 77
Commisso, Cristina, 131, *131*
Cope, Tanya, 167, 168, 171–2
Corder, Michael, 58, 60, 65
costume design
  Adam Zero, *32*, 33, 114–15, *120*, *121*, 123, 126
  Ballets Russes, 15, *15*, 27
  Checkmate, 29, 30, 36, *45*, 64–5
  Fire Dance, 27–8
  The Lady of Shalott, *154*
  Miracle in the Gorbals, 29, 30–1, 32–3, 103, *103*
  Narcissus and Echo, 25
  The Picnic, 25
  Rout, 17, *19*, 20
  As You Like It, 26–7, 38
Craig, Gordon, 27
Cranko, John, 166, 168
Crisp, Clement, 61
Crompton, Sarah, 94
Crow, Susie, 179, 181
Cullerne-Bown, Penny, 179
Cushing, Charles, 149, *149*, 160, 163

D

Dale, Margaret, 129
Day, Laura, 95, 100, 103, *103*, 184 n.3
de Valois, Ninette
  Academy of Choreographic Art, 12, *12*, 14, 16
  The Arts of the Theatre, 18
  career as a dancer, 13, 14, 16, 21
  Cephalis and Procris, 21
  collaboration with Bliss, 7, 8, 12, 28, 30, 56
  development as a choreographer, 14, 18, 19, 20, 21, 23, 24, 56, 58

as a director, 12, 13, 18, 19, 21, 24, 57, 61, 62, 65
early social and professional encounters with Bliss, 16–17
expressionism 20, 23
50th anniversary of *Checkmate*, *50*
founding of The Royal Ballet School and Companies, 7, 12–13
impact on English ballet, 12, 13, 57, 65, 108
Job, 17, 19, 23, 24, 82
and Karen Bliss, 178
La Création du monde, 19, 23, *23*, 24
The Lady of Shalott, 30, 169
photos of, *13*, *37*, *38*, *50*, *64*
The Picnic (The Satyr or The Faun), *25*
post-war creative innovation in dance, 14, 16, 20, 21, 56, 65, 108
The Prospect Before Us, 28, 88–9
The Rake's Progress, 50, 65
as a teacher, 20, 21, 63, 64
see also *Checkmate*; *Narcissus and Echo*; *Rout*
Dely, Matt, 130
design
abstract set design of *Checkmate*, 28, 30
Adam Zero, 28, 33, 109, 110, *110*, 118, 120, 127–8, 129, 130
Checkmate, 28, 29–30, 63
The Lady of Shalott, 153–4, *155*, 162, 163, *171*, 172
by Léon Bakst for Ballets Russes, 15, *15*, 27
Miracle in the Gorbals, 28, 30–3, *30–1*, 68, 73, 74, 82, 85
Narcissus and Echo, 23–8, *23*
see also costume design
Diaghilev, Sergei, 7, *13*, 14–15, 16, 27, 36, 38, 55, 57, 70, 138
see also Ballets Russes
Diversions (Music for Strings), 30, *139*, 140–1, 169
Dolin, Anton, *12*
Drew, David, 89, 130, 134
Drew, Roderick, *161*
Dukes, Ashley, 16–17, 19, 28
Duquette, Tony, 10, 148, 153, *154*, *155*, 163

E

education
ballet in, 166, *167*

Dance Mosaic, *170*, 171–2, 173
Leicestershire Schools Symphony Orchestra (LSSO), 164, 165–6, *165*, 168, 170–1, 175
Edwards, Leslie, 76, 121, *121*, 126
Egri, Valerie, 175
El Greco, 69–70, *69*
Eldridge, Grace, 166, 167, 169, 171, 175
Elgar, Edward, 70, 85
Eliot, T.S., 179
Elvin, Violetta, 61
Erickson, Betsy, 151, 160
Evans, Edwin, *12*, 16, 17, 18, 21, 24, 140

F

Farron, Julia, 61, 76, 120, *121*, 124
Festival Theatre, Cambridge, 14, 18, 20, 23–4, 28
Fire Dance, 27, 36, 140
Firebird, The, 15
Fleming, Victor, 139
Fokine, Mikhail, 23, 108, 152
Fomenko, Volodymyr, 130, 132
Fonteyn, Margot, 41, 167
Franca, Celia, *80*
Frankenstein, Alfred, 148, 149, 157
Fraser, Claud Lovat, 26–8
Fraser, Grace Lovat, 18, 26, 27, 28
French, Claire, *52–3*
Frontier, *139*, 141
Furse, Roger, 29, 33, 109, 110, *110*, 118, 120, 128

G

Gartside, Bennett, *63*
Gibbs, Armstrong, 144
Gielgud, Maina, 61
Gilmour, Maurice, 166, 168, 175
Girl in a Broken Mirror see New Parks Girls' School
Goossens, Eugene, 14, 15, 139–40
Gray, Jonathan, 168
Gray, Terence, 14, 18, 20, 23–4
Greek dramas, classical, 23
Grey, Beryl, *47*, 57, 61, 62, 63, *64*

H

Hamlet, 69, 108, 127, 129
Hammersmith Musical Society, 18
Haskell, Arnold, 12, 17, 20, 69, 93, 178

Hassall, Christopher, 141–2, 145–7, 154
see also *Lady of Shalott, The*
Helpmann, Robert
in *Adam Zero*, 108, 109, *109*, 110–11, 112, *113*, 114–15, *114*, *115*, 121, *121*, *123*, *124*, *125*, 126, *126*, *127*
in *Checkmate*, 41, *46*, 60, 65, 68
choreography for *Adam Zero*, 33, 108–9, 111, 118, 129
choreography for *Miracle*, 68, 77, 82, 89, 178
collaborations with Bliss, 7, 8–10, 24, 28, 68–70, 73, 109, 118
dance-dramas, 68–9, 77, 105, 108, 128, 129
hand gesture study, 69–70, *69*
impact on English ballet, 8, 24, 108–9
in *Miracle*, 70, 75, 76, *81*, 86–7, 89, 105
portrait, *68*
in *The Prospect Before Us*, 88–9
Helpmann Symposium, 111, 134, *135*
Highwood, June, *50*
Hockney, Mary, 166, 167, 168, 169, 172–3, 174–5
Hollander, Jacquie, 64
Hopkins, Antony, 24, 28, 142
Horrocks, Amy, 142
Howells, Herbert, 15
Howes, Frank, 85
Hutton, Karen, 170, 174, *174*
Hynes, Samuel, 80

J

Jackson, Buss, 77
Jacobson, Maurice, 144
Jacques-Dalcroze, Émile, 21
Jiesamfoek, Herman, *141*
Judson, Stanley, 21, *22*, 24, 28

K

Karsavina, Tamara, 15, *15*, 16, 17, 26, 27, 28, 36, 38, 140
Kerridge, Jeremy, 94, 96, 97, 100, 105, 184 n.3
Keynes, Geoffrey, 16–17
Keynes, John Maynard, 16–17
Kirstein, Lincoln, 77, 150, 152
Knight, Yvette, *100*

L

Laban, Rudolf von, 20, 182 n.60
Lady of Shalott, The
    Bliss's score, 116, 140, 144, 145–7, 155, 160, 162, 163, 170
    Christensen's choreography, 7, 8, 148, 149, *149*, 153, 156–63
    collaboration on, 142, 145–7, 154
    costume design, *154*, 155, *155*
    de Valois' plans for, 30, 169
    Duquette's design, 153–4, *155*, 162, 163, *171*, *172*
    earlier musical settings to Tennyson's poem, 142–4
    as a 'lost' work, 7, 150
    New Parks Girls' School production as *Girl in a Broken Mirror see* New Parks Girls' School
    performances of, 144, *144*, 147, 148
    premiere in California, 148–9
    San Francisco Ballet's production, 7, 8, 148–9, *149*, *152*, 153–7, *157*, *158*, *159*, *163*
    scenario/narrative, 144–5, 145–7, 154–5, 156
    South American tour, 148, *149*, *151*, *152*
    Tennyson's poem, 142, 144–5, 149, 150, 155, 156, 162
    Waterhouse's paintings of, 142, *143*
Lambert, Constant
    Adam Zero dedicated to, *116*, 117
    collaboration with Bliss, 117
    compositions for ballet, 14, 24
    as conductor, 17, 41, 56–7, 117, 140
    introduction to de Valois, 21
    as Music Director of the Vic-Wells Ballet, 19, 56–7
Lawrence, Brandon, *89*, *93*
Leicester Haymarket Theatre, 166, 170, 171
Leicestershire County School of Dance, 168
Leicestershire Schools Symphony Orchestra (LSSO), 164, 165–6, *165*, 168, 170–1, 175
Lopokova, Lydia, *12*, 16, 17
Lucas, Leighton, 139
Lustig, Graham, 57
Lynne, Gillian
    in *Checkmate*, 61
    as a choreographer, *88*, 89, *89*, 92–3

recreation of *Miracle*, 7, 89–105, *93*, *98–105*, 179
Lyric Theatre, Hammersmith, 18, 26

M

MacDonald, Elaine, *140*
Macfall, Haldane, 26–7
Mackay, Iain, *89*, *93*, 94, 96, 98, 99, *101*, 102, *102*, 104, 184 n.3
Mackay, Rory, *89*, *93*
MacMillan, Kenneth, 30, *139*, 141, 169
Makarova, Natalia, 61
Manen, Hans van, 166
Marinelli, Peter, 83
Markova, Alicia, 21, *22*, 28
Markova-Dolin Ballet Company, 139
Marshall, Norman, 20
Marston, Cathy, 24
Mascagno, Stefano, 150
Maslen, Max, *89*, *93*
Mason, Monica, 60, 61, 63, 64–5, *65*, *139*
Mason, Stuart, 164–5
Massine, Léonide, 28
Matthews, Delia, *88*, 94, 99, *101*, 102, *102*, 105, 184 n.3
May, Pamela, 41, *45*, 61, 88
McKnight Kauffer, Edward, 28–9, 30, 36, *38*, *39*, 42, *45*, 55, 56, 64
McMullin, Peter, 179–81
McNicol, Andrew, 111, 129, 134, *135*
Mendelssohn, Felix, 112
Mercury Theatre, 16, 17
Miracle in the Gorbals
    as a ballet/dance drama, 69, 92, 104
    Bliss's score, 24, 32, 41, 68, 69, 70–2, 74–7, 82, 84, 85–6, 96, 140, 178
    Burra's designs, 28, 29, 30–3, 68, *71*, 73, 74, 82, 85
    collaboration on, 68, 78, 83, 84
    conducted by Lambert, 72, 117
    costumes, 29, 30–3, *30–1*, 103, *103*
    Dance of Deliverance, 73, *74*, 75–6, 99
    dancers' experiences of, 88, 89, *89*, 92, *92*, 93, 94–105
    El Greco's influence in, 69–70, *69*
    the front cloth, 32, *71*, 74
    Gorbals setting, 32, 69, 79, 83, 85
    hand gestures, 69–70, *69*, 100
    Helpmann's choreography, 68, 75, 77, 82, 178

    Helpmann's performance, 70, 75, 76, *81*, 86–7, 89, 105
    Lynne as a choreographer, 89–90, 92–3, 94
    Lynne's recreation of *Miracle*, 7, 88–9, *90–1 see also* scenes from
    neoclassicism, 82, 83, 85
    pastoral-industrial tensions, 78, 82, 83–4, 85–6
    premiere, *72–3*, 77, *80*
    rehearsals for Lynne's recreation of *Miracle*, *88*, 89, *92*, 97
    scenario/narrative, 28, 73, 74–7, 82
    scenes from, 30–1, *81*, *84*, 86–7, *90–1*, *93*, *98–105*
    socio-historical contexts, 69, 78, 82, 84, 85–6, 93
    themes of spirituality and morality, 73, 78, 82–4, *84*, 93
Morales Anderson, César, 94, 101, *101*, 105, 184 n.3
Moreton, Ursula, *12*, *17*, 21, *23*, *25*, 28
Murphy, Paul, 96, 184 n.3

N

Nakano, Kimie, 130
Narcissus and Echo
    as a barefoot ballet, 23, 28
    Bliss's score, 12, 13, 16, 21, 23, 24, 28, 36, 140
    conducted by Lambert, 17, 140
    costume design, *25*
    descriptions of, 21–3
    design and staging, 23–4, *25*, 28
    as a 'lost' work, 13–14
    as a vehicle for Alicia Markova, 21, 23, 28
Neilson, Marie, 28
Neumeier, John, 141
New Parks Ballet Group, 168
New Parks Girls' School
    ballet and music performance as education, 166–8, *167*, 174–5
    costumes and setting, 172
    Dance Mosaic, 170, 171–2, *173*
    Hockney's choreography, 172–4, 175
    production of *Lady* as *Girl in a Broken Mirror*, 144, *144*, 164–5, *168*, 169–75, *169*, *171*, *172*, *173*, *174*
Newman, Claude, *39*
Newton, Joy, 18, 21

Nielson, Marie, 21
Nijinsky, Vaslav, *15*, 16, 23
Northern Ballet Theatre, 141
Novello, Ivor, 141
Novikoff, Laurent, 27
Nureyev, Rudolf, 64–5, *65*, 150
Nye, Palma, *32*, 120, *121*, *124*

O

O'Hare, Michael, 94, *105*, 184 n.3
Olovyannikov, Valentin, *93*
Owen, Wilfred, 83

P

Pacific Northwest Ballet, 152, 163
Paltenghi, David, *70*, *75*, *80*, 120, *124*
Petrushka, 15, 27, 108
Pinkett, Eric, 165, 168, 169, 171
Playfair, Nigel, 18, 26
Price, Roland, *50*
Prowse, Philip, 30, 139
Pugsley, Ralph, 173

R

Rambert, Marie, *12*, 16, 17
Rassine, Alexis, *124*
Ravel, Maurice, 16, 112
Reizenstein, Franz, 142
Reyloff, Paul, *39*
Richardson, Phillip (P.J.S.), 17
Rite of Spring, 15, 16
Rootham, Cyril, 142–4
Rosovska (Rozowska), Zoia, 27
Rout
    Bliss's score, 12, 14, 16, 19–20, 24, 27, 36, *138*, 140
    challenges for performers and musicians, 18, 19, 21, 27
    costumes, *17*, *19*, *20*, 21
    critical reception, 19–20
    de Valois' choreography, *12*, 13, 19–21, 140
    as an interlude for Ballet Russes, 14–15, 27, 36, 70, 140
    as a 'lost' work, 13–14
    performances, 16, *17*, 18–19, *19*, *20*, 28
    piano played by Bliss, 16, 18
    Stravinsky's influence in, 15
    Toller's poem, 17, 19, 28

Rout for Soprano Voice and Orchestra, 13, 138, *138*
Royal Ballet, 30, 62, 63, 65, 169
Royal Ballet School and Companies, 13
    Ballet for All, 167
Royal Ballet Touring Company, 166–7
Royal Court Theatre, London, 18, 28
Royal Offering, A, 141, *141*
Royal Opera House, Covent Garden, 110, 118, 129, 130
Russell, Francia, 163

S

Sadler's Wells Ballet, 7, 8, 12, 13, 30, 33, 50, 72, 77, 88, 89, 109, 118, 119, 129, 153, 176, 178
Sadler's Wells Ballet School, 129, 179
Sadler's Wells Royal Ballet, 49, 50, *50*, 55, 57–8, *57*, 61
Sadler's Wells Theatre Ballet, 178
Salem, Caroline, 168, 174, 175
Salem, Peter, 175
San Francisco Ballet
    and the Christensen brothers, 150–1, 152
    international tours, 149, *149*, 151–2, *151*
    production of *Lady*, 7, 8, 148–9, *149*, *152*, 153–7, *157*, *158*, *159*, 163
San Francisco Ballet School, 150, 151, 152
San Francisco War Memorial Opera House, 148
Sancha, Carlos, *177*
Sargent, Malcolm, 18
Saylor, Eric, 82, 83
Schorer, Suki, *151*, *152*, 157, *159*
Sellick, Christopher, 178
Sellick, Karen *see* Bliss, Karen (Sellick)
Shore, Bernard, 117
Shyryayev, Oleksandr, 131, *131*, 132, 134
Silver, Mark, 64, 65
Sinding, Christian, 27, 36
Somes, Michael, 41, *74*
Sorley Walker, Kathrine, 19, 20, 21–2, 127
Sowell, Debra, 152, 162
Spicer, Paul, 15, 18, 21
Stadttheater, Bremerhaven, 130, *131*, *132–3*
Stanford, Charles Villiers, 80–1
Stowell, Kent, *149*, 154, 160, 163
Stravinsky, Igor, 15, 16, 26, 27, 28, 70, 82

T

Tait, Marion, 94, 96, 103, *103*, 184 n.3
Tate, Phyllis, 144
Tchelitchew, Pavel, 33, 162, 183 n.32
Tennyson, Alfred, 142, 144–5, 149, 150, 155, 156, 162
Théâtre des Champs-Elysées, 39
Thomson, Virgil, 152
Tippett, Sir Michael, 165
Toller, Ernst, 17, 19, 28
Tudor, Anthony, 17, 108, 109
Turner, Harold, *39*, 41

V

Valois, Ninette de *see* de Valois, Ninette
Vanaev, Sergei
    Die Vier Jahreszeiten, 132
    reconceptualisation of *Adam Zero*, 117, 129, 130–5, *131*, *132–3*, *134*
Vaughan Williams, Ralph, 21, 82–3
Vic-Wells Ballet and School, *12*, 13, 19, 21, *22*, 28, 38, 56, 70
Vollmar, Jocelyn, *144*, *149*, 155–7, *157*, *160*, *161*

W

Wadsworth, Edward, 26
Wadsworth, Fanny, 26
Walton, William, 85, 142
Warren, Robert de, 141, *141*
Waterhouse, John William, 142, *143*
Wells, Kenn, *140*
Wheeldon, Christopher, 24
Whitman, Walt, 115
Wigman, Mary, 20, 182 n.60
Wilder, Thornton, 28, 109
Willis, Elisha, *102*, *105*
Wilshire, Adam, 89, *90–1*
Wordsworth, Barry, 58, 147
Worrall, Alexandra, *141*

Y

Yanowsky, Zenaida, 57, 63, *63*
Yeats, William Butler, 18
Yuan, Shang-Jen, *131*, 132, *132*

Published in 2026 by Unicorn
an imprint of Unicorn Publishing Group
Charleston Studio
Meadow Business Centre
Lewes
BN8 5RW
www.unicornpublishing.org

Text © see individual contributors
Images © see image captions

Front cover: Laura Day as a Red Pawn in *Checkmate*. The Royal Ballet School performance at The Royal Opera House, London, 2011. Photo: Johan Persson (ArenaPAL).
Back cover: Robert Helpmann as the Stranger with dancers of Sadler's Wells Ballet in *Miracle in the Gorbals* at The Royal Opera House, London, 1946. Photo: Roger Wood (Royal Ballet and Opera/ArenaPAL).

All rights reserved. No part of the contents of this book may be reproduced, stored in or introduced into a retrieval system, or transmitted, in any form or by any means (electronic, mechanical, photocopying, recording or otherwise), without the prior written permission of the copyright holder and the above publisher of this book.

Every effort has been made to trace copyright holders and to obtain their permission for the use of copyright material. The publisher apologises for any errors or omissions and would be grateful if notified of any corrections that should be incorporated in future reprints or editions of this book.

ISBN 978-1-917458-38-2
10 9 8 7 6 5 4 3 2 1

Copy-editor: Linda Schofield
Design: Felicity Price-Smith
Printed in Serbia by Publikum